Critical Essays on

CONSTANCE FENIMORE WOOLSON

CRITICAL ESSAYS
ON
AMERICAN LITERATURE

James Nagel, General Editor
University of Georgia, Athens

Critical Essays on

CONSTANCE FENIMORE WOOLSON

edited by

CHERYL B. TORSNEY

G. K. Hall & Co. / New York
Maxwell Macmillan Canada / Toronto
Maxwell Macmillan International / New York Oxford Singapore Sydney

Copyright © 1992 by Cheryl B. Torsney

G. K. Hall & Co.
Macmillan Publishing Company
866 Third Avenue
New York, New York 10022

Maxwell Macmillan Canada, Inc.
1200 Eglinton Avenue East
Suite 200
Don Mills, Ontario M3C 3N1

Macmillan Publishing Company is part of the Maxwell Communication Group of Companies.

Library of Congress Cataloging-in-Publication Data

Critical essays on Constance Fenimore Woolson/edited by Cheryl B. Torsney.
    p.   cm. — (Critical essays on American literature)
  Includes bibliographical references and index.
   ISBN 0-8161-7309-5
   1. Woolson, Constance Fenimore, 1840–1894—Criticism and interpretation. I. Torsney, Cheryl B. II. Series.
PS3363.C75   1992
813′.4—dc20
                               91–47111
                                   CIP

---

10   9   8   7   6   5   4   3   2   1

Printed in the United States of America

For my students

Contents

◆

CRITICAL WRITINGS AND APPRECIATIONS

REPRINTED CRITICAL ASSESSMENTS

General Editor's Note

◆

The Critical Essays on American Literature series seeks to anthologize the most important criticism on a wide variety of topics and writers in American literature. Our readers will find in various volumes not only a generous selection of reprinted articles and reviews but original essays, bibliographies, manuscript sections, and other materials brought to public attention for the first time. *Critical Essays on Constance Fenimore Woolson* is the first collection of essays ever published on this important nineteenth-century American writer, whose work is only beginning to receive the attention it deserves. The volume contains a sizable gathering of early reviews and nearly every important article published about Woolson. Among the authors of reprinted articles and reviews are William Dean Howells, Horace Scudder, Sybil B. Weir, Jay B. Hubbell, Ann E. Rowe, Rayburn S. Moore, and Victoria Brehm. In addition to a substantial introduction by Cheryl B. Torsney, which presents an overview of Woolson's career and critical responses to it, there are also four original essays commissioned specifically for publication in this volume, new studies by Sharon L. Dean, Joan Myers Weimer, Caroline Gebhard, and Carolyn VanBergen. We are confident that this book will make a permanent and significant contribution to the study of American literature.

JAMES NAGEL
University of Georgia, Athens

Publisher's Note

◆

Producing a volume that contains both newly commissioned and reprinted material presents the publisher with the challenge of balancing the desire to achieve stylistic consistency with the need to preserve the integrity of works first published elsewhere. In the Critical Essays series, essays commissioned especially for a particular volume are edited to be consistent with G. K. Hall's house style; reprinted essays appear in the style in which they were first published, with only typographical errors corrected. Consequently, shifts in style from one essay to another are the result of our efforts to be faithful to each text as it was originally published.

Introduction

CHERYL B. TORSNEY

Thanks to a growing number of scholars and university presses interested in reconstructing the canon of American literature, more readers are now familiar with the reputation and works of Constance Fenimore Woolson than there were even ten years ago.[1] Back then most attention to her work probably derived from a prurient curiosity regarding her celebrated relationship with Henry James, a relationship treated in two essays appearing in this volume, rather than from a distinct interest in Woolson's own writing.[2] Scholars and students gladly acknowledged her matrilineal middle name as though it might one day appear in "Trivial Pursuit," but few readers pursued her seriously: little criticism had been written on Woolson, and even the bare facts of her existence were elusive.

Constance Fenimore Woolson was born in Claremont, New Hampshire, on 5 March 1840, the sixth child of Charles Jarvis and Hannah Cooper Pomeroy Woolson, a niece of James Fenimore Cooper. When three of baby Constance's sisters succumbed to scarlet fever within weeks of her birth, the family escaped the tragedy by moving to the growing town of Cleveland, Ohio. Constance grew up in the Western Reserve, attending first Miss Hayden's School and then the Cleveland Female Seminary, before traveling to New York and Madame Chegaray's French School to be finished. As a girl Connie Woolson was a talented writer and singer, and an avid out-doorswoman known for her fondness for rowing and walking.

Following her father's death in 1869, Woolson cared for her ailing mother, traveling up and down the eastern seaboard, frequently to the Carolinas and to Florida, which she came to love, hoping to retire to a little cottage on the beach at St. Augustine. At her mother's death in 1879, however, Woolson sailed to Europe, never to return. She lived in Italy (Florence and Venice) and England, vacationing in Germany, Switzerland, Greece, and Egypt; and although she preferred a solitary existence, she had several close friends, including Henry and Alice James. Her first magazine

1

articles were published in 1870, but she did not begin writing novels until 1880, when *Anne* (published in book form in 1882) began appearing serially in *Harper's New Monthly Magazine*. In all, Woolson wrote numerous poems, travel sketches, and critical articles for magazine publication, and published separately a novel for children, four adult novels, a novella, a long poem, a volume of travel writings, and four collections of short fiction. She died, a probable suicide, in Venice on 24 January 1894, from a fall from a second-story window, and was buried in the Protestant Cemetery in Rome.[3]

At the time of her death, Woolson's fiction, especially, was known both in the capitals of Europe and in the cities and small towns of America. Even in Morgantown, West Virginia, a coal-mining and glass-manufacturing town with a relatively new university, Woolson's genius was recognized. Martha Brock, in "The Woman's Club and Its Predecessors," details the history and activities of the cultural group known in its earlier incarnations as "The Literary Club," "Conversazione," "The Bric-a-Brac," "The Shakespeare Club," and "The Ladies Friday Night Club," an organization whose engagement with literary topics led them to study Woolson.[4] Founded in 1891–1892, "The Woman's Club" spent its first year "delv[ing] in already half forgotten literature of our own land," for example, Wigglesworth's "Day of Doom," Barlow's "Hasty Pudding," Brockden Brown's novels, Jonathan Edwards's "The Freedom of the Will," and various works by Washington Irving.[5] They also attentively read the poetry of Phillis Wheatley. Later, the group moved on to Longfellow; "Cooper's best, 'The Leather Stocking Tales,' easily followed; then Poe's weird prose fancies, and Hawthorne's inimitable romances."[6] Brock continues: "These in turn led us to recent American fiction, in which we gave Constance Fenimore Woolson a high place."[7] Although Phillis Wheatley has found her way into anthologies of American literature, Woolson has just begun to do so. Apparently, to paraphrase Arthur Hobson Quinn, who noted that James's favorable assessment of Woolson's talent in his *Partial Portraits* sketch "Miss Woolson" is more accurate than that of the generations that followed, the opinion of the Woman's Club of Morgantown has proven more valid than that of the critics who have forgotten her.[8]

Woolson's works were in demand by her publishers and eagerly awaited by an admiring public. In addition to the Harpers, the house with whom Woolson is most often associated, the Appletons, one of Woolson's earlier publishers, courted the writer, encouraging her to supply them with a collected volume of poetry, which Woolson never attempted.[9] Woolson experienced with some consternation what she perceived as the Harpers' pressure to supply them with more to publish. For example, in a letter dated 12 June 1891, Woolson writes to her nephew, Samuel Mather: "They send me very satisfactory letters from Franklin Square, & are urgent for another novel. So I suppose I shall do some more fiction. But I must have a try at a play, too."[10] The following spring Mather invited Woolson to join him and his family at Newport for the summer, and although the temptation must have been great—she adored the Mather children, one of whom had been named after her, and she had not visited America since her departure for Europe in 1879—she may have feared the response of the Harpers, should the vacation cause a further delay in the writing of *Horace Chase*. She writes in a letter to Mather dated 8 February 1892:

> I can't come this summer simply because every well moment *must* be given to finishing the novel which begins as a serial in Harper's Magazine next December. I have already postponed it a whole year, owing to the tiresome condition of my health; never really ill, I may say, sadly enough with truth, that for a year I have not been really well. Unless I wish to make the Harpers lose all patience with me, I must keep my engagement fully & promptly this time. Therefore it is not by any means the moment for a home-coming, and a visit to you. How much writing do you suppose I should accomplish if my dear little Constance was within my reach; you & Flora might give me twenty writingrooms—but I should be out of them every five minutes to look at the boys, & see how they were amusing themselves![11]

At the beginning of the summer, Woolson had wanted to move from Oxford, where she had suffered from the climate, to an apartment in Venice, but as she wrote to Sam on 20 May 1892: "I *must* finish my novel before I can go anywhere."[12] *Horace Chase* was the last novel she would write.

Woolson was a valued talent, and not only among rural women's clubs and those publishers who provided them with books. The reviews of her novels and collections of short stories, published in the leading periodicals of the day (the *New York Times*, the *Nation*, the *Atlantic Monthly*, *Harper's New Monthly Magazine*, among others), are markedly positive despite some reservations, expressed most notably by William Dean Howells and the reviewer for the *Nation*.[13] More often than not the evaluations were glowing. In fact, the *New York Times* felt that Woolson's long poem, "Two Women," published serially in *Appleton's Monthly*, was significant enough to warrant a review and thus a break in its policy of not reviewing magazine verse.

From the reviewers' perspective, the poetic quality of Woolson's prose is perhaps the most alluring aspect of her writing throughout her career. According to the reviewer of her early *Rodman the Keeper: Southern Sketches* in the "Editor's Literary Record" of *Harper's Monthly*: "The sketches—for so Miss Woolson modestly styles them—collected in this volume place their author in the first rank of writers in this line [of realism]; nay, we know of no writer, English or American, whose short stories are so rich in description, so strong in their delineations of character, so opulent in narrative or dramatic interest, and so truly poetic in their settings and surroundings. Indeed, each of them is a genuine poem, noteworthy for the subtle delicacy of its fancy and for the weird and artistic indefiniteness of its denouement."[14] In an assessment of *Horace Chase*, the *New York Times* reviewer reflects on Woolson's earlier *East Angels*: "The 'atmosphere' . . . is its principal charm; the reader seems to be breathing the very air of the Florida of Miss Woolson's poetic imagination, and to pass his time partly in the deep shade of the fragrant forests and partly in the brilliance of the sandy, treeless wastes, and the sudden changes from one to the other seem actually to dazzle the vision of the sensitive reader."[15]

Like the Woman's Club of Morgantown and Henry James, who included his essay on Woolson in a collection that reprinted his essays on luminaries such as Maupassant and Turgenev, Emerson, and Stevenson, these reviewers considered Woolson among the finest talents of the day.[16] In various assessments she is compared to George Eliot, Anthony Trollope, and Bret Harte. Her reputation is expected to last. As the *Literary World*'s sympathetic review of *Horace Chase* concludes, just months after Woolson's death: "Although her *motifs* have not great variety nor her types exalted beauty, her work will long retain its charm."[17] The reviewer for the *Nation*, however, may have been more accurate in foreshadowing the general decline of Woolson's reputation: "Authority in literature is with the dead, but it is still too early to forecast the probabilities of Miss Woolson's surviving her generation."[18]

Woolson's popular reputation was based primarily on her fiction and poetry, but members of the literati also recognized her acute critical sense displayed in the "Contributors' Club" of the *Atlantic Monthly*. In these reviews Woolson revels in her anonymity, telling E. C. Stedman in a letter dated 30 September 1877: "Yes; I did write that about the 'Lass o'Lowrie's,' in the September Atlantic; but you must not tell. The pleasure of it is in the incognito; trammeled at once if names are known."[19] These critical appraisals reveal a discerning ear and eye. For example, in explaining what she interprets as Henry James's purpose in *The Europeans*, she writes: "In our raw American atmosphere, delicate and congenial lying has not yet been comprehended as one of the fine arts."[20] Later, she queries Jamesian style, prefiguring the concerns of many modern readers: "One peculiarity of style I have noticed, namely, the large number of what seem to me 'stage directions.' Thus, fourteen times in three consecutive pages, taken at random from those containing conversation, it is particularly noted down that they 'looked at' each other."[21] In reviewing Thomas Hardy, she quips: "Hardy always has one woman and three or four lovers; it is his idea of a story. In Desperate Remedies and The Hand of Ethelberta he has ventured off his ground and into the field where Wilkie Collins' banner, inscribed with the motto, 'Plots, not People,' floats supreme; and of course he has been slaughtered."[22] She did not feel free to write such criticism under her own name, sensing perhaps the pressures experienced by women earlier in the century to use pseudonyms to protect themselves from public scrutiny, and the opportunities offered by the Contributors' Club released a wickedly comic sensibility for which few give Woolson credit.

Both popular readers and those who recognized the scribblings of her anonymous pen deeply mourned Woolson's death under mysterious circumstances in Venice in 1894. News of her passing produced appreciations of her life and work both immediately and for years following, long before the trend toward critical reevaluation began in the thirties. In addition to the obituaries appearing in several Harper Brothers publications are two other notable tributes. The first, "Reminiscences of Constance Fenimore Woolson" by Linda T. Guilford, is printed here for the first time.[23] An 1848 graduate of Mount Holyoke College and Woolson's teacher at the Cleveland Female Seminary in the 1850s, Guilford details much of what we now know about Woolson's appearance, talents, and behavior as a young girl growing up in Cleveland. As fond of her influential teacher as her teacher was of her, Woolson had corresponded with Guilford throughout her life.

The second appreciation, long out of print, is excerpted from the curious second volume of *Five Generations*, edited by Woolson's niece, Clare Benedict.[24] An eccentric who lived most of her life abroad in European hotels, Benedict collected the writings of five generations of her family, beginning with the sisters of James Fenimore Cooper, constructing a genealogy that is conspicuously incorrect in its failure to include Woolson's younger brother, Charley, who may have committed suicide.[25] She set about lionizing her aunt by establishing a collection of Constance Fenimore Woolson memorabilia and providing the funds for constructing a building to house the collection at Rollins College, Winter Park, Florida, and writing and donating *Five Generations* to hundreds of college and university libraries. Benedict's volume on her aunt is a pastiche of Woolson's letters, notebook entries, poems, and short stories, with pertinent information on publication and specific provenance absent. A distinctly frustrating scholarly tool, Benedict's *Constance Fenimore Woolson* is nonetheless one of the only sources to reprint selections from Woolson's journals. The excerpt offered here from Benedict's introduction offers insight into the relationship between aunt and niece and into the fictitious Constance Fenimore Woolson that the niece constructed for the reading public, a fiction that, because of the paucity of scholarly work on Woolson, has been generally accepted.

Unlike Benedict's random compilation, this collection attempts to provide some method in considering Woolson's literary reputation. Beginning with Fred Lewis Pattee's few but telling paragraphs in 1915, I have assembled excerpts from critical assessments of Woolson's writing from every decade in the twentieth century except the first, in which appreciations rather than serious critiques appeared, given the recent date of the writer's death.[26] That this project was even possible—locating critical readings from each decade of the century—attests to an abiding interest in Woolson's art.

Several of the earliest critics, among them Pattee and Edward J. O'Brien, treat Woolson primarily as a transitional figure in the history of the short story. O'Brien characterizes her popularity as "baffling" yet admits that she "somehow commands our respect, so that we believe in her accomplishment, and feel that in a more settled environment which had long racial memories and a more implicit culture, she might have gone very far indeed."[27] But O'Brien's assessment is itself baffling, since many of Woolson's best stories are set in Europe, an environment affording, if nothing else, an "implicit culture." Pattee calls Woolson "one of the pioneers of the period," a comparison that was reiterated in the first full-length study of the writer, John Dwight Kern's *Constance Fenimore Woolson: Literary Pioneer* (1934).[28] In citing Woolson's contemporary popularity, Pattee states that her achievement pales by comparison to those who follow, like Grace King and Kate Chopin.[29] Another early assessment, however, compares Woolson favorably to another writer whose stock has risen with the revaluation of the canon: Ellen Glasgow. In John Hervey's view, Woolson's *For the Major* bests Glasgow's *They Stooped to Folly*, the former serving as his example of a work "warm with life and suffused with humanity" and the latter of "something got-up and frigid, clever to the ultimate but unconvincing."[30]

In 1934 John Dwight Kern published *Constance Fenimore Woolson: Literary Pioneer*, his University of Pennsylvania doctoral dissertation, which remains the only work to include a comprehensive bibliography of Woolson's own writings and one of only two studies to treat Woolson's oeuvre in its entirety.[31] This volume reprints Kern's valuable assessment of Woolson's "Miscellaneous Writings," which includes the only extant discussion of her poetry, thus providing a starting point for the scholar seeking to consider Woolson's work outside of the fictional arena.

Kern's dissertation adviser was Arthur Hobson Quinn, who devoted nine full pages to Woolson in his 1936 survey of American literature.[32] Like the other scholars of the thirties, forties, and fifties, whose works are excerpted here, Quinn was interested in establishing an American tradition and in describing Woolson's place within it. Like Kern before him, Quinn considers Woolson's work chronologically in relation to the biographical context, which he and nearly all other critics after him feel compelled to repeat in order to set the stage for a critical discussion.

Four years after Quinn's survey, the centenary of Woolson's birth brought a long, informative article from Lyon S. Richardson celebrating the anniversary and praising Woolson's accomplishment. He summarizes the facts of her life and the plots of her fictions, inaugurating a pattern that critical articles by Van Wyck Brooks, Alexander Cowie, Edward Wagenknecht, and Jay B. Hubbell would follow through the thirties, forties, and fifties.[33] Even while applauding Woolson's accomplishment, they all implicitly agree with Cowie: "She is now in the familiar category of the superior minor writer who is periodically 'rediscovered' by a sensitive critic or a zealous historian. No number of such discoveries, of course, can make her over into a major novelist. At best her art was extremely sensitive and delicate. . . . Yet vigorous action was not her forte."[34]

Rayburn S. Moore's Twayne series study of Woolson offers, as the earlier examinations had done, a biographical context for the criticism, but more than any other critique up to that point, Moore's presents, in addition to plot summary, a critical assessment of each work discussed.[35] Moore's concerns are traditionally formalist, so his readings focus on theme and character development, ending with an evaluation. Since his *Constance Fenimore Woolson* was published in 1963, he is also able to draw on the estimates of earlier readers of Woolson, integrating their appraisals into his own.

Rarely cited in Woolson criticism is another product of the sixties, Robert L. White's "Cultural Ambivalence in Constance Fenimore Woolson's Italian Tales," an early piece of what is now labeled "cultural criticism."[36] Unlike that of preceding critics, White's approach is neither literary nor biographical; rather, he attempts to present Woolson's Italian tales as documentary evidence of the middle-class American response to Italy. His early disclaimer reveals why his article is so seldom considered by Woolson scholars concerned with revitalizing Woolson's nineteenth-century reputation. White asserts: "Simply because her tales are so mediocre and lacking in individual lustre, they can all the more properly be viewed as an index to the culture which produced and ingested them."[37] Nevertheless, this work, one of the few to consider Woolson's late Italian tales exclusively, offers an insight into an all too typical later twentieth-century response to Woolson.

Although Anne E. Rowe's approach to Woolson, in her chapter on the writer in *The Enchanted Country: Northern Writers in the South: 1865–1910* (1978), resembles that of earlier critics who contextualize Woolson in the local color tradition, most critics of the seventies began to pursue Woolson from different angles, with the end result being an implied rejoinder to White.[38] It should not be surprising that Woolson's critics in the seventies were, for the first time, women and that these women should use feminist criticism to reread Woolson. Two years earlier, in 1976, Sybil B. Weir discusses Woolson's interrogation of the sentimental heroine in what Weir deems the writer's most successful piece: "What Woolson accomplishes in *For the Major* is to rescue the principle of self-sacrifice from the sentimental ideal."[39] In this novella the writer critiques both the South and the American ideal of womanhood, which "forces women to adopt a disguise of eternal adolescence."[40]

With the eighties Woolson criticism began to come into its own, using a variety of methodologies, including newer Marxist and cultural criticism, and revising older approaches, like genre criticism and biographical criticism, but with contemporary twists. Feminist critical approaches—both Anglo-American and French, formalist and psychoanalytic—continue to generate the most interest among recent scholars. My own project in "The Traditions of Gender: Constance Fenimore Woolson and Henry James" is twofold: first, to dispel the fiction that Woolson may have committed suicide over unrequited love for James, a myth that turns Woolson into a sentimental heroine herself and precludes serious study of her work; and second, to highlight, using Anglo-American feminist theory, the specific female-gendered character of her prose, as opposed to James's, which, though similar, is male gender inflected.[41]

In treating Woolson's Great Lakes stories, Victoria Brehm fits Woolson into a woman's tradition of frontier writing focusing on the theme of renunciation.[42] Unlike earlier critics, however, Brehm finds in Woolson's characters' martyrdoms and attending social isolation the key to their independence and their attractiveness for the late twentieth-century reader.[43] As Brehm explains: "She did write one story over and over, and it was about the cost and gains to women who refused to go along with the obligatory domestic femininity of their time."[44] A glance at Brehm's bibliography reveals her debt both to older examinations of local color writing and to more recent feminist approaches to nineteenth-century texts: Ann Douglas [Wood]'s "The Literature of Impoverishment" and Annette Kolodny's *The Land Before Her* and *The Lay of the Land*.

In addition to reprinting some of the key texts in Woolson criticism, this volume presents four commissioned pieces by readers who have developed their interpretations in response to theoretical trends in the profession; all are obligated to feminist theory, which, beginning in the late sixties and early seventies, gave credibility to rereading, as Cowie had called Woolson, "the superior minor writer who is periodically 'rediscovered' by a sensitive critic or a zealous historian."[45] The implicit assumption underlying all four of the commissioned works is, of course, that Woolson deserves, like Kate Chopin, Charlotte Perkins Gilman, and a host of other writers, admission to consciousness, to the canon, and thus to the classroom.

Joan Myers Weimer's " 'The Admiring Aunt' and the 'Proud Salmon of the Pond': Constance Fenimore Woolson's Struggle with Henry James" offers a perceptive addition to the criticism of the relationship between James and Woolson by asserting that although Woolson provided James with many ideas, the Master's "manipulative response to her writing . . . damaged her both as woman and writer." Weimer elaborates her argument using the Jamesian device of considering the two sides of a coin. First she undertakes a discussion of James on Woolson and then one of Woolson on James, highlighting James's ambivalence to his friend as a woman writer in his misreading of her novel *East Angels* in light both of his criticism of it in his *Partial Portraits* sketch and of his own *The Europeans*, which treats issues similar to those in Woolson's novel.

Sharon L. Dean, who cataloged Woolson's literary influence on James in her helpful "Constance Fenimore Woolson and Henry James: The Literary Relationship," undertakes to illuminate the familial roles played by many of Woolson's female characters in "Women as Daughters; Women as Mothers in the Fiction of Constance Woolson."[46] Using the work of Carol Gilligan and Nancy Chodorow in developmental psychology, Dean asserts that Woolson's biography supports their theories that affiliation provides the pattern for girls' development while boys strive for independence in the maturation process. Her fiction, too, explores the differing familial relationships between the genders: fathers and daughters, and mothers and daughters and sons. As Woolson's fiction develops, a pattern emerges: while the writer focuses on daughters and fathers earlier in her career, later she moves to discussing how sons abandon their mothers while daughters maintain strong ties.

Like Weimer, in comparing Woolson to a more famous male writer, and like Dean, in using Anglo-American feminist theory, Caroline Gebhard offers a strikingly new reading of Woolson's motivations and technique in "Constance Fenimore Woolson Rewrites Bret Harte: The Sexual Politics of Intertextuality." In "The Lady of Little Fishing," an early short story reprinted in *Castle Nowhere: Lake Country Sketches* (1875), Woolson attempts "to rewrite nineteenth-century American culture from a woman's point of view," Gebhard claims. Whereas in Harte's "The Luck of Roaring Camp" the woman's body only appears as a bloody corpse, Woolson's feminist revision presents a missionary who is enshrined as a saint at a Great Lakes mining camp. When she is discovered to experience erotic desire, however, the men feel betrayed, and "the transformation of a camp of hardened men into the pure joys of collective boyhood that in Harte's story is dramatized as a real possibility is shown up in Woolson's story as a sham." Woolson's story may finally be read as an allegory of how the nineteenth century's "cult of true womanhood" drains women of all energy and vitality. At the same time, however, the Lady's self-abasing groveling at the feet of the man she desires reveals a frightening power of desire that far exceeds that of the men.

Whereas Gebhard figures the men in "The Lady of Little Fishing" as exploitative capitalists engaged in extracting wealth from the land and in need of a saint to bless their activities, Carolyn VanBergen's use of economic metaphors is even more pointed in "Getting Your Money's Worth: The Social Marketplace in *Horace Chase*." In this essay, one of the very few to treat Woolson's last novel, VanBergen asserts that, like the Union and the Confederacy, male and female societies operate on different values systems, with men basing their economies on money and self and women favoring the commodities of information and self. Woolson's novels focus on which gender controls the marketplace and how one gets one's money's worth.

The new essays only begin to hint at the growing interest in Woolson's writing and the vital community of scholars at work. Research possibilities suggest themselves at every turn. Certainly critiques wait to be written, and those scholars skilled at deploying deconstructive methodologies, Bakhtinian readings, cultural analyses, French feminist interpretations, psychoanalytic explications, and Marxist approaches are encouraged to read and think about Constance Fenimore Woolson, for her work will certainly bear more scrutiny than it has received.

To date, most scholars have been enchanted almost exclusively by Woolson's short fiction. Yet, as Weimer and VanBergen point out here, the novels, though they have enjoined less immediate enthusiasm both today and in Woolson's own time, will abundantly reward study.[47] In addition to the novels, the poetry and travel writings await more thorough rediscovery. Finally, scholars still find themselves without such essential research tools as a definitive biography and an edition of Woolson's fascinating letters.[48]

After deciding to organize, the Woman's Club of Morgantown lost no time in expediting the formal necessities of writing a short constitution and electing officers, the rest of the club serving as a "Permanent Committee." As Martha Brock explains, "Having no taste for measuring our vitality by red tape, we sought always to keep the spirit in advance of the letter. We did debate somewhat as to the name, and concluded that 'no-pent-up Utica' should contract our powers, that nothing human should be foreign to our thought."[49] One can't help but think that Constance Fenimore Woolson would have endorsed this sentiment wholeheartedly, for as scholars both here and elsewhere have recognized, Woolson was an alluring and appealing yet puzzling personality whose works likewise attract, engage, and perplex. Scholars are only beginning to debate the terms of that attraction and engagement. Such discussions, both those reprinted here and those published for the first time in this volume, have proven that Woolson and the scholars themselves, like the early Woman's Club of Morgantown, have other measures of vitality than the red tape of current canonicity.

My debts, as always, are to many: my mother, Elsa M. Brenner, who *kvels* at my every small success; my young sons, Benjamin and Edward, who teach me lessons I never thought I'd learn; my friends, particularly Dennis Allen, who comment astutely on nearly everything I write; my husband, Jack R. Torsney, Jr., whose love and humor sustain me.

I would also like to thank the growing community of Woolson scholars, anchored, I believe, by the contributors to this volume. My students, especially Uma Satyavolu Rau and Cheryl Ware, and my research assistant, Sally Lynn Raines, have, in their own writing and enthusiasm for Woolson's work, further insisted that this book is long overdue. It is to them, the new scholars for whom Woolson is already a familiar name, that *Critical Essays on Constance Fenimore Woolson* is dedicated.

Notes

1. In addition to several articles, the last ten years have seen the publication of Joan Myers Weimer, ed., *Women Artists, Women Exiles: "Miss Grief" and Other Stories* (New Brunswick, N.J.: Rutgers University Press, 1988) and Cheryl B. Torsney, *Constance Fenimore Woolson: The Grief of Artistry* (Athens: University of Georgia Press, 1989).

2. See Cheryl B. Torsney, "Constance Fenimore Woolson and Henry James: The Traditions of Gender," in *Patrons and Protégées: Gender, Friendship, and Writing in Nineteenth-Century America*, ed. Shirley Marchalonis (New Brunswick, N.J.: Rutgers University Press, 1988), 161–83, and Joan Myers Weimer, "The 'Admiring Aunt' and the 'Proud Salmon of the Pond': Constance Fenimore Woolson's Struggle with Henry James." The former is reprinted here; the latter appears here for the first time. See, too, Rayburn S. Moore, "The Strange Irregular Rhythm of Life: James's Late Tales and Constance Woolson," *South Atlantic Quarterly* 41 (1976): 86–93, and Sharon L. Dean, "Constance Fenimore Woolson and Henry James: The Literary Relationship," *Massachusetts Studies in English* 7 (1980): 1–9.

3. For a discussion of Woolson's death, see Torsney, "The Traditions of Gender," 261–65, reprinted in this volume.

4. My thanks to Lillian J. Waugh, Ph.D., Director of Research, WVU Women's Centenary Project, West Virginia University Center for Women's Studies, for telling me about the Woman's Edition of *The New Dominion* magazine (30 December 1896), which contains Martha Brock's "The Woman's Club and Its Predecessors," 32–34.

5. Martha Brock, "The Woman's Club and Its Predecessors," *The New Dominion* magazine (Woman's Edition) (30 December 1896), 33.

6. Brock, 34.

7. Brock, 34.

8. See Arthur Hobson Quinn, *American Fiction: An Historical Survey* (New York: D. Appleton-Century, 1936), 342.

9. In a letter dated 31 March 1887 Woolson writes to her nephew, Samuel Mather: "Lately I have been asked both by the Harpers & the Appletons to allow the collection of all my scattered verses in a volume next year. I have declined both proposals" (Mather Family Papers). I am indebted to the Western Reserve Historical Society for permission to quote from these materials.

During her lifetime Woolson published dozens of poems, which John Dwight Kern classifies in his piece on Woolson's miscellaneous writings as "verses on persons; poems on nature and the seasons; love lyrics; verses on pet dogs; nonsense verse; poems on abstract themes; and miscellaneous verses." (See Kern, *Constance Fenimore Woolson: Literary Pioneer* [Philadelphia: University of Pennsylvania Press, 1934], 102, reprinted in this volume.)

10. Mather Family Papers. As early as 1877, in an unpublished letter to the writer and editor E. C. Stedman, Woolson had noted her temptation to write a play, but she feared that she would never succeed, having had no experience in the genre.

11. Mather Family Papers.

12. Mather Family Papers.

13. In a letter dated 30 July 1886, Woolson writes to her old friend John Hay, the writer and diplomat, that she is gratified by his opinion of her latest novel, *East Angels*:

I thank you the more for expressing your liking, because today brings me Mr. Howells' notice, in his "Study." I could not expect Mr. Howells to like "Margaret," for he does not believe in "Margarets,"—he has never perceived that they exist. But his writing as he has done, ex cathedra as it were,—from the literary chair of the magazine in which the story appeared,—strikes me as unfriendly; for the ordinary reader will not discriminate,—will not notice that it is Howells in his own person who is speaking; the ordinary reader will suppose that the magazine is coming out with a condemnation of its own contributor,—which is a course very unusual.

But your praise is more to me than Mr. Howells' dispraise; I have not cared for his opinions (literary) since he came out so strongly against what I consider a masterpiece— "Le Père Goriot." All I care for is the unfriendliness from one I have supposed a friend. (Alice Hall Petry, " 'Always, Your Attached Friend': The Unpublished Letters of Constance Fenimore Woolson to John and Clara Hay," *Books at Brown* 29–30 [1982–1983], 87)

Hay apparently wrote to assuage Woolson's feelings of betrayal, for in a letter of 23 February 1887 she writes:

> All you said, in your last letter, of Mr. Howells' criticism of "East Angels" was true, encouraging, & very kind. I appreciated it; & thank you for it. And it comforted me greatly. A really magnificent letter from Mr. Joseph Harper—in fact two letters— removed long ago any pain I might have felt. For you know it was not the criticism, but its appearance in *Harper's*, that troubled me. Since then Mr. Howells has said some generous things of "Castle Nowhere" & "Rodman."
>
> —Petry, 93

(Howells's reviews of *East Angels, Castle Nowhere: Lake Country Sketches*, and *Rodman the Keeper: Southern Sketches* are reprinted in this volume.)

Of the possibility of an enemy in the *Nation* office, Woolson wrote to Samuel Mather on 10 January 1883: "I think it very clever of Robert Chamberlain [probably a member of the powerful Chamberlain family of Cleveland] to divine a feminine influence against me in the 'Nation' office" (Mather Family Papers).

14. This and other references in this essay to reviews, appreciations, critical writing, and essays about Woolson are reprinted in this volume unless otherwise noted.

15. "Miss Woolson's Last Book," *New York Times*, 10 February 1894, 3. This description does not appear in the portion excerpted for this volume.

16. James's "Miss Woolson" has recently been reprinted in Henry James, *Literary Criticism: Essays on Literature, American Writers, English Writers*, ed. Leon Edel (New York: Library of America, 1984), 639–49, and in Weimer, 270–79.

17. "Horace Chase," *Literary World* (Boston), 24 March 1894, 85.

18. Review of *Horace Chase, Nation*, 29 March 1894, 233. This quotation does not appear in the excerpt of the article for this volume.

19. I am indebted to the Butler Library of Columbia University for permission to use this and other excerpts from the Stedman Manuscript Collection.

20. [Constance Fenimore Woolson], "Contributors' Club" (on James's *The Europeans*), *Atlantic Monthly* 43 (January 1879), 108.

21. [Woolson], "Contributors' Club" (on James's *The Europeans*), 108.

22. [Constance Fenimore Woolson], "Contributors' Club" (on Hardy's *Far From the Madding Crowd*), *Atlantic Monthly* 43 (February 1879), 262.

23. I am indebted to the Western Reserve Historical Society, Cleveland, Ohio, for permission to reprint the Guilford reminiscence contained in mss. 484.

24. Clare Benedict, ed., *Constance Fenimore Woolson*, vol. 2 of *Five Generations (1785–1923)* (London: Ellis, 1930).

25. Rayburn S. Moore, too, neglects to mention Charlie's existence. The youngest Woolson sibling and only son, Charlie was evidently a ne'er-do-well, who received his literary incarnation as Ettie Macks's brother, John, in Woolson's "The Street of the Hyacinth." In a letter to Samuel Mather on 16 January 1884, Woolson writes of her anguish over her brother's death and her attending illness:

> I presume all came from the shock of Charlie's death,—which made me suffer more than I have ever suffered in my life. I was so extremely unhappy for a number of weeks that I did not know where to turn. Charley [*sic*] left behind a letter, or rather two— a sort of diary—which he had written at different times during the summer. The diary showed suffering so piteous that it broke my heart. I cannot imagine any suffering greater than his was, at the last. I will say no more. I know you were sincerely attached to him; & to all your family, he was most grateful, for the kind acts which gave the only gleam of pleasure he had, during those last years. This diary of his only reached

me, of course, after his death. I have destroyed it, as he requested. Strange and mysterious are the ties of blood. I had seen so little of Charlie since he grew to be a man; we had been separated for so many years; & yet his death—out there in California—has made me perfectly desolate.

—quoted in Torsney, *Constance Fenimore Woolson*, 161, n. 6

As evidenced by this letter, Woolson herself was unsure about the spelling of her brother's name, perhaps a revealing detail.

26. Fred Lewis Pattee, *A History of American Literature Since 1870* (New York: Century, 1915), 317–18.

27. Edward J. O'Brien, *The Advance of the American Short Story* (New York: Dodd, Mead, 1931), 163.

28. Pattee, 318. See also Kern.

29. Pattee, 318.

30. John Hervey, "Sympathetic Art," *Saturday Review of Literature*, 12 October 1929, 268.

31. See n. 9.

32. See n. 8.

33. See Lyon N. Richardson, "Constance Fenimore Woolson, 'Novelist Laureate' of America," *South Atlantic Quarterly* 39 (January 1940): 18–36; Van Wyck Brooks, *The Times of Melville and Whitman* (New York: Dutton, 1947), 341–51; Alexander Cowie, *The Rise of the American Novel* (New York: American Book Company, 1951), 568–78; Edward Wagenknecht, *Cavalcade of the American Novel: From the Birth of the Nation to the Middle of the Twentieth Century* (New York: Henry Holt, 1952), 173–77; and Jay B. Hubbell, *The South in American Literature, 1607–1900* (Durham, N.C.: Duke University Press, 1954), 735–37. All these assessments of Woolson's art appear in this volume except that by Van Wyck Brooks.

34. Cowie, 568.

35. Rayburn S. Moore, *Constance Fenimore Woolson* (New York: Twayne, 1963).

36. Robert L. White, "Cultural Ambivalence in Constance Fenimore Woolson's Italian Tales," *Tennessee Studies in Literature* 12 (1967): 121–29.

37. White, 122.

38. Anne E. Rowe, "Constance Woolson and Southern Local Color," in *The Enchanted Country: Northern Writers in the South 1865–1910* (Baton Rouge: Louisiana State University Press, 1978), 54–73.

39. Sybil B. Weir, "Southern Womanhood in the Novels of Constance Fenimore Woolson," *Mississippi Quarterly* 29 (1976), 565.

40. Weir, 568.

41. Torsney, "The Traditions of Gender." See n. 2.

42. Victoria Brehm, "Island Fortresses: The Landscape of the Imagination in the Great Lakes Fiction of Constance Fenimore Woolson," *American Literary Realism* 22 (1990): 51–66.

43. For an earlier interpretation of Woolson's characters' self-sacrificing natures, see Evelyn Thomas Helmick, "Constance Fenimore Woolson: First Novelist of Florida," in *Feminist Criticism: Essays on Theory, Poetry, and Prose*, eds. Cheryl L. Brown and Karen Olsen (Metuchen, N.J.: Scarecrow Press, 1978), 233–43. Helmick writes: "Such unattractive, if not improbable, martyrs are perhaps part of the reason Miss Woolson's work is seldom read today" (238).

44. Brehm, 55.

45. Cowie, 568.

46. See n. 2.

47. See, too, Sharon L. Dean, "Homeward Bound: The Novels of Constance Fenimore Woolson," *Legacy* 6 (Fall 1989): 17–28.

48. Woolson's letters to Paul Hamilton Hayne were edited and published by Jay B. Hubbell, "Some New Letters of Constance Fenimore Woolson," *New England Quarterly* 14

(December 1941): 715–35. Alice Hall Petry has edited her letters to John and Clara Hay. (see n. 13). Leon Edel has edited and reprinted Woolson's four extant letters to Henry James in *Henry James: Letters*, vol. 3 (Cambridge: Harvard University Press, 1980), 523–62. Still, no one has yet edited and made generally available the large cache of letters from Woolson to E. C. Stedman, housed at the Butler Library, Columbia University, or the even larger collection in the Mather Family Papers at the Western Reserve Historical Society, Cleveland, Ohio.

49. Brock, 34.

REVIEWS

Recent Literature [Review of *Castle Nowhere: Lake Country Sketches*]

[WILLIAM DEAN HOWELLS]

The Lake-Country which Miss Woolson sketches is the region of the great inland seas, Superior, Huron, Erie, and the rest, and the term is allowably stretched to include that part of Northern Ohio in which the community of the Zoar Separatists prosperously doze their lives away. The ground is new, and Miss Woolson gathers from it a harvest out of which the grain had not been threshed long ago. Our readers already know three of her stories, Solomon, The Lady of Little Fishing, and Wilhelmina, which are the best in this book, and fairly suggest its range, for it is now poetically realistic in circumstance like the first and last, and now poetically fanciful like the second. Both kinds rest upon the same solid basis—truth to human nature; and because Miss Woolson has distinctly felt the value of this basis, we are the more surprised at her projecting such an air-founded fabric as Castle Nowhere. In this we are asked to suppose a wretch who beacons lake schooners to shipwreck on the rocks, and plunders them that he may keep in luxury the young girl whom he has adopted for his daughter, and who lives in an inaccessible tower on a secret isle of the lake. A subtle confusion of all the conceptions of right and wrong is wrought by this old reprobate's devotion to the child, and his inability to feel that any means to her pleasure and comfort can be bad; but we doubt whether this is an intended effect, and if it is, we think it not worth the writer's or reader's pains. Castle Nowhere is the least satisfactory of the stories; one is harassed from beginning to end by a disagreeable fantasticality.

The notion, in Peter the Parson, of the poor little ritualist who lives a missionary among the ruffians of the Northwestern lumbering town, and daily reads the service to himself in his empty chapel, is altogether better, though we wish the matter were less sketchily treated. Miss Woolson had something in Rose's unrequited love for the parson, and the tragic end it brings him to, worthy her most patient and careful art. The Old Agency is another good sketch, or study, tasting racily of the strange time and place. It is the ancient government agency building at Mackinac, about which linger the memories of the Jesuit missions, and in which, after its desertion,

Reprinted from *Atlantic Monthly* 35 (June 1875): 736–37.

an old soldier of Napoleon comes to spend his last days: the story gains color from its supposed narration by the Jesuit father Piret; for the French have had the complaisance to touch our continent with romance wherever they have touched it at all as soldiers, priests, exiles, or mere adventurers. St. Clair Flats is apparently a transcript from the fact, and with its portraits of the strange prophet, Waiting Samuel, and his wife, it is a not at all discouraging example of what our strangely varied American real life can do in the way of romance; it seems only to need the long-denied opportunity in fiction which some of our later writers have afforded it—none with greater promise of a successful interpretation in certain ways than Miss Woolson herself. Her story of Solomon is really a triumph of its kind—a novel kind, as simple as it is fresh. The Zoar Community, with its manners and customs, and that quaint mingling of earthy good-feeling and mild, coarse kindliness with forms of austere religious and social discipline, which seems to characterize all the peculiar German sectarians, has had the fortune to find an artist in the first who introduces us to its life. Solomon's character is studied with a delicate and courageous sympathy, which spares us nothing of his grotesqueness, and yet keenly touches us with his pathetic history. An even greater success of literary art is his poor, complaining wife, the faded parody of the idol of his young love, still beautiful in his eyes, and the inspiration of all his blind, unguided efforts in painting. His death, after the first instruction has revealed his powers to himself, is affectingly portrayed, without a touch of sentimentalistic insistence. It is a very complete and beautiful story. Wilhelmina, of which the scene is also at Zoar, is not quite so good; and yet it is very well done, too. Perhaps the reader's lurking sense of its protractedness dulls his pleasure in it. But it is well imagined, of new material, and skillfully wrought. The Lady of Little Fishing is as fine, in its different way, as Solomon. That is a very striking and picturesque conceit, of the beautiful religious enthusiast who becomes a sort of divinity to the wild, fierce fur-hunters among whom she pitches her tent, and who loses her divine honors by falling in love with one of them; and all the processes of this romance and its catastrophe are revealed with dramatic skill and force. It argues a greater richness in our fictitious literature than we have been able to flatter ourselves upon, or a torpidity in our criticism which we fear we must acknowledge, that such a story should not have made a vivid impression. It has that internal harmony which is the only allegiance to probability we can exact from romance, and it has a high truth to human nature never once weakened by any vagueness of the moral ideal in the author,—as happens with Mr. Harte's sketches, the only sketches with which we should care to compare it.

[Review of *Two Women*]

ANONYMOUS

It is not our custom to review at considerable length single poems or papers published in the magazines, except when there is that in them which renders their publication a matter of general interest. In the poem "Two Women," the first half of which appeared in the January number of *Appleton's Journal*, and the last half of which has just now come to us in the February number of that magazine, there is something, we think, which takes the piece out of the category of ordinary magazine work, and entitles it to special attention.[1] The poem is long enough, for one thing, to fill a little volume, if it were printed as it is the custom to print books of poetry; and while it is rugged, faulty, and in many respects defective, it is nevertheless strong, dramatic and full of the flavor of the soil. The two women who give it its name are types of two well defined classes of American women, but they are sharply drawn as individuals also, and their characters are presented with a boldness and a degree of distinctness which is possible only at the hands of a writer of very considerable dramatic power.

The style of the poem, the metre and the use of certain stiff forms of speech by the distinctively modern personages of the story, have the effect, in the first part of the poem, to give it an air of restraint, almost of stilted affectation, but as the emotions which are brought into play grow steadily more intense, this apparent incongruity disappears, and the reader accepts the form as altogether natural and fit. . . .

In writing thus of the poem with extracts from it, we are conscious of letting its chief beauty slip through our fingers. It is the dramatic quality of the piece which gives it value and that can be shown only in the poem as a whole. The faults with which it abounds—and some of them are serious ones—are emphasized in extracts, of necessity, but there are hints enough here of dramatic strength and fine character drawing to tempt the reader to read the whole piece, and it is with this purpose that we have written of it at so great length.

The poem is published anonymously, and it is hazardous to guess at its authorship perhaps; but no reader can read the story, we think, without

Reprinted from *New York Evening Post*, 15 January 1877. This review is pasted inside the cover of Woolson's personal copy of *Two Women*, in the archives of Olin Library, Rollins College, Winter Park, Florida.

discovering a near kinship between this piece of dramatic portraiture and the superb "Lake Country Sketches" which Miss Constance Fenimore Woolson published a year or two ago. The hand that sketched "The Lady of Little Fishing," "Peter the Parson," and the maiden of "Castle Nowhere" may well have painted this picture also. There are points of resemblance, too, between the prose stories and this poetic one, which strongly confirm our suspicion, and the blue-grass country, so lovingly dwelled upon here, has inspired Miss Woolson's verse on former occasions. Let us hope, at least, that "Two Women" is her work, the more because it may prompt many persons who have not yet given to the "Lake Country Sketches" the attention which they deserve to turn to them now, and make the acquaintance there of some of the very finest short stories recently published—stories as original, as fresh and as dramatic as Bret Harte's are.

Note

1. *Two Women* was published in a single volume by *Appleton's* later in 1877.

Editor's Table [Review of *Two Women*]

[E. L. BURLINGAME?][1]

The publication in book-form of Miss Constance Fenimore Woolson's poem, "Two Women," which attracted such wide attention upon its appearance in the JOURNAL last winter, makes the introduction here of an acute criticism, by one of our accomplished men of letters, timely and proper: . . .

It is safe to say that very few even of the most careless readers have read the poem without feeling in it a force and strength beyond the common, and wholly different from the common. It is equally safe to say that very few have not been struck by faults and crudenesses which they did not generally stop to define, but which were obviously present in such numbers as to have a distinct after-effect upon the whole. The sense of strength comes first; but it is not left unmingled. . . .

Miss Woolson has the strong desire—the instinct—of the artist, to get at the humanity under the conventionalities, whatever they are; to show, indeed, how independent it is of all conventionalities; to make these so subordinate to it as to show that in the light of a great human purpose or passion every surrounding takes on a hue from it—even becomes informed with its spirit, and loses for the time a disagreeable or obtrusive identity, to become part and parcel of an absorbing *action*. . . .

It is this intense artistic instinct which gives Miss Woolson a power that we perhaps estimate too highly, yet on which we should not hesitate to base a prophecy, were one needed for her. It has enabled her to put into the light and detached work that she has thus far done a strength such as has not informed any woman's writing, that we remember in some years of American magazine literature; and a force and freshness that has belonged to but a few men in that time. It is this trait that makes this first ambitious poem of hers a true poem, and that has made many eyes turn to her with renewed interest in possibilities which her former work suggested, and this has so strongly confirmed.

And having said this much—having registered our hearty belief in her powers, and in the likelihood of their fruition—it is with no spirit of carping, and with no coldness, that we go back to our opinion that it is an exaggerated or uncontrolled use of the method to which this very instinct leads, that is

Excerpted and reprinted from *Appleton's Journal* 2 (June 1877): 570–571.

the source of Miss Woolson's faults in this poem, as well as (in less degree) in the prose we have had from her before. . . .

The melody of Miss Woolson's verse suffers, too, from the exaggeration of her healthy contempt for the conventionalities. She will not polish or elaborate, but will let her thought, where it spoke out strongly, stand in its first crude expression rather than risk weakening it by change. In a very great degree her principle is right; a carping fastidiousness in these things is undoubtedly among the sins of the time, and has robbed us of no little strength.

It is not easy for a sincere critic to point at faults without presenting himself in the character of a man who, when he sees anything exceptionally strong and full of promise, immediately begins to pry after its weaknesses and littlenesses. Yet, to our mind, it would be hard to give a more real token of admiration for all Miss Woolson's powers, than to show how keenly they aroused us to wonder what element it was that kept their expression from being wholly complete and strong. The suggestions made may be right or wrong; but there is too much of the artist in the author of the poem to regard candid criticism upon it as other than a tribute to its promise. If there is the true poet in Miss Woolson, advice is superfluous which tells her that no time, no care, no earnest thought or labor, is too much to spend in perfecting her work; and that every flaw upon it should be more carefully studied, more diligently guarded against, than if it disfigured only mediocrity.

Note

1. This review, pasted inside the cover of Woolson's personal copy of *Two Women*, in the archives of the Olin Library, Rollins College, Winter Park, Florida, is unsigned. The name E. L. Burlingame, an editorial figure of the age, appears in Woolson's hand at the top of the clipping. Thus, although I cannot verify who was responsible for writing the Editor's Table, we can infer that Woolson knew who reviewed her long poem. *CBT*

Miss Woolson's "Two Women"

ANONYMOUS

Miss Woolson has won for herself an enviable place among the magazine writers of the day by her graceful stories. The demands upon her for these have been so great that she has for the past four or five years been kept hard at work, and her sketches are to be found in all the leading magazines. But those who know Miss Woolson are aware that her inclinations tend toward poetry rather than tale-writing.[1] In fact, in all her stories there are poetic touches and these give them their especial charm. But she cannot write poetry "to order," and the urgent appeals of the most pertinacious editor cannot draw from her a poem when she is not in the mood. Nor will she allow a poem to pass from her hands until it has been revised again and again with a pencil that has "her heart in it." Such of her poems as have been given to the public—especially those of a narrative character—have attained wide circulation. In all of them the dramatic element is strong. The late Charlotte Cushman,[2] having met with two or three of Miss Woolson's poems in the magazines, was so struck with this quality that, without having the slightest knowledge of the author until some time afterward, she used them in her "Readings" and always with great success.

Notes

1. Woolson actually preferred reading and writing fiction and criticism to poetry (see "Introduction," n. 4). In a letter dated 20 December 1890, she confided to her friend John Hay: "I have all my life, until recently, been in too much of a hurry to love poetry. Now I find myself going back to it as a cordial and peace giver" (Alice Hall Petry, " 'Always, Your Attached Friend': The Unpublished Letters of Constance Fenimore Woolson to John and Clara Hay," *Books at Brown* 29–30 (1982–1983), 102).
2. Charlotte Cushman (1816–1876), a gifted and renowned American actress, performed both male and female roles in America and Europe.

Excerpted and reprinted from *Cleveland Morning Herald*. This newspaper, edited by George A. Benedict, the father-in-law of Clara Woolson Benedict, Woolson's sister, provided Woolson with several early publication opportunities in the form of anonymous columns about the New York scene published between December 1870 and February 1871. This review, too, was apparently saved by Woolson, in the pages of her personal copy of *Two Women*, in the archives of Olin Library, Rollins College, Winter Park, Florida.

[Review of *Rodman the Keeper: Southern Sketches*]

Anonymous

The sketches—for so Miss Woolson modestly styles them—collected in this volume place their author in the first rank of writers in this line; nay, we know of no writer, English or American, whose short stories are so rich in description, so strong in their delineations of character, so opulent in narrative or dramatic interest, and so truly poetic in their settings and surroundings. Indeed, each of them is a genuine poem, noteworthy for the subtle delicacy of its fancy and for the weird and artistic indefiniteness of its dénouement.

Excerpted and reprinted from *Harper's New Monthly Magazine* 61 (June 1880): 153.

[Review of *Rodman the Keeper: Southern Sketches*]

[B. PHILLIPS]

Miss Woolson is perfectly familiar with Southern life and scenery. The faculty of describing locality may be easily acquired, but where the author shows real genius is in that finer appreciation of Southern women. Miss Woolson evinces a very touching sympathy for her Southern sisters, who, after the war, were often placed in the saddest plights, and what the author has written about them is full of tender grace.

Excerpted and reprinted from *New York Times*, 11 June 1880, 3. The reviewer can be identified by an unpublished letter in the Lee Kohns Memorial Collection of the New York Public Library dated 16 August [1880] in which Woolson thanks the recipient for the favorable review.

Some Recent Novels
[Review of *Rodman the Keeper: Southern Sketches*]

[Thomas Sergeant Perry]

Miss Woolson's volume of short stories about Southern life is an interesting proof of the abundance of unused material in our unwieldy country, that is simply awaiting the novelist to put it into shape and give it standing. Florida and South Carolina are the regions that have inspired this author, and the local coloring is well given. At times, however, some of the people who are introduced give the reader quite as much an impression of strangeness as does any wonder of semi-tropical vegetation; and this we must regret, for the writer of fiction should above everything set people before us whom we can at least understand. The cantrips of Miss Gardis Duke, for instance, which are only matched by the scornful airs of Miss Bettina Ward, the minx-like heroine of Rodman the Keeper, read like what one finds oftener in poor novels than in real life. This young person, Miss Duke, is a little chit, who, in extreme poverty, imitates the splendors of her former opulence, and gives the rough edge of her saucy tongue to two of her lovers, Union officers, who just after the late war are stationed near her house. She invites them to dinner, and then, when they are gone, she burns up the shabby finery in which she had received them. " 'So perish also the enemies of my country!' she said to herself." Certainly, this little cat is not a very impressive person, and it is not easy to interest one's self in such a lump of affectation; but Miss Woolson seems to take her at her own pompous valuation, and to see heroism in her imitation of tawdry novels. Finally, she steps down from her pinnacle of conceit, and marries one of the officers, and we have no doubt that by this time she has satisfactorily taken vengeance for everything that happened during the war.

Sister St. Luke, after a tornado has swamped the boat in which were two young men, sees them clinging to a distant reef. As ignorant of the art of navigation as of the game of baccarat, she wades through water waist-deep, gets into a little boat, and sails out to them in a terrible wind. This

Excerpted and reprinted from *Atlantic Monthly* 46 (July 1880): 124–25.

she does although morbidly timid. In fact, she could more easily have thrown a hawser a mile or two and have hauled them in to shore.

King David, on the other hand, is a life-like account of the sufferings of a Yankee school-master among the freedmen, whom he in vain tries to educate. In this sketch there is no exaggeration; no inclination toward the use of melodramatic devices, such as are only too apt to make their appearance in the other stories. Miss Woolson certainly deserves credit for her perception of the picturesque contrasts that the South affords. She has at least pointed out a region where much can be done, and where she can herself do good work if she will keep "closer to the record."

Southern Sketches

ANONYMOUS

The word "Sketches," which the author gives them, by no means does justice to the careful study and fine finish that have gone into their workmanship. She [Woolson] is a genuine artist, and knows just how to bring her material into attractive shape. Her insight is keen, her touch firm but delicate; her sense of fitness so sure, her critical faculties so trained, that she sees instinctively what to write and what to leave unwritten, and the result is—the kind of stories that people like to read. . . . They are all of the South, and though the writer is a Northern woman they more thoroughly represent the South as it is than anything of the kind that has been written since the war. Not the political aspect, nor the questions that have vexed the very atmosphere of the country; but the present desolation, the depression, the pathos, the loss and the anguish, the wounded pride, the ruined homes, the stricken hearts.

Excerpted and reprinted from *Literary World* (Boston), 3 July 1880, 223.

Miss Woolson's "Rodman the Keeper"

Anonymous

Poetry and rhetoric are not necessarily antagonistic elements; but in a mind where they are not perfectly fused they are apt to interfere sadly with each other. Thus, in Miss Woolson's "Southern Sketches," a rhetorical vein appears every now and then and spoils the illusion produced by the vividly poetic descriptions of Southern life and scenery. We dare not positively assert that Southern girls, when wrought up sufficiently, may not make use of such hollow phrases as the following: "Shall I forget these things? Never! Sooner let my right hand wither by my side!" etc., but if they do, they are not so genuine in their grief or in their wrath as Miss Woolson would have us believe. So, also, when that semi-savage little mongrel Felipa, a girl of twelve who wears a boy's trowsers, remarks, apropos of these same trowsers: "The son of Pedro being dead *at a convenient age*, and his clothes fitting me, what would you have? It was a chance not to be despised,"—we are again incredulous. It is *per se* a delightful little touch, but it is utterly untrue. The humorous idea that Pedro's son died just at the proper age to bequeath his trowsers to her, or rather the consciousness of its being humorous, which is plainly indicated in the above quotation, implies a complexity of thought which is out of keeping with Felipa's primitive nature. In the case of Felipa, however (who is a charming creature, or, we rather suspect, a charmingly elaborated sketch from some living original), this is the only lapse from psychological realism. The passionate attachment of the little savage to the beautiful, fair-skinned Northern lady, her hunger for praise and her resolute despair at being repulsed, are in themselves very pathetic, and the pathos is nowise weakened by the half-humorous manner in which the story is related. . . .

The most artistically complete of these ten stories is "Miss Elizabeth," which abounds in delightful situations. Miss Daarg's interview with the prima donna is especialy [*sic*] admirable. "Rodman the Keeper" strikes us as being a little superfluously fantastic in some of its minor details; thus, for instance, we cannot help smiling at Rodman's heroism in refraining from smoking because his fourteen thousand comrades under the sod could not partake of the same enjoyment. The best writing (if

Excerpted and reprinted from *Scribner's Monthly Magazine* 20 (August 1880): 633–34.

comparisons were not so odious) is probably to be found in the "South Devil," which is brilliantly tropical and lingers long in the memory. In fact, the whole book makes a strong impression and refuses to be forgotten.

[Review of *Anne*]

ANONYMOUS

This book seems to be written with the purpose of reviving the plot, which is fast going out of date in the modern novel. *Anne* is a story in which something happens. Indeed, so much happens, and there are so many people to whom it is happening, that the first impression is one not unlike that received by a traveler who objected to Milan Cathedral on the ground that it had so many spires. His mind carried away more detail than cathedral. We think better of this hesitation, however, and find the story, as a whole, harmonious and clear. It begins with remarkable vigor. We would rather not say, if we could help it, that the finale does not sustain the promise. No one sketches so firmly and freshly as Miss Woolson the lake country life, its pathetic solitudes, its unsung poetry. Some of the finest work done in America has been done by her hand. She dropped below her own originality when she brought us back to the summer boarding-houses, when she murdered the heroine's rivals, and led us reluctantly through the sensational scenes of a court-room and the columns of New York reporters. Let her leave such things to Wilkie Collins, or perhaps to less than he. She has better to do. To one point more we must demur a little. We should wish for a writer of her force and growing influence a diminished acquaintance with or interest in the tricky [*sic*] of her own sex. Her women dress for dinners and flirt after tea. They tell of their "offers" and make small secret of their unrequited affections. Woman is the hunter, man is the game, and to hound him down by organized fascination makes life worth living. . . . The best thing about the story is its clear and fearless delineation of the action of a great passion upon a perfectly sincere nature. Anne is as true as a magnet, and as constant as the tides, not only because she has a more even temperament than the other women, but because she is more natural. Her confession of love at the end of the trial of her lover, when that confession alone can save his life, is an original and powerful stroke. Her reply when, by a cruel combination of chances, temptation is added to the exigencies of her lot, has the magnificent morality of honesty, beside which the little pretense and evasion of mere virtue is a poor thing.

Excerpted and reprinted from *Literary World* (Boston), 15 July 1882, 227.

[Review of *Anne*]

ANONYMOUS

Indeed, seldom has any biographer traced the personal and mental development of a real individual and the influences that contributed to it with greater minuteness and fidelity to life than they have been traced by Miss Woolson in the case of the ideal Anne. The result is a consistency and continuity of character that leaves us in no doubt as to her personal identity. Anne is always Anne. Strong, pure, loving, faithful, and true in her early girlhood, so she ever remains; self-sacrifice, self-surrender, and a protecting care for others were her earliest and her latest characteristics; the budding virtues that with her rare beauty and grand physique constituted the charm and promise of her childhood, grew with her years and expanded with her growth, and became the crown and glory of her noble womanhood. If we thus insensibly find ourselves thinking and speaking of Anne as if she were "a being breathing thoughtful breath," it is due to the glamour of Miss Woolson's art, which stamps the impression of reality on incident and character, and invests the persons of her creations with genuine human qualities and attributes.

Excerpted and reprinted from *Harper's New Monthly Magazine* 65 (August 1882): 478.

Miss Woolson's "Anne"

ANONYMOUS

Though Anne is not a brilliant woman, nor at first beautiful, yet interest never flags in her and her fate,—not even in the uninspiring surroundings of fashionable people at a country resort. It is true that the opening chapters are the freshest and most charming; the scene is so new and so admirably portrayed. Somehow, Miss Woolson can introduce old turns of plot and yet not offend. There is the heroic conduct of Anne on the brow of the precipice. There is the old plot of a wonderful voice that develops in the heroine. We wonder how many women writers there are who can resist giving their heroine a wonderful voice! But these are incidents—they do not sway the movement of the plot seriously. The real reason for Miss Woolson's impunity is that she puts them in a new way. Altogether, the appearance of "Anne" may be regarded as a fact worth special notice. For Miss Woolson adds to her observation of scenes and localities an unusual insight into the human heart. Sometimes one is ready to say that a fragment, and not an inferior fragment, of the mantle of George Eliot is resting on her capable shoulders.

Excerpted and reprinted from *Century Magazine* 24 (August 1882): 630.

Recent Novels
[Review of *Anne*]

ANONYMOUS

'Anne' will be pronounced a convincing proof that the author's forte is the short story, not the novel. It is, in fact, but a succession of short stories linked together by the presence of the one central figure of Anne herself, but with no logical dependence one upon the other. Change the names, and the successive stages of the wandering plot might each stand by itself. The first half-dozen chapters of the book are indeed remarkable. It was a rare opportunity to have discovered so new a field, in the little lonely military station on the far island of the North. In one sense only a colony, and yet already provided with a past in the traditions of the great fur-trading company and of the deserted mission, its little handful of strangely contrasted people afforded unique material for fiction. The comedy or the tragedy of life there must be on a narrow scale, but it suggests combinations and possibilities quite beyond the common routine of American novels. Miss Woolson has unfortunately given it to us only in a few fragmentary sketches, and carries off her heroine to the very commonplace scenes of city boarding-schools and country boarding-houses, to suffer under the tyranny, equally commonplace, of a grim maiden aunt. Even then there was a chance for fine discriminating work in showing how the world would look to the eyes of a clear-headed girl coming to it from such a simple, unconventional life, but the author only chooses to heap incident upon incident till nothing short of murder will suffice for a climax. That the book will not bear looking at as a whole is a fault not solely of American novels. Too few show careful plan from beginning to end, or in the balance of each part with all others.

Excerpted and reprinted from *Nation*, 31 August 1882, 182.

[Review of *For the Major: A Novelette*]

ANONYMOUS

By confining herself to much narrower limits than in "Anne" this, the most promising of our women novelists, has made "For the Major" a complete and well-balanced story, without weaknesses and with a gradual leading up to the explanation of the plot. Miss Woolson excels in drawing the character of women who are thoroughly charming and yet not too good "for human nature's daily food"; and here again we find in Sara Carroll a young lady who has her brusque side and her unaccountable aversions, her arrogance, if you will, and her apparent lack of heart, but who is nevertheless most delightfully true to the best that one finds in the best of women. In the step-mother, Mme. Carroll, the little foibles of women that men make the most sport of, such as artificial enhancement of the looks, are by a stroke of true genius attributed to the dutiful desire of a wife to keep herself just as her husband wants to find her. It may be said that, commonly speaking, women dress fashionably, rouge, and dye their hair for other women more than for men, since it is the women, not the men, whose criticisms they fear and whose tribute of praise they oftenest receive; but Miss Woolson shows a woman whose efforts in that way are truly and only "for the Major." For Major Carroll, the ex-Confederate and small magnate of Edgerley, lives also his daughter Sara, a finer, higher, firmer character than his second wife, but not more interesting. The simple story of the gradual bereavement of his mind is told with the utmost fineness and pathos; the coming of a good-for-nothing son of Mme. Carroll by an earlier marriage is managed so as to excite curiosity without anticipating the truth. Sara's complication through his means is natural and original. Perhaps we could have wished for her a more decidedly individual husband than the Rev. Frederick Owen, but the future of curates is conventionally safe, and the naturalness is not impaired by the wedding between the one charming girl of a Southern village and the one irreproachable, and yet intelligent and cultivated, young man. Some very delightful touches describing the Edgerley folks generally—like and yet unlike people of the Middle States—justify those who see many points of analogy between Miss Woolson and the late George Eliot. "For the Major" has none of the

Reprinted from *New York Times*, 16 June 1883, 3.

brilliant descriptive chapters of "Anne"; it is not so ambitious a story, yet its roundness, ease, and spiritual beauty raise it above the level of the longer novel. Apparently more trifling, it is really a better piece of literary work.

[Review of *For the Major*]

Anonymous

Miss Woolson's new story, *For the Major*, will be an agreeable surprise to her admirers because of its revelation of the increased range of her powers. In *Anne* she had exhibited the culmination of the phenomenal realistic power of which there had been large promise in her previous efforts; but in it, as in them, there was a lack of that rich imaginativeness and nice sense of artistic proportion (or perhaps we should say a disregard for them) which are essential elements of the higher forms of romantic fiction. Not so in *For the Major*. For while it is to the full as realistic as *Anne*, it manifests a quality of the imagination that is not visible in that fine tale—a certain psychological clairvoyance which enables the author to place herself so completely *en rapport* with her imaginary creations as to merge her identity in theirs, and to reflect their individuality in what seems their most contradictory and at first glance inexplicable motives and actions. In other respects, also, although it may not be pronounced as "of imagination all compact," the imaginative power predominates. Moreover, its accessories are disposed with a more perfect regard to art than in *Anne*, and its actors are placed in situations which are less strained, and are productive of more poetic and more impressive effects. The portrait of Madame Carroll, whose character and motives are left sufficiently enigmatical at the outset to pique the curiosity and baffle the penetration of the reader, but which develop with the progress of the story into a subtle and very beautiful illustration of the strength that exists in weakness, is one of the most original and most perfect conceptions in modern literature, though not sufficiently exaggerated, perhaps, to win the popular recognition and favor that have been accorded to such skillful exaggerations as Mrs. Nickleby, Sarah Gamp, the Marchioness, and Becky Sharp. If Woolson would rival the popularity of the great artists in that field of character-painting, she must learn like them to heighten nature by that shrewd touch of exaggeration which they so well know how to apply. Doubtless she will prefer, as we think most wisely, to continue to depict character without recourse to the easy device of exaggerating its peculiarities, and will be satisfied to develop her powers in the line of her own native genius.

Reprinted from *Harper's New Monthly Magazine* 67 (July 1883): 316–17.

American Fiction by Women
[Review of *For the Major*]

[HORACE SCUDDER]

The story is a very ingenious one, and skillfully managed. The reader, at the critical moment when he would naturally turn impatiently away from this very artificial woman, is drawn to her by the revelation of her redeeming quality. In fact, the reader and the stepdaughter are in much the same category, only that the daughter is in the secret before the reader is. It is, however, the ingenuity of the story which makes the strongest impression upon the mind, and thus one is led to doubt if the whole conception be not too artificial to be thoroughly good art. We noticed in Anne something of the same tendency in Miss Woolson to make too much of the machinery of her stories, and we hope that it will not increase in her work. With a good story, built upon the large lines of nature, Miss Woolson would have more leisure to give to the realization of her characters, and the reality would be more enduring because more natural.

Excerpted and reprinted from *Atlantic Monthly* 52 (July 1883): 119–21.

Recent Novels
[Review of *For the Major*]

Anonymous

It was skilful art to put the young lovers a little out of the centre of the picture, to keep them back from the foreground; but the closing chapter is a mistake. The repetition of the marriage ceremony with an uncomprehending old man is a theatrical incident out of keeping in a story otherwise so well balanced. If it were actually necessary, then it upsets the whole plot, for no law recognizes the deed of an imbecile. It is made out as a satisfaction to Mme. Carroll's own feeling, but that does not help the matter. A woman might have her fancies, but the rector should have been able to convince her, on the one side, that, sincerely believing herself a widow, she had been purely and truly married in the sight of God; and, on the other, that no law of man would be satisfied by a clergyman's blessing given in a bed-chamber without certificate and without witnesses. Better to have left her, as the world believed her, a true and faithful wife.

Excerpted and reprinted from *Nation*, 9 August 1883, 120.

For the Major

ANONYMOUS

It will readily be conceded that *For the Major* is its author's most perfect production. After one has finished reading it, the temptation is strong to go back and take further note of the delicate humor, and those touches, slight but full of meaning, which show how close an observer she is, even in so small a matter as this of a breezy morning, when, "on the many knolls of Far Edgerley the tall grass, *carrying with it the slender stalks of the buttercups*, was bending," etc. For a specimen of fine individualizing, what could be better than the description of Sara? And for crystalline clearness of style, the two pages where that quaint, old-world child, Scar, who reminds us of one of Sir Joshua Reynolds's child-portraits, comes in? If *Anne* placed the author in the highest rank among women writers of today, *For the Major* gives further proof of her right to be there.

Excerpted and reprinted from *Literary World* (Boston), 11 August 1883, 261.

East Angels

ANONYMOUS

It must be owned that at first the unnatural calmness of the rare, pale Margaret was exasperating, and we were half ready to wish that she might for once lose her balance; but when the nobility of her brave, indomitable spirit began to dawn upon us, we felt that here was a woman whom no appeals of passion would swerve one hair's breadth from rectitude. Renouncing self, and knowing what desolation and heart-hunger must be her portion, she stands for the sanctity of the marriage obligation which she took upon herself, and holds it sacred, though her husband has set it at naught and made the bondage almost unbearable. Miss Woolson's treatment of this subject is a scathing rebuke to the many authors who have made marital infidelity, separation, and elopements their favorite theme—bringing all their sophistry and special pleading to bear on the case by way of excuse or palliation. . . .

Merely as a story *East Angels* is admirable; as fine in its workmanship as *For the Major*, it is yet a long way in advance of that; in some respects resembling *Anne*, it is fortunately without the sensational element which toward the close was such a blemish and disappointment in that book; for its pure, moral atmosphere, its discriminating portraiture, its picturesqueness and coloring, its mellowness and tranquility, and its literary finish, we must regard *East Angels* as Miss Woolson's best novel.

Excerpted and reprinted from *Literary World* (Boston), 24 July 1886, 243.

Recent Novels by Women
[Review of *East Angels*]

[HORACE SCUDDER]

In Miss Woolson we have a novelist of another order. It is not merely that the material in which she works is different; she is a casuist in her morality. Her latest novel is a study of interesting cases, and she expends a wealth of incident in conversation in setting the cases before the reader, so that there may be no element in the problem not fairly taken into account. Her anxiety to get in all the evidence, and to get it in dramatically, leads her, we think, into excess of invention. In this story of East Angels, two characters, for example, Middleton Moore and Manuel, are not only superfluous, they are in the way. Her conversations are needlessly repetitious; we could get at the relations of people to each other without the endless variations upon these relations. It sometimes seems as if Miss Woolson had made careful studies of all the doings and sayings of her characters, and then could not bear to relinquish this or that clever passage, and so had printed everything, instead of selecting those scenes which were typical, and making them tell the story.

There are also certain artistic laws which she presses too hard. The law of contrast, for instance, so valuable in a sharp definition of character, is used by her to a somewhat exhausting extent. Garda's husband dies apparently for no other reason than to give new opportunities for the contrast of Garda with Margaret, and Adolfo and Manuel are constantly bringing out each other's colors. Everywhere is shown a lack of reserve power; the situations are stretched to their utmost capacity, and though there is a prodigality of interesting detail, the reader cannot help wishing that the author had spared herself somewhat, and not been so scrupulous in her art. We can almost imagine Miss Woolson throwing herself back in her chair, upon the completion of the task, and saying, I am nearly worn out, but not one of you can say I have neglected you.

And yet, when we come to the heart of the story, when we consider the relation which Evert Winthrop, Margaret, and Garda bear to each other, we cannot help feeling that Miss Woolson's naturalness of manner and carefulness of art have failed in making us really believe in the situation. This Undine of a Garda is a little too incredible. We may not lay our finger

Excerpted and reprinted from *Atlantic Monthly* 59 (February 1887): 267–68.

upon any one weak spot in Miss Woolson's construction of her, but she is too perfectly irresponsible to be altogether true. For one thing, we believe such a nature would have had a more distinct infusion of passion. Then the heroism of Margaret has a tension which impresses us painfully. We do not ask that she should be less noble and self-sacrificing, but that the reader should not be made quite so uncomfortable at sight of her. Nor do we think that Winthrop's behavior toward her is any more the outcome of his nature than is hers toward him. She hides herself from him with a persistency which does not deceive the reader, and could not deceive Winthrop; he rushes at her in a style which irritates the reader even more than it disturbs Margaret. The real manliness which we have no doubt he possessed would have made him stop short of such petulance of passion as he betrays.

In brief, Miss Woolson in her over-anxiety to elaborate her characters has missed, it seems to us, the more obvious laws of their being; the result is a highly refined artificiality of sentiment, which scarcely consists with the admirable naturalness of those scenes in which no profound intention lurks. Little by little the book is built up; it is immensely clever in its separate passages; the minor characters, who have no great moral exigency to serve, are delightfully truthful; the negroes are hit off with great dexterity, and the crane becomes a real *dramatis persona* by virtue of his distinctness of character. It is only when one comes to regard the novel as a whole that one feels how ingenuity has been racked, and casuistry made to take the place of clear, honest, generous handling of human relationships. We are reluctant to believe that Miss Woolson is going to refine away her unquestionable power, and strain her art into forced service. Certainly we do not fear that she ever will fall into careless ways. She has secured great pliability of workmanship; why can she not use this power in some swiftly accomplished tale, where the quickness of movement will save her from undue subtlety of motive?

A Romance of Florida
[Review of *East Angels*]

Anonymous

You go to Florida when you read "East Angels," and pass your day in lazy bliss at Gracias á Dios. You look over the snow-white belt of sand at the blue sea, and watch the pelicans plunging into the water, or overhead follow the man-of-war birds or the curlews winging their way, or you saunter inland through the pine barrens, the ground all carpeted with the brown spines, with their clumps of palmetto and palms, or if you be on the side of the lagoon you gaze at the forests of impenetrable mangroves. . . .

Perhaps "East Angels" is a trifle long, longer than is absolutely necessary, and this not so much due to elaboration as a repetition of incidents, but it is for all that the work of a most accomplished artist. We do not know, however, whether Miss Woolson's success is as great in an extended romance as in a more compact one.

Reprinted from *New York Times*, 6 June 1886, 3.

Editor's Study
[Review of *East Angels*]

[William Dean Howells]

Of the ladies of East Angels several are freshly and singularly charming, whom the reader will like if he is a man, and there is at least one very heroic, whom she may adore if she is a woman. Margaret Harold, martyr-wife of that chief of scapegraces Lansing Harold, is a figure that ought to console such of her sex as have heart-hungered for grand and perfect women in fiction perhaps ever since George Eliot drew Romola. She not only dedicates her life to the invalided age of the unloved husband who has insulted her by the precept as well as the example of gross indifference, she not only very rightly drives from her the man she loves, but she proposes to the young widow who jilted him that she shall try to get him back and marry him, and promises that their children shall be a consolation to her. If this is not enough for the worshippers of grand and perfect women, we cannot imagine what they want more.

For ourselves we will confess that it is too much, and that we are better satisfied with the man who guesses this plan for his consolation, and finds it revolting, though he is too much in love with Margaret Harold to feel its absurdity. It was perhaps the supposed necessity of keeping the chief person exemplary and sublime which caused the error. Neither Margaret nor Winthrop her lover appeals to our sympathy, perhaps because we cannot believe in them; they form for us the one false note of the book. . . .[1]

Garda is a masterpiece, and the triumph of the book. For our own selfish pleasure we prefer a novel where there is less going and coming, and there are fewer people, and the webs of so many different lives are not intertangled. Yet we are obliged to own that the small isolated group is less life-like, and that if Miss Woolson can paint a multitude of figures so well, that is a sufficient reason for her introducing them. The story is full of delightful moments, of interesting moments, and there are great moments in it. But, above all, there is, except in the heroine, the respect for probability, the fidelity to conditions, human and social, which

Excerpted and reprinted from *Harper's New Monthly Magazine* 73 (August 1886): 477–78.

can alone justify the reading or writing of novels; there is the artistic conscience, and the other conscience without which art is merely pernicious.

Note

1.   See Introduction, n. 13.

[Review of *East Angels*]

Anonymous

In 'East Angels' there is nothing so fresh or remarkable as are the opening scenes of Miss Woolson's 'Anne.' The movement is intentionally languid, fitted to the surrounding, but, through a too scrupulous regard for conformity, the effect on the reader is similar to that wrought upon the heroine, Garda, by the sight of her hammock in the tropical afternoon—it invites drowsiness. Little penetration is needed to discover some of the reasons why a novel with so many pleasant pages is tedious, requiring in the reading a mental effort which is not repaid. The unfolding rose is a more interesting object for contemplation than the perfect flower; the bud that in spite of anxious care should continue to be a bud, refusing either to bloom or to die, must eventually excite irritation or indifference. . . . Garda Thorne is the perpetual bud. On first acquaintance she piques curiosity; even if the author does not suggest possibilities of development, the reader instinctively looks ahead with expectation. But Garda passes through the fires of life, her selfishness unimpaired, her capacity for sleep undiminished, and, though it is not mentioned, probably fulfils the only possibility of young girlhood which we all scorn to contemplate—grows fat. In the delineation of these characters, it is clear that Miss Woolson understands what she means to do, and the fault is comparative worthlessness of design, not defective execution. In representing the passionless, shallow, selfish Garda as a child of the South and of Nature, she is perhaps at fault; aside from her habit of dozing in the sun, Garda is a daughter of the long-conventionalized North.

Excerpted and reprinted from *Nation*, 11 November 1886, 396–97.

Editor's Study [Review of *Castle Nowhere: Lake Country Sketches* and *Rodman the Keeper: Southern Sketches*]

[WILLIAM DEAN HOWELLS]

The reader of Miss C. F. Woolson's short stories, lately reprinted in two volumes, must have felt the mastery which she shows in them: and perhaps pausing from the pathos of "Solomon" or "Wilhelmina," or from the fascination of "The South Devil," he may have let his thoughts run to the vast amount of work which other Americans have done in that kind. This work, indeed, is so great in quantity and so excellent in quality that we are tempted to claim a national primacy in short-story writing; and we do not easily content ourselves with the belief that we have merely done better in writing short stories than in writing long ones. The rest of mankind might dispute our claim, and our novelists, but for the modesty native in novelists, might refuse our conclusion as injurious. We will not insist upon either; perhaps neither is true; and if this is the case, we should like to hold Miss Woolson's charming volumes responsible for both. One of her books groups under the title of *Castle Nowhere* nine stories of the great lake country, from the southern shores of Erie to the further coasts of Superior; the other, called *Rodman the Keeper*, is a series of studies and brief romances of the South, from Florida northward to the Carolina mountains. The collections are different and alike in their fidelity to the physical and social conditions of these diverse regions; these are sometimes involved in romantic mists, and sometimes they are unsparingly distinct, but the sensitive and sympathetic spirit of the author, her humanity, her passion for nature, her love of beauty, and her delight in color, characterize all. Several of the stories in time past have given us very great pleasure, especially the "Solomon" and the "Wilhelmina," which we have mentioned, and which are pictures of life in the community of the Separatists at Zoar, in Ohio, and "The Lady of Little Fishing," a romance placed beyond the reach of the gazetteer on an island of Lake Superior; and we have been reading them over again with a satisfaction not diminished by the greater intelligence which the ten or fifteen years passed since their first publication may be supposed to have brought even to a critic. In fact, their

Reprinted from *Harper's New Monthly Magazine* 74 (February 1887): 482.

assemblage under one cover somehow throws a new light on all the stories, and one sees, or seems to see—it is best not to be positive—that their final value, or the merit that they have in supreme degree, is to have caught and recorded in very clear and impressive terms the finest poetry which stirs in the heart of wild, new countries. This poetry is a religious aspiration or possession, often grotesque and delusive, but always touched with sublimity and sanctified by impulses of unselfish sincerity. The reader will feel it most in the study of "St. Clair Flats" and in the pathetic romance of "The Lady of Little Fishing"; but a sense of it imbues and qualifies nearly the whole book, which assumes a historical importance from it, as "Rodman the Keeper" and the companion pieces achieve vastly more than their aesthetic interest by eternizing that moment of heart-break and irreconciliation in the South when its women began to realize all their woe and loss through the defeat of their section in the war. Something more and something better than the literary instinct helped our author to the perception of things which give both of these books their uncommon claim to remembrance; she has made them necessary to any one who would understand the whole meaning of Americanism, or would know some of its most recondite phases by virtue of qualities which are felt in all her work, and at which we have hinted. These qualities, which are above artistry, to our thinking, need not make one indifferent to that; one would lose a great deal that is beautiful and valuable if they did. Miss Woolson deals with nature and with human nature in a fresh way, or at least a way of her own, which is at once simple in its kindliness and conscious of the limitations of all human judgment, where it ceases to be a question of suffering, sin, love, and hate, and becomes a question of sufferer, sinner, lover, and hater, with their relation to the frame of things, and to that material aspect of the universe, which now seems so deaf and blind to humanity, and now so full of poignant sympathy. The landscape is apt to grow sentient under her touch, which in the portrayal of that beautiful and deadly Florida swamp in "The South Devil" is really life-giving: the wicked, brilliant thing becomes animate. In this a writer who has since evolved for herself one of the most interesting phases of realism is romantic, but her epoch is distinctly marked by her forbearance in another respect: she does not extort an allegory from the malign morass, as Hawthorne must have done in obedience to the expectation of his time, nor suggest a psychical significance in it, as the romance of a little later period would have done. It is a merely animal life which "The South Devil" lives.

Recent American Fiction
[Review of *Jupiter Lights*]

[HORACE SCUDDER]

M̲r. Parkman touches a responsive chord when he concludes: "The realism of our time has its place and function; but an eternal analysis of the familiar and commonplace is cloying after a while, and one turns with relief and refreshment to such fare as that set before us in Mrs. Catherwood's animated story." We do not quote this as reflecting upon the art employed by Miss Woolson, for this writer, though closely occupied with the experience of men and women of her own day, has distinctly an adventurous spirit, and follows her heroes and heroines through the mazes of their minds only as some succession of incidents gives reason for such a pursuit. We have followed her writing with interest and pleasure heretofore, and our observations upon her art have been directed chiefly to what we may regard as due to an excess of literary conscience. Her latest book, however, is a somewhat disturbing one. We do not find the best of Miss Woolson in it except in the portraiture of the minor characters and in one strong theme, which is indeed the central theme of the book, but so confused with other issues as to be less effective, we think, than if it had been allowed a simpler expression.

The story of Jupiter Lights is briefly as follows: Cicely Abercrombie, a little devil of a Southern girl, married John Bruce, a Northern soldier. He was madly in love with the girl, and carried her by storm after a brief siege. They had a child, and then Bruce died. In a few months the widow herself fell madly in love with a handsome, gay Southerner, Ferdinand Morrison, and married him with a willful perversity which was not in the least weakened when it turned out that Ferdie, as everybody in the book feels bound to call him, had an hereditary tendency to a mixture of insanity and delirium tremens. In one of his moments of aberration Ferdie struck Cicely, and slung little Jack out of his crib, breaking his arm. He then disappeared to the convenient remoteness of Valparaiso, to wait till the novelist wanted him for dark and dreadful purposes.

Not long after Ferdie had gone to South America, Eve Bruce, the sister of Ferdie's predecessor, arrived at Romney, the dilapidated home of the Abercrombies, on the coast of Georgia, with the intent of taking possession

Reprinted from *Atlantic Monthly* 65 (January 1890): 126–28.

of Jack. She knew nothing of his early adventures with his step-father. She did not even know that he had a step-father, much less that Ferdie had gone, temporarily, out of sight. She was a willful young woman in her own right, who looked upon herself as ill used by this Southern girl who had stolen her brother, and she was drawn to Romney only by the hope of getting control of little Jack. She could not understand Cicely,—nobody can,—and found her sister-in-law even more of an enigma when she learned for the first time of Ferdie's behavior, and discovered that it seemed to intensify the wife's admiration and love.

It was now time, in the development of the novel, for Ferdie to reappear. He came. He was as handsome as he could be, but Eve, forewarned, discovered certain marks about the corners of his mouth which confirmed Cicely's tale. All went well for a time, but suddenly Cicely presented herself to Eve in the night, and advised her that the crisis had come. They dressed Jack and fled, the crazy Ferdie in full pursuit. Cicely with Jack succeeded in reaching a boat; Eve was behind, and Ferdie between her and his victims. She had a pistol, which she fired, and saw the man fall. Cicely, meanwhile, had fainted in the bottom of the boat, and Eve, with the strength which terror imparts both in fiction and in real life, shoved the boat off, and rowed to a neighboring island. The fugitives made their way to Savannah, always with the fear of seeing Ferdie behind them, and thence fled to the shores of Lake Superior, to seek the protection of Paul Tennant, the half-brother and whole admirer of the reprobate Ferdie.

The moment Paul appears, the sagacious reader foresees that destiny has provided him for Eve. But Eve herself did not at first discover this, nor did Paul. Meanwhile, letters and dispatches kept the party informed regarding Ferdie's condition. He had been shot—so the word came—by two negroes, who had escaped, but his wound was healing. He grew better; then suddenly he died, and the whole party, without Paul, returned to Romney. Paul followed shortly after, insisting upon marrying Eve, who fled to avoid him. She took refuge finally in a religious house, and was about to take the veil, when Paul reached her with important information, broke through all the barriers which separated him from his love, "and took Eve in his arms."

This is, of course, but the dead shell of the story; the living animal is quite another matter. The real theme of the book may be stated succinctly as an aphorism: Woman's love is absolute abandonment of self. The illustration in Cicely's case is clear. She loved Ferdie with such blind devotion that though he were to slay her, yet would she trust him; it was only her other love for Jack and his little life that forbade her to be a sacrifice. The real torture is for Eve. It must be premised that the reader is not informed at the time that Eve shot Ferdie. He may surmise it, but for the purposes of the story it was necessary that for a long while Eve alone should know it. Until she reached Paul she did not know whether she had killed Ferdie or not. Then he began to recover, and her own spirits rose. When he died she was madly in love with Paul; in fact, she began to discover what Cicely's love for Ferdie meant. At last she told Paul of her act, as before she had told Cicely, and then fled. As we have seen, Paul pursued her. He loved her in spite of the fact that she had killed his brother. But Eve, with a woman's wit, divined surely that in time, if he married her, he would come to loathe her. She would not make him miserable, and so she left him again. The important news which Paul finally brought to her was that she did not kill Ferdie, after all. He recovered from the slight wound she had inflicted, and died from the effects of a debauch. She was therefore free to love and be loved.

Although the main theme of the book can be stated as above, the endless variations on the theme bring the reader to the point of distraction. What Cicely thinks of Eve when Cicely is in her senses and when she has brain fever; how the relations of the two women are affected by Eve's saving Jack from drowning; how Eve feels before she tells her crime,—her crime consisting in shooting a man who was dead sure to kill his wife and her child; how she feels after she has told it to Cicely and before she has told Paul; how she wavers between a fear of Cicely's telling Paul and a resolve to tell him herself,—all these and many other complications make up a network of emotional torture which may be exact enough for psychological purposes, but is very confusing to the reader of a piece of fiction. One is under the harrow from beginning to end, and the final sensation, when the author lets him know that all the heaped-up trouble has no actual basis of fact, is not so much relief that Eve can now have what she wants as irritation that characters and reader alike have all been suffering needless agony.

Miss Woolson's ingenuity does not fail her in this book, but it is put, we must think, to extreme tests. There is such a succession of narrow escapes, so many dreary attacks upon the comfort of all concerned, so constant a conspiracy against a sane, wholesome experience of life, that a sensitive mind awakes at last out of a sort of nightmare aggravated by mosquito bites. The relief is gained by the undeniable humor expended on the characters of Judge Abercrombie, Hollis, the several darkies, and above all on Mrs. Mile, the nurse, who is a genuine success. We fear that Miss Woolson's interest in casuistry and her ingenuity of invention are leading her farther and farther away from large pictures of human life into the windings and turnings of fictitious pathology. We may add that there are many passages in the book which read as if they were random notes jotted down by the novelist, and one comes to have a feeling that the author as well as the reader is exhausted from time to time with the effort to keep up with the half-crazy heroines.

A Southern Romance
[Review of *Jupiter Lights*]

ANONYMOUS

It might be unfair to the reader to give the plot in full. All that need be said is that Miss Woolson has made a good plot and filled it with incident. It may be criticised toward the end. There are two love stories, for the half-brother falls in love with Eve, and she with him, but the supposed murder stands between them. We may quarrel with Miss Woolson for not ending her romance on this side of the ocean. The pursuit of Eve to Italy by Paul is superfluous, and the forcing of the religious house where she is "in retreat" is a trifle absurd, particularly as she causes Paul to knock down a priest and a small and respectable English person during his efforts to see his beloved. These be rather too heroic methods, and they do not belong either to our century or to that artistic spirit which we have occasion to admire so often in the novels of this talented woman.

Excerpted and reprinted from *New York Times*, 29 December 1889, 2.

Jupiter Lights

Anonymous

Miss Woolson's latest novel will add little, if anything, to her reputation. She cannot write poorly, and her pictures of human life and nature at Abercrombie's Island, south of Savannah, and at Port aux Pins on Lake Superior, are well finished; but the chief characters of *Jupiter Lights* are a poor set. The long narrative of Eve Bruce's morbid feelings about the worthless "Ferdie," at whom she shot to save his wife and child from his insane rage, is extremely wearisome, and the device of making Cicely's husband die of a debauch after his recovery from the wound is a weak one for any but a third-rate writer.

Excerpted and reprinted in *Literary World* (Boston), 4 January 1890, 41.

Recent Fiction
[Review of *Jupiter Lights*]

ANONYMOUS

Miss Woolson must have been dominated by an evil spirit when she conceived the central situation of 'Jupiter Lights.' It is more easy to believe that she was "possessed" than that she deliberately chose to write a long novel about the stupid and obstinate attachment of a silly woman for a man who, every few months, became insanely drunk, beat her, turned her out of doors, and tried to kill both her and her child. In real life we occasionally hear of such instances of infatuation, but never that the fascination which men of Mr. Morrison's unpleasant habits exercise over their wives extends to other people, particularly to the wife's relations. In real life the wife's relations are generally coarse enough to combat her clinging affections, and, when possible, to deliver the husband over to the police. Such matter-of-fact behavior would, however, never do for high-flown romance. . . .

All this is sheer romantic nonsense, and in every problem of conduct the people involved are as nearly irrational as possible. Their misunderstandings and their false way of looking at facts are so exasperating that there is danger of overlooking what is worth telling and well told, of including all in a sweeping condemnation. Miss Woolson is very familiar with the country round about the Jupiter Lights of the North and of the South, and with the people who dwell there. Her description of scene and local character is the straightforward expression of close and sympathetic observation. By dwelling upon these pictures the reader may soothe his indignation against the preposterous people struggling in a sea of self-inflicted trouble.

Excerpted and reprinted from *Nation*, 13 March 1890, 225.

Miss Woolson's Last Book
[Review of *Horace Chase*]

ANONYMOUS

The book ends happily—as happily as such a book can end. It is a sombre tale, in spite of its many bright touches of comedy. Its minor characters are many and well sketched in Miss Woolson's own charming manner, but there is an excess of hysteria, or something akin to it, and an over amount of eccentricity in the people. Jared Franklin attempts suicide in his last illness, and Ruth plainly threatens to kill herself unless her sister will let her tell her husband just what she has done. Maud Muriel Mackintosh, the masculine sculptress, who smokes a clay pipe and never uses any model that is not absolutely commonplace, believing that truth can only be found in the general average; Miss Billy Breeze, Mrs. Kip, Achilles Larue, Malachi Hill, and old Etheredge are all humorous creations, but it does not seem that the author has got very much fun out of them after all.

On the whole, "Horace Chase" is a sad book, but it is worth while to read it, quite apart from the facts that it is its author's last novel and that its publication closely follows the announcement of her sudden and violent death in Venice.

Excerpted and reprinted from *New York Times*, 10 February 1894, 3.

Recent Novels [Review of *Horace Chase*]

Anonymous

Nothing too harsh could easily be said of Chase's wife, judged by the revelations of her conduct, her speech, and even the tendency of her thought; yet Miss Woolson abounds in explanatory excuse. She says that her heroine is "essentially feminine," and rejoices that this delightful essence had not been "refined away by overdevelopment of the mental powers, or reduced to a subordinate position by ascetic surroundings." The evidence of Miss Woolson's novels is that she estimated women by the effect they may have upon men, and regarded them always leniently if they attracted what she calls "masculine adorers." By the modern movement, the so-called emancipation of women, she appears to have been quite unimpressed. Perhaps she thought the clamor for rights all a humbug, regarding it as only a clever device for extorting further privilege from men. Presumably, she was hostile to the movement, and, in her last novel, has put her hostility on record in the person of the grotesque sculptress, Maud Muriel Mackintosh.

Excerpted and reprinted from *Nation*, 29 March 1894, 233.

Horace Chase

The interest always belonging to the work of Miss Constance Fenimore Woolson is deepened by the tidings of her death. *Horace Chase*, her last story, is upon the whole characteristic of its author, although dealing with a hero who is far from being her ideal. Her keen perception of details, her sensitiveness to beauty, and her humor find full scope in describing the life of the agreeable, rather indolent Franklin family and indicating the peculiarities of their neighbors. . . .

With all Miss Woolson's realism and searching wit she was a romanticist. Her central theme was passionate love even when, as in this book, there was a great deal of amusing byplay and comment. No character of marked elevation belongs to the group portrayed in *Horace Chase*. The easy-going Franklins are strong chiefly in their family affections. They have principles indeed, but principles so interpreted according to their temperaments that their story is a picture interesting rather than inspiring.

Miss Woolson's palette always abounded in color, her drawing was vivacious, and her sketchbook was full of studies. Thus, although her *motifs* have not great variety nor her types exalted beauty, her work will long retain its charm.

Excerpted and reprinted from *Literary World* (Boston), 24 March 1894, 85.

Miss Woolson's Italian Stories [Review of *Dorothy and Other Italian Stories*]

ANONYMOUS

Probably there is no magazine writer of a recent day more regretted by the company of faithful magazine readers than Constance Fenimore Woolson. She had the faculty of making her characters odd as well as actual, and although there are passages in some of her novels that seem almost to foreshadow the tragic fate of the author, they are relieved by a truly brilliant humor that lends to her work the richness so often lacking in the modern novel; it is so much easier to make a book all of ponderous gloom or else of sudsy lightness than it is fortunately to combine strength and wit. This reprint of magazine stories stands the test of a second reading. None of them falls below, and two of them, "A Transplanted Boy," and "A Waitress," rise above the average of the author's accomplishment.

Excerpted and reprinted from *New York Times*, 1 December 1895, 31.

Recent Fiction [Reviews of
The Front Yard and Other Italian Stories
and *Dorothy and Other Italian Stories*]

ANONYMOUS

The volume of Italian tales by the late Miss Woolson displays her amiability and grace more abundantly than her stronger qualities. All the stories are about Americans long domiciled in Italy, pursuing art, society, and climate, and enjoying that idleness which is cheaper and less invidious in Europe than at home. They are easy-going, pleasant people, their national traits surviving exile, and their ridiculous or contemptible aspects so softened by the author's kindliness and humor that the absurd appears a little pathetic and the ignoble not altogether base.

In the whole of Miss Woolson's work, for instance, though there is no shirking of physical passion and the dire complications for which it may be responsible, there is not a hint of coarse sensuality or a touch of grossness. On the other hand, her lovers do not become phantasma through attenuation of the force of physical attraction. In 'Dorothy,' the second volume of Italian tales and her last work, most of her lovers are fervent and persistent rather than fiery. . . . The lover may belong to any nation, but he is always, as it were, on the wing: at the slightest tiff with his adored one he takes the first express, and, prodigal of railway fares, exhausts his ire in an inconsequent whirl over Europe. These stories, even as the life from which they are drawn, are more pleasing than exciting, and depend for charm on the congeniality between scene and temperament.

Excerpted and reprinted from *Nation*, 12 December 1895, 433; and 27 February 1896, 181.

CRITICAL WRITINGS AND APPRECIATIONS

◆

Contributors' Club[1] [Review of *Esther Pennefather* by Alice Perry]

[CONSTANCE FENIMORE WOOLSON]

There are some books so very bad that they are good. To be very bad, a book must have originality in badness; when it has that, we can stand reading it, as we look with some interest at the woman who has dressed herself in man's clothes and climbed down a skylight at midnight to rob us, but with none at all at the common thief who, in ordinary daylight, has stolen articles from the garden clothes-line.

Esther Pennefather strikes me as the most utterly ridiculous book of the season. And yet it has originality, a few very fine passages, and, with all its absurdity, a promise, to my mind at least, of better things in the future. Its originality is in its subject, which is that of the singular power one woman sometimes has over another. All the men may as well now retire, and read their newspapers; since *they* do not believe this. They are perforce retired from this book by the writer herself, since there is not in the whole volume a single man worthy of the name; nothing but a chorus of women, chasing each other madly along, doing the most extraordinary things for the most senseless reasons, from the first page to the last. Practical people may say at once (and end the matter) that there is no such power; but the fact remains that there *is*. Let questions be asked, and it will be discovered that there is scarcely a woman of strong, self-reliant nature who has not at some time or other been followed and besieged, with almost dog-like humility, by some other woman, whose affection she never asked for, whose adoration she did not want. Mothers, surrounded and fenced off by their children, do not excite this worship; wives, not often. It is almost always the women who are not tangled in domestic ties who receive it; it is thrown at them whether they wish it or not. And, generally, they do not wish it; in fact, it almost seems a necessary part of the performance that the worshiped one should remain indifferent, and care nothing for the worshiper.

Esther Pennefather must inevitably excite inextinguishable laughter; I have observed that the critics who have noticed it at all have politely advanced the supposition that the author was very young, and then, hiding their smiles behind their tall hats, have hastily retired. But I want to bring forward one

Reprinted from *Atlantic Monthly* 42 (October 1878): 502–503.

passage on the power of love, one of the few passages that redeem the book, and give, to my mind at least, a promise. "There is no one who has a right to take back love. There is nothing one's friends can do, no meanness, no cruelty, no forsaking, that gives us a right to forsake them. Ah! what would become of us if God loved us as we love our friends? I believe, I believe without doubt, that *love is redemption*. We can love to the very end even those not worthy of love in this world, and we can carry that faithful love at last to the feet of God himself, and lay it down there, and he will give us back our own. No one can sin *forever*, whom *one* heart loves faithfully and purely; in some time that we cannot tell, love will gain its own." Now it seems to me that there is a height of beauty and nobleness in that passage to which many a popular book, in all its sparkling pages, never attains.

To go back to the original subject, namely, a woman's adoration of another woman. There is such a thing. I myself have seen tears of joy, the uttermost faith, and deepest devotion, in mature, well-educated, and cultivated women, for some other woman whom they adored; have seen an absorption for months of every thought. But—but! there is a monotonous certainty that follows on, which arouses to laughter the unregenerate masculine mind and makes it deny the whole (which is a mistake; it *is* there), namely, the certainty that once let loose an agreeable *man* in this atmosphere, and, ten to one, the whole cloud-structure topples over, its battlements dissolve, and the dwellers come out and act like everybody else—only more so. Those to whom I have referred are all married now, and happily married; they no longer care in the least for each other. And yet I know that there come moments when they sit apart and think of that old adoration which was so intense and so pure, so self-sacrificing and so far away.

Note

1. William Dean Howells began the Contributors' Club of the *Atlantic Monthly* in January 1877. This regular feature, which offered anonymous reviews and commentary by well-known writers, was a Woolson favorite, as she admits to the writer-editor E. C. Stedman in a letter dated January 1879: "I like the Club; naturally; because I am generally in it!" In response to Stedman's later attempt to identify one of her reviews, Woolson confirms his suspicion on 30 September 1887: ". . . but you must not tell. The pleasure of it is the incognito; trammeled at once if names are known" (Edmund C. Stedman Papers, Rare Book and Manuscript Library, Columbia University).

Contributors' Club [Review of *Far from the Madding Crowd* and *A Pair of Blue Eyes* by Thomas Hardy]

[CONSTANCE FENIMORE WOOLSON]

Why is it we do not hear more about Thomas Hardy? We discuss Tour-guéneff, in translations too, until he is threadbare; we dabble in Cherbuliez, likewise in translations for the most part; but this original Englishman we leave alone. Yet it seems to me that he is well worth attention, and a stronger writer in many respects than either Black or Blackmore. Haven't we all read his five stories? Or what is the trouble?

To my mind, Far from the Madding Crowd is as fine a piece of work as anything in fiction we have had from England in ten or fifteen years,—I make no exceptions; A Pair of Blue Eyes is an especially sweet little love story; Under the Greenwood Tree, a lesser sketch, is a rural picture so realistic that we know all the characters as neighbors, when we have finished it; and, as an offset, Desperate Remedies and The Hand of Ethelberta are failures.[1] The best one, Far from the Madding Crowd, is a sheep story. The few characters, Bathsheba and her lovers and the little knot of farming people, move in a circle of meek sheep-faces from beginning to end. It opens with a vigil among lambs, followed by the tragedy of the ewes, where the young dog, who in his mistaken zeal has chased two hundred of the gentle creatures over the precipice to their death, is discovered standing alone, surveying his work, on the brow of the cliff, "against the sky, dark and motionless as Napoleon at St. Helena." Of the three lovers, one is a shepherd by profession, and comes on and off the scene either with lambs dangling from his shoulders, or grinding shearing-tools, or shearing sheep, or washing them, or something of the kind, from first to last. The second, although not a shepherd, is even more sheep-surrounded, poor fellow! The first time he tries to speak to the dark-eyed Bathsheba (a sheep-like name that too, and not unconnected with the ancient story of "one little ewe lamb," as told by Nathan the prophet), she is busy with the flock. He offers himself to her at a "sheep-washing," continues his suit at a "sheep-shearing," makes his second offer at a "shearing-

Reprinted from *Atlantic Monthly* 43 (February 1879): 260–62.

supper," and, after she is left a widow, renews his addresses at a "sheep-fair." Times and seasons in this book are stated as follows: "It was now early spring, the time of going to grass with the sheep"; or, "It was the first of June, when the sheep-shearing season culminates." All through the story the mild woolly creatures accompany us. But what a strong tale it is that is set in these pastoral surroundings! The moment Troy, the soldier, steps on the scene, his scarlet coat contrasting with the green fields, we know how it is to be. Here is a man at last who has nothing to do with sheep; but rather "sword exercise," as when he spits the wandering caterpillar, that has crawled by chance across the front of Bathsheba's bodice, on the point of his flying circling sword, or severs a lock of her hair unfelt, with its swift and radiant edge. He tells her openly how beautiful she is! The others have not dared to say it; but Troy dares everything. This handsome soldier, to whom "the past was a yesterday; the future, to-morrow; never, the day after," one who, "perfectly truthful towards men," lies "like a Cretan toward women," wins Bathsheba, of course, from her slow, sheep-entangled suitors. He marries her, and—tires of her. Such men are always tired of their wives up to the age of forty or forty-five, when, if the wife has been patient meanwhile, they come back to her like schoolboys, and are good forever after. But Bathsheba is not patient. Tragedy now appears in the episode of Fanny. It seems to me that the chapter called On Casterbridge Highway, describing the inch-by-inch progress on foot of the dying girl, trying to drag herself over the three long miles to the poorhouse, her attempt with the crutches, her encounter with the homeless dog, and especially her woman's invention of pretending that the end of her journey was but five fence-posts distant, and then, having dragged herself past the five by means of this self-beguilement, pretending it was but five posts more, and so on, is powerfully pathetic. And powerfully dramatic, too, the chapter where, all her sufferings over and in her poorhouse coffin, she comes back to conquer her splendid rival at last, and win again her recreant lover, by achieving "the one feat alone—that of dying"—which could make her powerful.

Hardy's descriptions of scenery are like no others with which I am acquainted, unless Thoreau's; I do not maintain that they are better than others, but they are certainly his own. They are not in the least poetic; nothing could be farther from what is known as "beautiful writing." Here are no "pearly," "opaline," "amethyst" tints at all. He selects generally rather sober times and scenes, and then describes them so that we actually see them. His landscapes have no moral meanings, for one thing. His sunsets and his thunder have no suggestions to offer respecting oblivion, remorse, or the infinite; his storm is simply an atmospheric disturbance, his fog a wet cloud. Here are some Thoreau-like bits. "A list of the gradual changes on a moor betokening the approach and arrival of winter. The retreat of the snakes. The transformation of the ferns. The filling of the pools. A rising of fogs.

The embrowning by frost. The collapse of the fungi. An obliteration by snow." And this of the hue of very young tree-leaves: "a yellow beside a green, and a green beside a yellow." Of early morning: "It was so early that the shady places still smelt like night-time." Of nightfall: "He lingered till there was no difference between the eastern and western expanse of sky." The fog described in the Madding Crowd makes your own trees drip outside the window. And when this severely plain style rises at all, it is to such fine sentences as these: "To persons standing alone on a hilltop during a clear midnight, the roll of the earth eastward is almost a palpable movement. The sensation may be caused by the panoramic glide of the stars, or by the wind, or by the solitude; but whatever be its origin, the impression of riding along is vivid and abiding."

But if the descriptions of scenery are good, those of the English farm-laborers are better; they seem to me the best we have had yet. For the dialect here is not simply an uncouth tongue, relying for its effect upon barbarous mispronunciations, but a quaint use of familiar, old-fashioned words and idioms, which seems to be taken bodily from actual life. Note the following: "There, 't is a happy providence that I be no worse, so to speak it, and I feel my few poor gratitudes." And this: "I knowed the boy's grandfather, a truly nervous man even to genteel refinement. 'T was blush, blush with him almost as much as 't is with me—not but that it's a fault in me." "Not at all, Master Poorgrass," said Coggan. " 'T is a very noble quality in ye." They discuss church and chapel. "Chapel-folk be more hand-and-glove with them above than we be," said Joseph, thoughtfully. "Yes," said Coggan. "If anybody goes to heaven, they will; they've worked for it. I'm not such a fool as to pretend that we who stick to the church have the same chance; but I hate a feller who'll change his ancient doctrine for the sake of getting to heaven! No, I'll stick to my side, and fall with the fallen." When the old master's age is doubted, they soothe the ancient man as follows: "Ye be a very old aged person, master; and ye must have a wonderful talented constitution to be able to live so long." The earl's wife dies, and after several hours have passed, they remark musingly, "She must know by this time whether she's to go up or down, poor creature!" And here is an unapproachable bit: "Gabriel Oak is coming it quite the dand! When I see people strut enough to be cut up into bantam-cocks, I stand dormant with wonder, and says no more." The men discuss whether or not their mistress is in love, and one says, "But last Sunday, when we were in the tenth commandment, says she, 'Incline our hearts to keep this law,' says she, when 't was 'laws in our hearts we beseech Thee' all the church through! Her eye was upon *him*, and she was quite lost, no more than a mere shadder at that tenth, a mere shadder!"

If Far from the Madding Crowd is a sheep story, A Pair of Blue Eyes is a tale of tombs. It is too bad to make sport of one of the sweetest little love-stories of the day, but there certainly is an omnipresence of "Jethway's tomb" which is gravely comic. There are three live lovers; and Jethway's tomb. The latter has an unpleasant way of shining "with singular weirdness." The first lover woos Elfride in the churchyard, while sitting on this tomb. The second lover, also with her in the churchyard, observes the tomb, and, after a while, finds out something of the truth. He questions her and she attempts to prevaricate by murmuring that the lover is dead; but, as she has already confessed to the love-making, he not unnaturally wishes to know "how in the name of Heaven a man can sit upon his own tomb!" Upon being informed at last, and falteringly, that there were two, he remarks with gloom that he hardly thinks *he* could have accepted the attentions of a new lover "while sitting upon the poor remains of the old one." He goes alone for an evening walk, again selecting "the churchyard"; he sits and regards "the white tomb." Meanwhile Jethway's mother having appropriately selected that day and spot to come by and be killed, lover number two is the one to discover the body, of course, and end the chapter sepulchrally. When poor discarded number one returns from India, it is in this churchyard again that Elfride promises to meet him. She does not come; but, has he not the companionship of Jethway? At last, when he meets her with number two, and is informed in so many words of their betrothal, the scene this time is a family vault into which by chance they have all descended. There are two fine breezy descriptions of churchyards in the book, with the merits and demerits of the style of graves in each; and there is a quaint account of masons at work in a vault among ancient coffins, which, in unlettered prose, rivals Hamlet. Last of all, when the two lovers, after long absence and alienation from Elfride, find out their errors, and after attempting to deceive each other by an affectation of utter indifference, meet at the railroad station in the early dawn, each hastening to her on the wings of the wind, they notice a singular dark car attached to their train; and it accompanies them all day. Once, by some mistake, it is detached, and they have to wait for it. "What a confounded nuisance these stoppages are!" one says, fretfully. When they reach the end of their journey, the dark van stops too; it turns out to be a funeral car, and from it is borne a coffin,—the coffin of Elfride. Struck dumb, they follow in silence, two miserable men, each, however, sure in his heart that she loved him to the last; sure! She was such a sweet, loving little creature! And then they learn that it is a countess who is being borne on before them, and that Elfride has been for five months the wife of the earl! The story ends in a vault,—her vault now; they visit it together the day after the funeral, only to find there the earl, who is number three, and before them both, and who loved her better than they all.

Hardy always has one woman and three or four lovers; it is his idea of a story. In Desperate Remedies and The Hand of Ethelberta he has ventured off his ground and into the field where Wilkie Collins' banner, inscribed with the motto, "Plots, not People," floats supreme; and of course he has been slaughtered.

In all his writings he quotes, as far as I can discover, but two American authors, namely, Hawthorne and Walt Whitman.

Note

1.   Thomas Hardy published *A Pair of Blue Eyes* in 1870, *Under the Greenwood Tree* in 1870, *Desperate Remedies* in 1871, and *The Hand of Ethelberta* in 1876.

Contributors' Club [Review of *The Europeans* by Henry James]

[CONSTANCE FENIMORE WOOLSON]

Mr. Henry James's Europeans is, to me, his best work, so far; always excepting two or three of his short stories. For his peculiar style of mere hints as to such commonplace things as reasons, motives, and causes seems to me better adapted to a short story, which is necessarily a sketch or condensation, than to the broader limits of a novel, where we are accustomed to more explanation and detail. It is true that Charles Reade, also, seldom tells us what his characters mean, intend, or think, but only what they say or do; leaving us, as James does, to study them as we study our living neighbors, who carry no windows in their breasts. But the difference here is that Reade's characters always do such tremendous things, and so incessantly, that their mere bodily activity sufficiently defines their mental processes; whereas Mr. James, as far as possible, has *his* people do nothing at all.

What atmosphere could possibly have been contrived more quiet than the wide, cool Wentworth homestead, and its little cottage opposite, from which, as scene, the story scarcely wavers, save for that one glimpse of the Acton mansion, emphasized and slightly colored by its "delightful chinoiseries." The two Europeans arrive, and, after one sharply drawn picture of their dislike for the Boston horse-cars, they depart to this Wentworth home, and stay there through to the end of the tale. No one does anything; a drive for Madame Münster and a drifting about in a skiff for Gertrude are about all the action allowed. So quiet is the story in this respect that when, in the eleventh chapter, the baroness goes to see Mrs. Acton, and goes on foot, the description of her "charming undulating step" as she walked along the road is a kind of relief to us, and mentally we all go with her, glad of the exercise and movement and fresh air. Mr. James has advanced in his art; in *this* story of his there is absolutely no action at all. What is there, then? There is contrast of character, and conversation.

I suppose it will be allowed without question that we are all far more interested in the baroness than in the other characters. Felix is, to me, a failure, in spite of his felicitous name; or rather he is a shadow, making no definite impression of any kind,—like Mirah in Daniel Deronda. His "in-

Reprinted from *Atlantic Monthly* 43 (January 1879): 106–108.

tense smiling" does not save him; does not give him body, any more than the brilliant rainbow gives body to the spray at Niagara Falls. Gertrude is not a failure; but she is not sufficiently explained. Minute details concerning her are given, such as for instance, that "her stiff silk dress made a sound upon the carpet" as she walked about the room; yet she remains from first to last like a tune which the composer has as yet but briefly jotted down. *He* knows it; but *we* do not. There is no mystery about it, however; it is only that he has not written it fully out,—that is all. Mr. Wentworth is excellent throughout; we see him, we are acquainted with him, sitting there "with his legs crossed, lifting his dry pure countenance from the Boston Advertiser." There is no indistinctness in the outline; he is a figure clearly and carefully finished; some of James's finest art has been given to him. Clifford and Lizzie are good, the latter an amusingly accurate picture of a certain type of very young American girl,—pretty, coolly self-possessed, endowed with a ready, unappalled, and slightly-stinging native wit; a small personage whose prominence and even presence amaze and secretly annoy the baroness, who is not accustomed to consider and defer to the opinions of "little girls" in her graceful and victorious progress through society.

Mr. Brand is the good, slow, serious, clean young man, with large feet and a liking for substantial slices of the excellent home-made cake of well-regulated households, whom many of us know. There is an unregenerate way (which Mr. James shares) of looking at these young men, which sees only their ludicrous points. Light-natured fellows like Felix (or what we suppose Felix is intended to be) are always laughing at them. Even when poor Brand gives up the girl he loves, and stiffens his resolution by offering, in his official capacity, to unite her to his rival, a ludicrous hue is thrown over the action, and we all unite in an amused smile over the young minister and his efforts, which, judged soberly, is unfair. The "Brands" always seem to me to belong to a soberer age; they are relics of plainer and more earnest times, and out of place in this American nineteenth century, where everything is taken lightly, and where ridicule is by far the most potent influence. During the war, the Brands had a chance: they marched to the war with tremendous earnestness; nobody minded their big feet on the plain of battle; their slowness was mighty, like a sledge-hammer. Their strong convictions fired the assault; they headed the colored regiments; they made, by their motives and beliefs, even small actions grand. The whole nation was in earnest then; the Brands found their place. But now they are left to themselves again, and are a good deal like mastodons, living by mistake in a later age, objects of amusement to the lighter-footed modern animals, and unable to help it.

The baroness is, however, *the* character. She is the "European,"—the contrast; she is the story.

In the first description of her personal appearance, I do not think Mr. James was quite fair; he followed Tourguéneff, and pictured the irregularities of her features and personal deficiencies so minutely that I, for one, have never been able to forget it, or to think of her as in the least handsome. Now the baroness *was* handsome; she was an extremely charming woman. We have all met women of that sort; I mean women who had irregular features, but who yet, by their coloring, their grace, or some one single and wonderfully great beauty, kept us from noticing when with them whether their noses were classical, or their mouths large or small. If in real life this is a truth, it should be a truth doubly remembered and guarded in books, where necessarily the warmth of the personal presence is lost. Mr. James might have stated that her face was irregular, judged by rule, but he should have dwelt upon what beauties she *did* have, so that they would make a vivid impression; just as, in real life, they would have domineered vividly over her lacks, if she had entered the room where we were sitting. She is *his* creation; *we* don't know her. He should have answered for her in this respect, and started us fairly.

What was the baroness's fault? The moral of the story?—if there is any. Acton was deeply in love with her; yet he would not quite marry her.

According to my solution, the fault was (and the moral) that she lied; and, in our raw American atmosphere, delicate and congenial lying has not yet been comprehended as one of the fine arts. This is my idea of what Mr. James means.

George Eliot says, in speaking of Gwendolen's mood early one morning, "It was not that she was out of temper; but that the world was not equal to the demands of her fine organism." So likewise it was not that the baroness spoke untruths; but the American world was not equal to the accomplishments of her fine organism, or the habits bred in older and more finished society on the other side of the Atlantic.

Mr. James's delightful style is even more delightful than usual in this story. Mr. Wentworth's "thin, unresponsive glance"; Mr. Brand, "stiffly and softly" following; the "well-ordered consciousness" of the Wentworth household; Clifford Wentworth's "softly growling tone," indicative, however, merely of "a vaguely humorous intention" (how good that is!); and, best of all, the last visit of the baroness to Mrs. Acton, and the conversation between the two women, Madame Münster at last giving up in despair, as she perceives that all her delicate little points of language and tone are thrown away, and feeling "that she would *never* know what such a woman as that meant,"—these are perfect, and make us, for a while, impatient with less artistic stories.

One peculiarity of style I have noticed, namely, the large number of what seem to me "stage directions." Thus, fourteen times in three consecutive pages, taken at random from those containing conversation, it is particularly noted down that they "looked at" each other. As "Gertrude looked at her a moment, and then, 'Yes, Charlotte,' she said simply"; "Gertrude looked at

Lizzie Acton, and then looked away"; "She looked down at him a moment, and then shook her head." They "look at" each other "a moment," and "then" speak, uncountable numbers of times. Generally, in print, *cela va sans dire*. I don't mean that this is a fault at all; but certainly it is a characteristic peculiarity.

Monthly Record of Current Events

ANONYMOUS

The death of Constance Fenimore Woolson is deplored by the entire literary fraternity of this country. We speak of her literary associates rather than of the army of readers who followed her with delight, because they were probably more sensible of her refined and painstaking literary art. She had such a high conception of her art that she thought no pains too great in whatever she undertook. She respected her public, and never offered it crude work. Her conscience was never set at ease by popularity, and to the last her standard was not popular favor, but her own high conception of her office as a writer. Her short stories, probably all of them, were written over again and again, and some of her novels were rewritten as many as five or six times, and she followed her productions into print with the same longing to revise that Coleridge felt for his poems. She was never satisfied, and her example was a constant protest against hasty and slovenly composition. This patience in creative genius is not common, and it always gave Miss Woolson a certain distinction. It is sometimes supposed that original strength is impaired by too much revision, but there is no doubt that the work of this novelist gained in beauty, ease, and finish by her labor on it. The processes by which writers reach their results differ. Some write slowly, determine the idea and its form of expression before committing anything to paper, and make the needed choice and exercise the exclusion as they go along, so that the first draught is essentially the best they can do. But others pour out their thoughts on paper with little regard to selection and refusal, and trust to repeated revision for the ultimate form. The danger in the latter course, if the writer becomes popular, is that he grows careless and sloppy. It is to the honor of Miss Woolson that no temptation of good pay for easy work ever impaired her conscience or lowered her standard. She valued her art. It is in this aspect that we speak here of the loss to us in her departure. To attempt an estimate of her as a novelist would be impossible in this space. She was among the first in America to bring the short story to its present excellence, that is, the short story as a social study in distinction from the sketch of character and the relation of incident. . . .

    . . . There lived among our writers no one in fuller sympathy with

Excerpted and reprinted from *Harper's New Monthly Magazine* 88 (May 1894): 966–67.

American life and character, none prouder of her country and all that is best in it, and no one who brought to the task of delineating them a clearer moral vision and a more refined personality.

Reminiscences of
Constance Fenimore Woolson

Linda T. Guilford[1]

It is with hesitation the pen is taken up for these remembrances of the true woman, and the true artist who so suddenly went out of life little more than a month ago. The unveiling of a beautiful picture or a perfect statue is a part to thrill the hand of the most unappreciative actor.

The slender, blue eyed maiden stands before me a pupil in the Cleveland Seminary. I hear her low cultured voice; the scene in the silent, attentive class room when she read her compositions is vivid yet, but she was so averse to personal notoriety, so refined and high bred in nature, that one would only talk of her with hushed tones within the sacred precincts of the family circle.

Rejoicing in the beauty and color, reveling in scenes of the Orient and Mediterranean,—pouring out unstinted love to friends, conscientious to her art and devoted to it, her life was full of the joy that springs from such fountains perennial. It was, certainly, no morbidness in herself that many of her stories with their bright-hued setting of skies and woods, of warm vales and hills have a stern necessity that shuts out a fully happy ending. Unselfish in word and thought, it was not from her own heart that she drew those varied portraits of intensely selfish women, who, in crass unconsciousness of their own character occasion the tragedy in nearly every one of her novels. Revelations of her real self come out in her letters studded with discriminating sketches of character and playful narratives of her own experiences. They are the sparkles of a sunny soul that found a congenial environment in the Italy she loved, in the Venice she chose of all places for her abode. But how true she was to her early friends and home! "Many thoughts arose," she wrote once, "on reading your book. One was my (still fixed) impression of the immense size of the old grove and the Water Cure woods.[2] I have traveled far and wide since then, but I really think I never found any forest so wild and so vast as the Water Cure woods. A vision rises before me of the Cleveland Seminary with its furnace heated air, its crowds of girls, the early spring flowers among the trees." . . .

Excerpted from Mss. 484, by permission of the Western Reserve Historical Society, Cleveland, Ohio. Some of the spelling and punctuation have been regularized for clarity.

In another reminiscence she says: "I have been rowing during the autumn on the Avon, Shakespeare's Avon, such a pretty little river winding among the soft green English fields. Flora Payne and I used to row on the meandering Cuyahoga, I am afraid one cannot row there now."[3]

One of the delights of her residence at Oxford was the boating. "I can row as often as I like by having a boy or man to steer. Then when I have had my four or five miles of what is, to me, the most charming exercise in the world my steersman can row me home."

It is touching to know that the faithful gondolier devoted to her was nigh at the fatal spot where she fell, and tenderly bore her to her home. . . .

How thoroughly her heart was in nature is felt in this account of a stroll at Oxford.

"This beautiful Indian summer day I walked across the fields beside a little brook, to a rustic ferry across a branch of the Thames. A cord hangs down from a tree, you pull it, and it rings a bell in the ferryman's house on the other side, then he comes over in a punt and takes you across for a penny." . . .

Far reaching plans of study were in her mind as she wrote later:

"The older I grow the more curious I am about the modes of thought and the literature of other countries. The Russians and Spanish fascinate me, and now that I have had a glimpse of the East I am curious about the Persian and East Indian writers. When I am eighty (if alive) I shall probably be trying to get hold of the Sacred Books of the Chinese or of Tibet. See what we are reduced to, we who have not the joy of children."

Her friendships with noted men and women were many (Henry James used often to send her spritely telegraph messages in substitute for talk). With Addington Symonds in Italy she formed a most delightful acquaintance. That she herself was more charming than her books was a common testimony; and the multitude of letters and messages sent here since her untimely death proves her place in the hearts of those who knew her. Her own comments on literary men and their works are never without point, and she did not hesitate to dethrone the idols of her correspondents.

"Do not fancy that I admire Tolstoi whom you quote, I do not in the least, save as a novelist. I think him half mad as I know much of his life from a lady who lived for years in his family. He wears a colored shirt and makes shoes in his drawing room. He digs in his fields. But the drawing room and the house are very handsome. Madame Tolstoi has a large fortune. He makes the shoes so badly that no one can wear them and he only spoils so much leather and the farm laborers are obliged to do over secretly all the work he does in the field. What good does it do to any one on earth for him to go barefoot? He was notoriously immoral for years, and after he was married he had, I dare not say from memory how many children—I think twenty-two. Madame being strong and very rich has lived through it, for she has nothing to do with the children, nurses, tutors, and governess, taking the entire charge. This is a nice record for an Apostle who has lately preached to the world in his old age that all men should live like monks. I write this because there is a very incorrect idea of him abroad in the English speaking world."

In reference to another popular favorite we have this: "There is much talk in London about 'Plain Tales from the Hills' and 'Soldiers Three' by a young fellow named Rudyard Kipling. As I have been in Egypt I have only just read them. They are original, and strong after a fashion. Still I am disappointed. They do not, in my opinion, equal Bret Harte's early tales. But of course the English are much struck with them as they have not many Bret Hartes." "The English are limited I grant, but what they do take hold of, they hold with a will. At present it is Stanley. All London was at his feet when I passed through. They take hold of other things too besides men. They've got poor Egypt fast."

Her love for children and for pet dogs were two of the shy traits which did not appear on the surface to strangers.

"I am always delighted," she wrote, "when children climb into my lap of their own accord; I am recalling all my fairy stories." On another occasion after the birth of a little niece, she confesses that "Oxford, and rooms, and writing a novel, are poor things compared to a baby." Again she can in any circumstances "always read Matthew Arnold's poetry and have a little dog-gie," and a pet dog she loved and talked with in her quaint fashion to the last.

This love had a commemoration in the last "English Illustrated Magazine" which gave with the portrait of a famous Oxford dog, the copy of a note which Miss Woolson had tied to his collar after a visit.

Affectionate messages to her nephews are not without illustration. "The boys, I suppose, are still devoted to soldiers. Robert Louis Stevenson plays with tin soldiers and makes great forts of sand and clay to this day. The funniest part of it is, that he has no children. He plays these soldier games with his wife."

After the travels in Egypt in 1889–90 her enthusiasm over it never flagged. "The winter," she wrote in May, "was a magnificent one and I fell almost gorged with new impressions and Oriental color. I lost my heart completely at Cairo and I was strongly, Oh! so strongly, tempted to go to Constantinople for the summer; it is the summer resort of the Cairo people. Then I should have returned to Egypt for another winter. But after all enough is as good as a feast and with Corfu, Athens, and Egypt, I had all I could carry. I am even yet a little intoxicated with the beauty and the color. What brought me back was the strong wish to do a year's steady work in absolute seclusion."

Her account of a Cairo acquaintance leads her to a subject on which she had a right to definite opinions.

"In Cairo I often saw Brugsch Bey,—he is the man who discovered the Pharaohs, you know. He has some idea of going to America to lecture. I think the career of Miss Edwards over there stirred him up.[4] I would see that he did not believe that women could be very profound students in anything, though, of course, he did not actually say so to me. I think we can be, only our education must begin a hundred years before we are born. It means that it will take several generations of study and training before our girls can equal our boys in scholarship, or, rather, before our women can equal our men. Brugsch is a German and thinks the sex not capable of deep investigation or endued with the scientific spirit. When he spoke rather slightingly of Miss Edwards' knowledge about Egypt he merely meant he had no faith in her because she was a woman—I fancy he knew nothing of her personally. Of course I do not agree with Brugsch. I think the feminine mind inferior to the masculine at present, simply because our girls have not for centuries been solidly educated as boys have been. The Woman's Colleges are movements towards rectifying this state of things. Girls do so much need a more thorough education. I seldom hear my own sex talk long without noticing the lack of broad, reasonable, solid views." "But," she repeats, "training is all that is needed." . . .

Never with all her love for stories and sunny climes did Miss Woolson cease to be truly American, and she thus describes an evening in Cairo.

"Eugene Schuyler gave a house-warming on Easter Monday.[5] A lady present invited me to her rooms in the evening and I went. As I entered the parlor the piano was sounding forth the strains of 'Tenting on the Old Camp Ground.' A company, of whom Elihu Vedder the artist was one, were singing the chorus and from that we passed to 'Rally Round the Flag' and 'Marching through Georgia.'[6] It was very strange under the shadow of the Pyramids, as it were. I belong to the generations, you know, who felt those years (of the war) as they have felt nothing since." . . .

At one time she made a thorough study of early Italian art, taking painter by painter. As a byplay her fancy speculated on one of Titian's portraits—unknown, called "The Young Man in Black." She made out of him an imaginary career, not to his credit and her friends were invited to his defense. It was in prospect of the departure of acquaintances that she wrote, "It seems I should be the only American in Florence this year left alone with my Young Man in Black (The Rascal) and Botticelli."

The sore sense of loss while the tragic ending of her beauty-giving life is so recent makes it painful to dwell on that end. All who knew her loved her too much to think of her simply as a writer, though her place in literature is quite as secure as that of her famous uncle.

At the last she said very little. Perhaps the finely balanced brain suffered in her excessive weakness under the terrible disease which has proved fatal to so many. The physician's orders that she should not be left alone had reference to the fear that she might not be able to ring her bell, as she disliked another person in her sleeping room. She did this, however, and asked the nurse for some milk in a particular cup. While this was being brought no one will ever know just what happened. After perhaps three minutes' absence the attendant returned to find the couch vacant and the room empty. There was only a small white heap on the pavement below, and, before morning, the wires were carrying under sea and over land a sad message that needed no explanation wherever the English tongue is read.

Whoever has been in the Protestant Cemetery at Rome, just outside the picturesque ancient gate to Ostia, and under the imposing presence of the pyramid of Caius Cestius, must have a deep impression of the spot. The quiet seclusion near the imperial city walls, the greenery and sweet blooms above the resting places of so many whose names sound along the years, the tall monument telling in silent massiveness through all the ages of Christendom of human mortality and human love, make it a place where one would choose to be laid, "life's fitful fever over" to sleep well.

There by the dust of Shelley's heart is hers amid an illustrious company. After a service in the chapel, said by a mourning friend, her flower-laden coffin was lowered to its final place amid the tears of loving hearts from two hemispheres. Violets are planted over it for the leaves are ever green under the sky of Italy and we may imagine that Anne, and Margaret, with all the attendant creations of that busy fancy from Little Silver in "Castle Nowhere" to the filial Maso in Pisa will keep watch and ward over the grave.

Notes

1. A graduate of Mount Holyoke College, Linda T. Guilford was Constance Fenimore Woolson's teacher at the Cleveland Female Seminary during the early 1850s. Woolson corresponded with Guilford throughout her life.

2. Water Cure Woods, a large Cleveland area forest. In a letter to Guilford, Woolson writes: "I have travelled far and wide over the world . . . but I really think I have never found any forest so wild and so vast as the Water Cure Woods!" (Clare Benedict, ed., *Constance Fenimore Woolson*, vol, 2 of *Five Generations (1785–1923)* [London: Ellis, 1930], 42).

3. Flora Payne (1840?–1893) childhood friend of Constance Fenimore Woolson, married William Collins Whitney in 1869. The Whitneys became lights of New York, Washington, and European society during the last quarter of the nineteenth century. A lawyer by education, William Whitney played roles in both Cleveland administrations.

4. Miss Edwards is undoubtedly Amelia Blanford Edwards, popular novelist and traveler, who, after voyaging up the Nile in 1873–1874, abandoned novel writing, developed the idea of the Egypt Exploration fund, and popularized Egyptology. Her American lecture tour of 1889–1890 was highly successful. In her own day she was called "the first woman

Egyptologist." (See especially John David Wortham, *The Genesis of British Egyptology, 1549–1906* [Norman: University of Oklahoma Press, 1971], 106–109.)

5. Eugene Schuyler (1840–1890) was a diplomat, historian, and writer. When Woolson visited Cairo in 1890–1891, he was serving as the American consul-general.

6. Elihu Vedder (1836–1923), a painter and illustrator, lived most of his life in Rome although he returned frequently to America, where his work was well received.

Introduction, *Constance Fenimore Woolson*

CLARE BENEDICT

What seems to me to be completely absent is an appreciation—however inadequate—of Constance Fenimore Woolson's remarkable and unforgettable personality. It was said of her that she had never failed to win a person if she desired to do so, for her charm was potent and well-nigh irresistible. There were many who came under the spell and the spell was lasting.

Endowed by nature with a passionate and even stormy temperament, together with a keenly analytical mind, she possessed at the same time such rare insight and tact, combined with a broad liberality of outlook, and had, moreover, such intense sympathy with and understanding of all forms of suffering, whether physical or mental, as well as all moral and intellectual aspirations, that she was able to draw out of people the best that was in them, while giving them in return the most inspiring and comforting comprehension. As her sister wrote of her: "She always helped people; knew, not only just what to say and do, *but just how they felt!*"

Having to combat many serious ills in the course of her comparatively short life, yet she invariably rose above them, and made a success—virtually—of everything that she undertook.

She was a delightful talker, but also an excellent listener, her humour was kindly, her observation almost phenomenal. She disliked mediocrity, weakness and inaction, just as she adored originality, courage and strength. She was the soul of generosity, and never deserted a friend.

Like all creative artists, she suffered from periodical fits of acute depression, but her powers of enjoyment were correspondingly high, and her interests were many and catholic.

She had an intense love of nature, of wild-flowers and ferns (having been at one time an expert botanist), of walking, of boating, of dogs, of fine acting, of colour in nature and art. Her love of music was perhaps greater than all these; in her youth she had had a beautiful and well-trained contralto voice, but increasing deafness had obliged her to turn to pictures for some measure of that mental delight and stimulus which she had formerly derived

Excerpted and reprinted from Clare Benedict, ed., *Constance Fenimore Woolson*, vol. 2 of *Five Generations* *(1785–1923)* (London: Ellis, 1930), xiii–xvi. Sincere and repeated efforts to contact the copyright holder have been unsuccessful.

from music. Her courageous determination in so doing was but another proof of her strong character.

Of her love of reading it is unnecessary to speak—it was with her a veritable passion. It used to be said of her in jest that she had read everything of importance before she was twelve years old!

She was fond of society under certain conditions, and she never tired of studying human nature in all its various manifestations. She was always sought after in every circle in which she moved, and among her devoted comrades were men and women whose names were eminent in literature, art, learning, diplomacy, science and the Great World.

Holding a curiously low opinion of her own personal appearance, she was nevertheless considered by others to be unusually attractive, physically. She had a fine carriage and poise of the head, beautiful hands, and a delicate, almost transparent complexion, moreover there was about her an air of distinction which no likeness has fully reproduced.

Her attachment to the South and above all to Florida, remained unbroken to the very end, in spite of her later enthusiasm for Italy and the Orient, nor did she ever forget that "Isle of the North" where she had been so happy in her childhood and youth and which she subsequently described so vividly in the opening chapters of "Anne." As she says of herself in what was almost her last letter written by hand: "I often think that though I stay abroad, I *remember* better than anyone else."

Her last wish, written down as a "Reflection" on the Christmas Eve before her death, as she gazed from the Lido at the incomparable scene before her, seems to me to epitomize in a wonderful way her lofty mind and character.

"I should like to turn into a peak when I die, to be a beautiful purple mountain, which would please the tired, sad eyes of thousands of human beings for ages."

Note

1.   Clare Benedict, the daughter of Clara Woolson Benedict, was Constance Fenimore Woolson's niece and frequent companion.

REPRINTED CRITICAL
ASSESSMENTS
◆

[From *A History of American Literature Since 1870*]

FRED LEWIS PATTEE

Constance Fenimore Woolson's *Rodman the Keeper*, 1880, undoubtedly was a strong force in the new Southern revival. During the eighties Miss Woolson was regarded as the most promising of the younger writers. She was a grand niece of Cooper, a fact made much of, and she had written short stories of unusual brilliance, her collection, *Castle Nowhere*, indeed, ranking as a pioneer book in a new field. Again was she destined to be a pioneer. In 1873 the frail health of her mother sent her into the South and for six years she made her home in Florida, spending her summers in the mountains of North Carolina, Virginia, South Carolina, and Georgia. During the rest of her life her stories were studies of Southern life and Southern conditions. Only *Anne* of her novels and two late collections of Italian tales may be noted as exceptions.

It was in *Rodman the Keeper*, a collection of her magazine stories of the late seventies, that the North found its first adequate picture of the territory over which had been fought the Civil War. The Tourgee novels, which had created a real sensation, were political documents, but here were studies carefully wrought by one who did not take sides. It showed the desolation wrought by the armies during the four years, the pathos of broken homes and ruined plantations, the rankling bitterness, especially in the hearts of women, the helpless pride of the survivors, and the curious differences between the Northern and the Southern temperaments. It was careful work. Contemporary opinion seemed to be voiced by the Boston *Literary World*: The stories "more thoroughly represent the South than anything of the kind that has been written since the war."

Necessarily the standpoint was that of an observer from without. There was no dialect in the tales, there were no revealings of the heart of Southern life as in Harris and Page and the others who had arisen from the material they used, but there was beauty and pathos and a careful realism that carried conviction. A sketch like "Felipa," for example, is a prose idyl, "Up the Blue Ridge" is the Craddock region seen with Northern eyes, and the story

Reprinted from Fred Lewis Pattee, *A History of American Literature Since 1870* (New York: Century, 1915), 317–18.

that gives the title to the book catches the spirit of the defeated South as few writers not Southern born have ever done.

For a time Miss Woolson held a commanding place among the novelists of the period. After her untimely death in 1894 Stedman wrote that she "was one of the leading women in the American literature of the century," and again, "No woman of rarer personal qualities, or with more decided gifts as a novelist, figured in her own generation of American writers." But time has not sustained this contemporary verdict. Her ambitious novel *Anne*, over which she toiled for three years, brilliant as it may be in parts, has not held its place. And her short stories, rare though they may have been in the day of their newness, are not to be compared with the perfect art of such later writers as Miss King and Mrs. Chopin. She must take her place as one of the pioneers of the period who discovered a field and prepared an audience for writers who were to follow.

[From *The Advance of the American Short Story*]

EDWARD J. O'BRIEN

Constance Fenimore Woolson . . . is more difficult to classify. As a regionalist, her special field is the shore of the Great Lakes. But she also wrote creditable stories of indeterminate setting, tales of reconstruction days of the South, and vividly realized pictures of Italian life. It is on the shores of Lake Superior, however, and among the French *habitants* that she sets the scene of her most characteristic stories. She does not always avoid the reproach of sentimentality, and she was influenced by every fashion to achieve admirable pastiche, so that influences as diverse as those of Bret Harte and Rose Terry Cooke and Henry James have deeply affected her. And yet this baffling transitional figure somehow commands our respect, so that we believe in her accomplishment, and feel that in a more settled environment which had long racial memories and a more implicit culture, she might have gone very far indeed.

Excerpted and reprinted from Edward J. O'Brien, *The Advance of the American Short Story* (New York: Dodd, Mead, 1931), 162–63. Sincere and repeated efforts to contact a copyright holder have failed.

Sympathetic Art

John Hervey

Constance Fenimore Woolson . . . beside being a niece of Fenimore Cooper, was in her own right one of the finest novelists that America thus far has produced. Her story, "For the Major," was perhaps a novelette rather than a novel, but in this day its theme would have been expanded into double the length she allowed it, for the novelist of the 'eighties seldom, as a practice, beat out her materials so thin as is now the vogue. . . .

I have been constrained to sketch the story of "For the Major" because, while it is one of the little masterpieces of American fiction and will so remain, it is, presumably, nowadays read by few people, as is the case with "Anne," "East Angels," "Jupiter Lights," and Miss Woolson's other works, despite the fact that as social studies and on the score of literary art they have been surpassed by none of our women novelists of later days. What makes "For the Major" live, what gives it its enduring charm, is its perfect sincerity and exquisite sympathy. It is written with a quiet humor that abounds in touches worthy of Jane Austen, with an extraordinary insight and clairvoyance, a lightness of touch that is unfailing. . . .

Now, one can imagine without great difficulty the story of Miss Woolson retold in the manner and with the accent of Miss Glasgow. Nothing would be easier, to so expert a craftsman as the gifted author of "They Stooped to Folly," than to turn it into just such a book as that one is. Without exception, there is not a character in "For the Major" that would not lend her or himself to the uses of satire with complete facility and once they had been exposed to its attacks what rags and tatters of sheer futility they would become. After the spectacle of Aunt Agatha, of Mrs. Dalrymple, of Milly, as that implacable and caustic pen has portrayed them, one shivers to think of the fate of little Madame Carroll, of the Major, and of all the rest—particularly the clergyman, whose abjectness would no doubt leave him no lower depth to which to sink. . . . Miss Woolson, however, saw them with a difference and she invested them all with the garment not of hatred but of pity. Little Madame Carroll, especially, that living lie— with what infinite mercy, what a penetrating and beautiful sympathy she surrounds her, making of her not a puppet but a living, breathing, suffering,

Excerpted and reprinted from *Saturday Review of Literature*, 12 October 1929, 268.

human being, clothed with a luminosity and a passion that elevate her, at last, into a tragic figure in the high Greek sense.

A novel is, after all, only a story: what the author, what the reader, makes of it. But in the end it remains either sincerity or a simulacrum. Either it is warm with life and suffused with humanity or it is something got-up and frigid, clever to the ultimate but unconvincing.

Miscellaneous Writings—1870–1879

John Dwight Kern

The verse of Miss Woolson shows less interest in local color than any other form of her writing. It is true (as has already been pointed out) that she wrote a few poems about the lake country and about the South, but most of her verse is free from that interest in setting which is a feature of her best creative work. Almost all of her poems were written while she lived in this country; that is, before her progress as a writer convinced her that her talents were better adapted to fiction. But the fact that her verses were published in the leading magazines of the time indicates that they are not without merit. Miss Woolson had the ability to employ various metrical forms with some skill and the desire to express herself in poetic language; but she belongs, unfortunately, to that class of poets (not uncommon at the time) who substitute piety for inspiration and sentimentality for deep emotion.

These poems can be classified in accordance with the following scheme: verses on persons; poems on nature and the seasons; love lyrics; verses on pet dogs; nonsense verse; poems on abstract themes; and miscellaneous verses. Most of these poems were separately published, though a few of them appeared among Miss Woolson's prose works and others have been printed only recently in Miss Clare Benedict's *Five Generations*.

Among the poems addressed to persons, the first (and also the author's first published poem) is an anonymous tribute to "Charles Dickens. Christmas, 1870,"[1] revealing that early interest in Dickens which found expression in several of the less important short stories. In the story, "St. Clair Flats," there is, curiously enough, a sentimental poem on "Cleopatra."[2] Another poem addressed to an individual is called "On a Homely Woman, Dead,"[3] and indicates that solace for homeliness on earth can be found in a heavenly beauty. Miss Woolson pays her respects to fellow craftswomen in sonnets "To George Eliot"[4] and "To Jean Ingelow."[5] One of the most interesting of this group of poems is an elegy entitled "In Remembrance,"[6] written shortly after the death, on August 11, 1878, of Henry James Montague, the English actor who became famous on the New York stage. The verses are unsigned and Montague's name is not mentioned, but since the poem is included in

Excerpted and reprinted from John Dwight Kern, *Constance Fenimore Woolson: Literary Pioneer* (Philadelphia: University of Pennsylvania Press, 1934), 102–108.

Miss Woolson's own bibliography, and since there are references in it to the actor's career and to his burial in Greenwood Cemetery (in Brooklyn), the authorship and subject of the elegy are established beyond a doubt. Miss Woolson addressed several poems to members of her own family and close relatives: three stanzas on "Plum's Picture,"[7] to her niece, Clare Benedict; and verses, "In Memoriam. G. S. B.,"[8] on the tragic death of George Stone Benedict, husband of the author's younger sister, Clara.

Six of Miss Woolson's poems relate to nature and the seasons. The first of these, "The Herald's Cry,"[9] is a New Year's poem, celebrating the winter season and moralizing about the dead past. The verses entitled "Floating. Otsego Lake, September, 1872,"[10] describe the departure of summer from the vicinity of Cooperstown. In the poem "February"[11] an artist declaims on the dullness of that month, but intimates that with his art, combined with his love, he will transform both the present and the future. Two poems on plants, "Heliotrope"[12] and "Four-Leaved Clover,"[13] are sentimental treatments of the advantages of nature over art. The didactic verses on "Indian Summer"[14] point out a parallel between the prodigals of nature and the prodigals among men.

One of the favorite subjects of poetry—love—is the theme of seven rather uninspired lyrics. "Love Unexpressed,"[15] for example, complains that people on earth do not adequately express the love they feel for others; in heaven, thinks the author, all this will be different. Perhaps the best of the love lyrics is that called "The Heart of June,"[16] which contains a lush imagery rather unusual to its author. It is just possible that the verses entitled "The Haunting Face"[17] are addressed to some lover whom the writer could not forget. There is also a possibility that the lines on "Memory"[18] are to some extent autobiographical; as these verses—

> . . . perhaps that love we spurned
> For one that proved unreal

—might be interpreted as indicating that the author scorned love in her search for a literary career. Two lovers are the characters in "October's Song,"[19] a silly poem in which October indicates its preference for brown eyes as against blue or gray. The poem called "Mizpah. Genesis XXXI. 49"[20] is an invocation, with a personal note, asking the Lord to watch between loved ones who are absent one from the other. "I Too!,"[21] evidently written in a despondent mood, expresses the desire of the author for such happiness as even the birds and the butterflies seem to enjoy.

The fondness of Miss Woolson for dogs, apparent in many references contained in her letters and fiction, is also expressed in three of her poems. The amusing "Complaint of Pete Trone, Esq.,"[22] in which the author's little black-and-tan terrier states his desires, takes the form of a "dog-gerel petition." "Tom"[23] tells the story of how a dog saved a baby from the fire after a number of men had struggled vainly to extinguish the flames. This poem has long been a favorite for purposes of declamation. The verses to "Gentleman Waife"[24] celebrate the death of the faithful little dog who, it will be remembered, accompanied Miss Woolson on her "Voyage to the Unknown River."

The Old Stone House contains several examples of clever nonsense verse. The "Ode to Chicago,"[25] for instance, is a humorous exposure of the various pronunciations of the name of the lake metropolis. "A June Lyric"[26] is a bit of extravagance in the manner of a coxcomb who thinks himself a poet. The eight verses of "A June Rhapsody"[27] show that their author was a humorist of some ability:

> The lovely month of June has come,
>   The sweetest of the year,—
> (I've heard this somewhere;—never mind!)
>   The meadows green and sear;—
> Sear's not the word; there's something wrong,—
>   I fear my muse will drop
> The fire of genius' flowing song,
>   And so I'd better stop!

The last of these nonsense verses is a parody[28] of Tennyson's "Brook," poking fun at the inveterate punning of Miss Woolson's brother.

A number of Miss Woolson's poems deal with abstract themes, treated usually in a moralizing fashion. The influence of Browning is apparent in the poem "Ideal. (The Artist speaks.),"[29] in which the speaker concludes that he should paint the ideal rather than the real, on the theory that "the ideal shall become the real." The thoroughly genteel tone of all of Miss Woolson's works is in accord with the artistic theory expressed in this poem. In the verses called "Commonplace"[30] the author undertakes a defense of Philistinism that is probably a direct result of her coldness towards Matthew Arnold. A moral screed entitled "The Greatest of All is Charity"[31] is directed principally against sharp-tongued and proud-hearted women. Several lines of the poem called "Two Ways"[32] are reminiscent of the younger Margaret Fuller's "Dryad Song." Like her contemporary, Miss Woolson finds in her heart the assurance of immortality. "Hero Worship"[33] is an uninspired plea to accord the highest respect to "the living whom we love" as well as to the few illustrious dead. The discovery of a faded paper on which the author had written in her youth is responsible for the sentimental musings on the evanescence of knowledge contained in the verses entitled "Forgotten."[34] The various manifestations of grief at the death of loved ones are recorded with true poetic fervor in the untitled lines beginning:

> Far back within the cycles of the past,
>   A train of centuries rolls,

From out whose cloudy borders came the day
    Of memory for all souls.
How long it seems, a thousand years ago!
How dark and weary, if we did not know
A thousand years are but as yesterday within His sight,
Seeing that it is past like one brief watch within the night![35]

Some of Miss Woolson's verses, because of their variety of theme and treatment, do not fit conveniently into any of the previous classifications. Among these miscellaneous poems is " 'Only the Brakesman,' "[36] a narrative in nineteen stanzas of irregular hexameters expressing, by means of a dramatic monologue, the circumstances attending the death of a railroad worker and the consequent grief of his mother. In the verses addressed "To Certain Biographers,"[37] the writer seems to have anticipated the type of criticism that has been directed against the modern school of "debunking" biographers. Her position is that writers should emphasize the virtues rather than the blemishes in the lives of famous men. She does not seem to realize that the unpleasant "mud-slinging" against which she inveighs is a natural reaction from the Parson Weems school of biographical whitewashing. Among the various types of poetry which Miss Woolson attempted is a good example of social verse, entitled "An Intercepted Letter."[38] These lines are an amusing description of life and customs at Narragansett, one of the fashionable resorts of the time. The intense religious convictions of Miss Woolson are displayed in some pious and uninspired lines based on John 17:15, beginning:

Not out of the world, dear Father,
    With duties and vows unfulfilled,
With life's earnest labors unfinished,
    Ambition and passion unstilled;[39]

Among the miscellaneous poems are a number of verses first published in the volumes edited by Miss Clare Benedict. These include: "Gettysburg. 1876,"[40] a poem reminiscent of Lincoln's Gettysburg Address; "Martins on the Telegraph Wire,"[41] a decidedly feminine rhapsody on the human qualities of birds; "We Shall Meet Them Again,"[42] expressive of the author's assurance of increasing her circle of acquaintants and cementing the bonds of friendship in the next world; and "Alas!"[43] the poet's expression of dismay at her inability to parade the pageant of her bleeding heart before the world.

Notes

1. *Harper's Bazar* (December 31, 1870), III, 842.
2. *Appleton's Journal* (October 4, 1873), X, 423.
3. *Harper's Bazar* (April 1, 1876), IX, 210.

4. *The New Century for Woman* (May 20, 1876), No. 2, p. 1.
5. *Ibid.* (July 8, 1876), No. 9, p. 67.
6. *New York Evening Post*, Friday, October 18, 1878, p. 2.
7. Benedict, III, 650.
8. *Ibid.*, III, 649. Miss Benedict indicates that the poem was originally published in *The Churchman*, but a careful search through the files of that journal has failed to reveal it.
9. *Lippincott's Magazine* (January 1872), IX, 98.
10. *New York Evening Mail* (Saturday, September 14, 1872), VIII, 1.
11. *Appleton's Journal* (February 8, 1873), IX, 210.
12. *Harper's New Monthly Magazine* (July 1873), XLVII, 274.
13. *Harper's Bazar* (July 8, 1876), IX, 443.
14. *Appleton's Journal* (October 17, 1874), XII, 500.
15. *Ibid.* (March 9, 1872), VII, 273.
16. *The Galaxy* (June 1872), XIII, 816.
17. *Appleton's Journal* (December 6, 1873), X, 723.
18. *Ibid.* (November 8, 1873), X, 597.
19. *Harper's New Monthly Magazine* (October 1872), XLV, 753.
20. *Appleton's Journal* (June 1877), II (n.s.), 539.
21. *Ibid.* (September 1877), III (n.s.), 270.
22. *The Old Stone House*, pp. 130–131.
23. *Appleton's Journal* (May 20, 1876), XV, 656.
24. Benedict, I, 233–34. Miss Benedict indicates that this poem is reprinted from *The Animal Kingdom*, a privately printed pamphlet or periodical of which I can find no record.
25. Pp. 110–11.
26. Pp. 113–14.
27. P. 118.
28. P. 292.
29. *Atlantic Monthly* (October 1872), XXX, 461.
30. *Lippincott's Magazine* (February 1873), XI, 59–60.
31. *Harper's Bazar* (February 8, 1873), VI, 90.
32. *Atlantic Monthly* (June 1873), XXXI, 669–70.
33. *Harper's New Monthly Magazine* (October 1873), XLVII, 727.
34. *Ibid.* (July 1876), LIII, 216.
35. *The Old Stone House*, pp. 324–26.
36. *Appleton's Journal* (July 1876), I (n.s.), 47–48.
37. *Ibid.* (September 1878), V (n.s.), 376.
38. *Harper's Bazar* (September 7, 1878), XI, 578.
39. *The Old Stone House*, pp. 254–55.
40. Benedict, III, 224–45.
41. *Ibid.*, II, 81–82.
42. *Ibid.*, II, 545–47.
43. *Ibid.*, II, 495–96.

[From *American Fiction: An Historical and Critical Survey*]

ARTHUR HOBSON QUINN

Miss Woolson's later short stories were concerned largely with European scenes. After her mother's death in 1879, she went to England and the Continent, staying most frequently in Italy. Her first short story written abroad, "Miss Grief,"[1] is of special interest because the central character is a woman who dies of privation rather than change her powerful but crude drama to suit the critical judgment of a popular author. Curiously enough, it was not included in either of the two collections published after her death, *The Front Yard and Other Italian Stories* (1895) and *Dorothy and Other Italian Stories* (1896), for it is one of the best. The similarity of this theme to some of those used later by Henry James is also noteworthy, since it was in 1880, under his guidance, that she grew to know Florence, her favorite among Italian cities. In these later stories, the American characters are the most important; sometimes indeed they are the only ones. The European scene remains the background, but it is an integral part of the narrative. Sometimes, as in "The Street of the Hyacinth,"[2] it is the belief that she can paint which brings an American girl to Rome, but it is her poise and courage under disappointment that lend distinction to the narrative. In "The Front Yard"[3] not only the scene but also the Italian characters form a contrast to the American. This is a fine study of a New England woman, Prudence Wilkin, who has married an Italian and who takes care of his family after his death, including a terrible old woman, the grandmother of his first wife. Living in Assisi, Prudence is oblivious to its meaning. To her life is not beauty but duty. The one thing she longs for is a "front yard" such as she had had in New Hampshire, but each time she saves up enough to start one, she makes a new sacrifice for her adopted family. Courage and fixity of purpose make the Americans in the later stories memorable. The way Mrs. Azubah Ash, an elderly woman, rises to command the situation after her son has killed his rival in "Neptune's Shore,"[4] the clear grit of the fourteen-year-old lad in "A Transplanted Boy,"[5] who plays a man's part, without heroics; both are revelations of a power that showed no sign of weakening.

Reprinted from Arthur Hobson Quinn, *American Fiction: An Historical and Critical Survey* (New York: Appleton-Century, 1936), 340–42. Reprinted with permission.

When the social scene is important, her Americans are never the vague uncertain figures of Henry James. Even the expatriated Americans like Mrs. Churchill in "A Pink Villa" are real. But what distinguishes Miss Woolson's stories from the usual magazine fiction is the way she can fix a character with one brief sentence. "No vulgar affluence oppressed Isabella. She had six hundred dollars a year of her own and each dollar was well bred." Her art is a fine art; one returns to her fiction for the sheer joy in well-controlled creation. She knew her own limitations as well as those of her characters. For the daring female of literature she had no respect, and she puts the case for her own manner brilliantly in one of her short stories, "At the Chateau of Corinne." In her delicate and distinguished art, she and Miss Jewett represented at its height that ability to guide with a firm hand the steeds of imagination and introspection which carried the so-called feminine impulse in American fiction very far toward perfection. Henry James in his *Partial Portraits* chose to place her with George Eliot, Trollope, and Turgenev and his judgment was sounder than that which has apparently forgotten her. But at the time of her death (she fell or threw herself from her window in Venice in 1894), she was recognized as one of the most consummate artists in that great epoch of the novel.

Notes

1. *Lippincott's Magazine*, May, 1880.
2. *Century Magazine*, May–June, 1882.
3. *Harper's Magazine*, December, 1888.
4. *Harper's Magazine*, October, 1888.
5. *Harper's Magazine*, February, 1894.

Constance Fenimore Woolson, "Novelist Laureate" of America

Lyon N. Richardson

The centenary of her birth is here. Were one to follow some of various printed accounts, one might accept either 1938 or 1948 as the centennial year. But it is wiser to follow her scholarly biographer, John Dwight Kern, and set the date as 1940. Using source material in *Five Generations*, by Miss Clare Benedict (Miss Woolson's niece), Kern quotes from the mother's journal: ". . . in the early days of March, came Number Six (Constance). . . . When she was but two days old, scarlet fever appeared in our family, and in three short weeks, three of our dear little ones entered Paradise." The *Grave Stone Records* of Claremont, New Hampshire, record that year as 1840.

Domestic sorrows account for Miss Woolson's far-flung literary scenes. In 1840, when the six children became three, the two eldest and baby Connie surviving, the family left Claremont, in the beautiful valley of the Connecticut River flanked by New Hampshire hills, and moved to the infant city of Cleveland, Ohio. Here, as the years passed, Miss Woolson's horizon widened, and came to include the Tuscarawas Valley, the Lake Superior region, and Madame Chegaray's school in New York City, from which she was graduated when she was eighteen years of age.

Again sorrow came. The roots in Cleveland soil were severed one by one. Her eldest sister, the wife of Samuel Livingston Mather, and the next eldest, the young widow of a deceased minister of Grace Episcopal Church, both died; and Connie, born the sixth child, became the eldest surviving. The death of her father in 1869 was the determining factor which turned her into the path of literary work; the following year, when thirty years of age, her first descriptive articles were published. In 1871 George S. Benedict, one of the publishers of the *Daily Cleveland Herald* and husband of Constance's younger sister Clara, was killed in a widely-reported railroad drawbridge accident along the Hudson River near Hamburg, New York. Fate had cut the several roots; the losses and the uncertain state of her mother's health led Constance and Mrs. Woolson to the South. There was Asheville in summer, and St. Augustine in winter, with several excursions or periods of residence

Excerpted and reprinted from *South Atlantic Quarterly* 39 (January 1940): 20–36. Published by Duke University Press, Durham, NC. Reprinted with permission of the publisher.

in Charleston, in Tennessee, Georgia, and other places. Miss Woolson continued to write short stories; when Northern materials faded, she began to use
the Southern locales.

Sorrow came a third time to change her way of life when her mother
died in 1879, and Miss Woolson and her sister, Clara Benedict, sailed in
November for Liverpool. After leisurely wandering on the Continent, she
chose Italy for residence—Florence, and Rome, and finally Venice—with
long excursions in summer to Switzerland and Germany, and two periods of
residence in England. Rome became for her the "most magical" city, London
the "most interesting," Vienna the "most brilliant," and Venice the "most
divine." In Europe she wrote her five novels, all of them stories of the South
or of the Mackinac region, as well as a number of short stories of Americans
in Italy and of Italian peasant life.

As the years progressed, her intense enjoyment of music was taken from
her by hardness of hearing, but the art galleries and literature and life in
Venice remained to delight and to comfort. On January 19, 1894, she
dictated her last letter, explaining that she was "in bed with influenza."
Accounts of the next five days vary. There is one statement that typhoid
fever developed. Certainly for some time she had been melancholy, as her
letters indicate. Her early teacher and intimate correspondent, Miss Linda
T. Guilford, in some manuscript "Notes in Memory of Miss Woolson," at
the Western Reserve Historical Society, refers to "the terrible disease which
has proved so fatal to many."[1] Another close friend, Mrs. Marie L. Thomp-
son, in an unpublished letter from Florence, February 12, 1894, to a member
of her family, mentions a "second acute attack of influenza" and "the brain
fever which formed a part of her last illness." On January 24, at a moment
when it is reported she had sent her nurse from the room to bring some
milk, Miss Woolson fell or leaped from her bedroom window to the street
below, and never regained consciousness.

Although Miss Woolson did not turn to authorship until she was nearly
thirty, her heritage was uncommonly literary. Before his marriage, her father,
Charles Jarvis Woolson, somewhat "bookish," had planned to publish a
newspaper in Charlottesville, Virginia, and at one time was part owner of
the *New England Palladium*, of Boston. His marriage brought obligations
best satisfied by engaging with his father in the manufacture of stoves at
Claremont, but the nuptials which deflected his life from journalism only
modified his daughter's literary background, for his wife was Hannah Cooper
Pomeroy, of Cooperstown, New York, niece of James Fenimore Cooper and
an heir to the Cooper tradition which Constance came to cherish. From
Athens she wrote in 1890: ". . . I can truthfully say that the only American
author universally known in France, Germany, Italy, Austria, & Switzerland,
is Cooper. Old, thumbed translations, in the language of the country, I have
found everywhere, even in small villages."

Some of Miss Woolson's own girlhood lies recorded in her book for children, *The Old Stone House*, published in 1873 under the pseudonym of "Anne March." There were paintings and music, and there was literature especially, to interest the children. In one scene in the book, the children, organizing themselves for play, willingly yield the delight of a torchlight procession to play "Editor's Sanctum," each child supplying a poem, a story, or an essay. On another occasion they celebrate the Fourth of July with a drama of their own composition, featuring Israel Putnam as hero, the spy Nathan Hale as the villain, and Bunker Hill as a scene of glorious action. Literary expression was a normal part of Miss Woolson's childhood activities.

Miss Mary Lyon, founder of Mt. Holyoke College, unwittingly did her best to rob Miss Woolson of her most inspiring literary tutor, for she counseled her protégée, Miss Guilford, not to come to Cleveland to teach; there was a well-established school for girls in near-by Willoughby which seemed to the president of Mt. Holyoke adequate for the region. Disregarding the advice, Miss Guilford arrived in Cleveland in 1848, as principal of a new girls' seminary, with twenty-one students. Six years later the school was merged with the Cleveland Female Seminary, under the direction of Dr. Samuel St. John, Professor of Geology at Western Reserve University. Miss Woolson later recalled happily her associations with Dr. St. John and Miss Guilford, writing to the latter when *East Angels* was published: ". . . it is from you that I first learned how to write. Do you remember the wonderful and ceaseless pains you used to take with our compositions?" Miss Guilford remembered the Connie Woolson of this period as blue-eyed, with wavy light-brown hair, fun-loving, dignified and cultivated of manner, eager to tramp the wooded swells of land southeast of Cleveland and to row on the winding, looping Cuyahoga River. Years later Miss Benedict remembered her in maturity as possessed of "a passionate and even stormy temperament," with capacity for acute depression and high powers of enjoyment. She loved wit, and was deeply sympathetic, yet she was intolerant of mediocrity.

Despite business reverses, father Woolson insisted that he and his family enjoy the luxury of long vacations. In Cleveland he continued his efforts to supplant fireplaces with stoves, and added merchandizing and banking to his interests. Unhappily, he placed too much faith in a partner, and, later, fire destroyed many hopes. But the family spent a number of summers on Mackinac Island—Connie's first voyage was made in 1855—and there were trips into Wisconsin and two-week excursions by horse and buggy through northern Ohio.

These vacations became Miss Woolson's first literary capital. In 1870 her descriptive articles and stories began to appear, and soon she was contributing to *Scribner's Monthly, Harper's New Monthly Magazine,* the *Atlantic Monthly,* and the *Galaxy.* Books of short stories were popular in the latter part of the century and her stories of the Great Lakes region were published in book form in 1875 under the title, *Castle Nowhere: Lake-Country Sketches.* Poetry, mainly short narratives, also appeared in magazines, but she never allowed a collection of her poetry to be made, though in an unpublished letter from Villa Brichieri, Florence, she mentions that both Harper and Appleton had asked her to allow her scattered poems to be published in a volume. Only her single long poem, *Two Women: 1862*, originally published in *Appleton's Journal*, was later reprinted separately as a book (1877).

The quality of freshness characterizes Miss Woolson's regional stories of the Lakes; in the spirit of discovery the reader approaches the characters, the localities, and the periods. Traveling by horse and carriage, Miss Woolson came to know the Zoarites of a rural German Separatist community in the Tuscarawas Valley of Ohio—"The Happy Valley." And by horse and carriage Miss Woolson introduces us to the story of Wilhelmina, who is in love with Gustav, who has joined the ranks in the Civil War. When he returns home with worldly views and is a bit dissatisfied with Wilhelmina, her mother persuades her daughter to marry baker Jacob, who is a widower with five children, and so sound in his rigidities and simplicities and insistence that he is soon left a widower again. Here also we are introduced to the story of Solomon and his wife. Solomon is an outlander by birth, having spent his early life near Painesville, Ohio; by occupation he is a miner, but at heart he is an artist. After repeated failures, he dies in the comforting illusion that he has finally achieved an acceptable portrait of his wife. The German settlers did not like Miss Woolson's stories about them, but they were of a clan who would also frown on Solomon's paintings as a waste of time, and perhaps symbols of the sin of vanity, images sprung from an addled mind.

Proceeding up the Lakes in memory, she turned her pen to "The Wine Islands of Lake Erie" and to the extraordinarily descriptive "St. Clair Flats." In the Flats, near Detroit, a region of marsh and reeds cut by labyrinthine channels in which she glided, she met on a bit of land the religious fanatic, Waiting Samuel, and his obedient wife. Then on and up to "Fairy Island"— Mackinac—wonderful and startling, for, amidst the virgin wilderness, lay an old town, fallen in decay, with dingy warehouses, once full of furs, now empty.

Odd, eccentric, and stray characters often lurk along the fringe of wildernesses, where their idiosyncrasies have driven them from populous areas; and they may be the more easily observed where few men tread. Miss Woolson recorded them. At Fort Mackinac, in "Jeannette," a young Boston physician, in spite of his sophisticated rationalizations, is falling an unwilling victim to his love of an impetuous native maid of French, Indian, and English ancestry; but though the young man's reason fails to guide him, her instinct easily rescues them—for she gives her hand to a local fisherman. Over on the shores of Lake Superior, in a small mining camp, little Peter the Parson, whose sobriquet gives title to the story, lonesomely carries on in full ritualistic detail the services of the Episcopalian Church, as though his were a rectory in rural England; a thief in the guise of a religious revivalist ridicules him as a cowardly, impotent fellow in the midst of a camp of strong men, yet

Peter is bold enough to die in an attempt to save the miners from the sin of murdering the revivalist when the latter's thieving designs become known. And on the southernmost of the twenty-three islands known as the Twelve Apostles, in the western end of Lake Superior, at Misery Landing, George is made the center of a dramatic story of the power of external conditions on human behavior; though urged to forsake his environmentally adjusted life for a larger but foreign world, he cannot leave his familiar haunts.

The most absorbingly romantic of her Great Lakes stories are "The Lady of Little Fishing" and "Castle Nowhere." The first is a chronicle of religious experience on Little Fishing Island, in Lake Superior, among a camp of men. The Lady enters as a voice of God and Conscience, and her commands to walk in the ways of righteousness are observed until she falls in love with one of the men; then, contemptuous of anything less than mystery, all of them fall again into their ungodly ways. Fred Lewis Pattee has awarded this story a rank far above that of Bret Harte's "The Luck of Roaring Camp," which it somewhat resembles in its basic idea. Castle Nowhere is hidden in the wilds bordering the northern end of Lake Michigan. In it lives old Fog, who has fled to this uninhabited region after killing a man, and who occasionally salvages cargoes washed ashore from ships he has lured to destruction by setting up false lights. To atone for his early crime, he has devoted his life to a little girl, and has reared her in Castle Nowhere with elaborate regard for her innocence. Her marriage to a young man of good breeding temporarily enjoying life as a woodsman, who accidentally discovers the castle, is occasion for a visit to Beaver Island, on which dwell a Presbyterian minister and a colony of Mormons—"as reckless a set of villains as New World history can produce," men who steal nets and wives, and, like Fog, lure boats onto hidden rocks.

*   *   *

Even Miss Woolson's descriptive sketches were done with a conscious literary philosophy. She did not believe that artists should try to express action with their lines, or that writers should try merely to paint pictures with words. Thus there is story-value and motion in her most descriptive of Southern writings, "The South Devil." Among her writings, it is for Florida what "St. Clair Flats" is for the Great Lakes country. In the company of approaching death, and finally with death itself, she takes the reader through the South Devil swamp, beautiful, odorous, oppressive, poisonous, deadly, with claret-colored pools, lilies, tall cyprus trees, birds, and snakes and other venomous creatures.

*   *   *

The literary tasks Miss Woolson set for herself were never easy. Her notebooks are filled with germinal ideas; themes, scenes, situations, and characters were matters for cogitation. These thoughts she kept for reference, waiting the while to discover which of them were so closely associated with her inner nature that they would develop into adequate representations of life. Her work was never of the surface; her characters were never conceived as puppets moving in the restricted areas of mechanically devised plots, although she did in her novels rely too much on coincidence.

*   *   *

From unpublished letters, a picture of her later years—the years of all her novels and of half her short stories—may be discerned. Her investments brought her income enough to pay rent to the landlords; but she felt financially dependent on her literary earnings, which were modest. She was worried about the state of her health, for the extended periods of illness limited her production. Still, she could not work rapidly even when she was well, for there was a basic aversion to ordinary slipshod writing which kept her always in the field of her utmost capacity. She marveled at the literary productiveness of Mrs. Margaret Oliphant and other English women of her day, but she could not imitate them.

To some extent, she felt the lack of family life, and tried various substitutes, including frequent change of scene and, at one time, a trial at renting and furnishing a villa in Florence. There was always her profession, but it was a profession requiring life-experiences, and she was restricted in her use of four themes which her feminine contemporaries employed so easily to win popular favor. I have mentioned her domestic limitations. Neither could she win the popular triumphs of Frances Hodgson Burnett and Mrs. Humphrey Ward, for she could not write of life in the factories or of evangelism along waterfronts. Muddled revaluations of the social and religious concepts fermenting in the minds of the middle class of the latter nineteenth century did not interest her. Asked her opinion of *Robert Elsmere* at a time when its religious theme made it internationally popular, she wrote that she could find "nothing the least new in it"; it was merely Matthew Arnold "a little widened," and though she admired Arnold's poetry, she could not relish his prose. Finally, popular triumph by glorifying the sex-emancipated woman was not for her; that theme and its exponents violently displeased her. Of Louise de la Ramée she wrote from Villa Brichieri, Florence: "Ouida (of whom you speak) has left Florence for good. She says she was not appreciated here. She is now in England—where, let us hope, appreciation surrounds her richly. She made a goose of herself here by falling in love with a young Italian 20 years younger than herself. She thought he wd. marry her (he is a Marchese); but he did not. While the affair was going on, Ouida (who is 55) wore her hair braided down her back in two long tails, tied with blue ribbon, & attired herself in short white frocks, with juvenile sashes. If he did not notice her sufficiently (in company), she wd. sit down and pout, & swing her feet like a child. (N. B. Her feet are her only beauty.)"

Russian novels she appreciated. In one letter she mentions having read all of them that had been translated in French. To her, Turgenev's novels were by far the best, though she thought Dostoevski's *Crime and Punishment* "extraordinary," and while she disliked the personality of Tolstoy and thought him "insane, in a mild form," she admired *Anna Karenina* second only to the novels of Turgenev.

In her own chosen fields, in her short stories she drew careful delineations of life modified by natural environments in the country districts of America, and of those who lived in the foreign atmosphere of Italy. Metropolitan life meant nothing to her. In her novels, she expressed the moods of those who are not oriented, and of those who are not realizing the fullness of the natural experiences of life. Like the Hawthorne of *The House of the Seven Gables*, she worked in the retreats of minds made angular by frustrations which they could not analyze. She worked most painstakingly, with recuperating vacations in Switzerland, Germany, Austria, and England. No picture reveals more clearly her method and infinite pains than the one she drew of herself at Villa Brichieri, Florence, in an unpublished letter written one August 22: "Perhaps you will be interested in hearing how I arrange life? I am called at 4½ a.m. I take a cup of tea, & go out to walk at 5. Come in at 6, or soon after. Bath; breakfast; cool linen attire. Then my stand-up desk, where I remain until 7 p.m. with a half an hour's rest at noon. The whole house, after having been thrown open at dawn, is hermetically closed about 8; windows, blinds, inside shutters. Only one little ray of light is allowed to enter, & this illumines my desk. In that way, while it may be 90° outside, we can keep it at 74–76 within. At evening, dinner; the house is thrown open again; & the evening is spent on my high-up terrace, under the splendid stars, & overlooking the wide view."

Note

1.   "Notes in Memory of Miss Woolson" seems to have been an early draft of Guilford's "Reminiscences of Constance Fenimore Woolson," reprinted in this volume. Both versions appear in ms. 484 of the Western Reserve Historical Society archives.

[From *The Rise of the American Novel*]

ALEXANDER COWIE

An author able to elicit the high praise of so austere a critic as Henry James may be assumed to have mastered important elements in the technique of writing.[1] Praise from such a quarter would indeed for some people be presumptive evidence that the writer was more skilled than readable. Yet Constance Fenimore Woolson was not only an able craftsman but also in the 1880's and 1890's a popular writer, especially with that relatively superior audience comprised in part of readers of magazines such as *Harper's*, in which many of her stories first appeared. Her popularity of course has long since waned, and she is now in the familiar category of the superior minor writer who is periodically "rediscovered" by a sensitive critic or a zealous historian. No number of such discoveries, of course, can make her over into a major novelist. At best her art was extremely sensitive and delicate. True, she undoubtedly won many readers by the sensational, even melodramatic, materials which she sometimes ineptly introduced into her work. Yet vigorous action was not her forte: it is vain to look in her work for any suggestion of the broad powers of her illustrious kinsman (her mother was a niece of James Fenimore Cooper). The structure of a long narrative she never mastered. It is her distinction, rather, that she skilfully employed some aspects of that type of impressionistic technique which was one of the principal interests of the more serious post-Victorian novelists. She also added to the domain of the local-color writers who were prominent in the seventies and eighties.

Miss Woolson was born in New Hampshire, educated in Ohio, "finished" at a school in New York City, lived for several years in the South (Florida and the Carolinas), and traveled extensively in Europe.[2] She practiced writing at an early age, producing rapidly a considerable number of tales and sketches, the more successful of which are set in the Great Lakes country, where she spent her childhood. Her first volume of short stories, *Castle Nowhere: Lake Country Sketches* (1875), reprinted a number of pieces that had won favorable comment upon their first appearance in *Harper's, Lippincott's, The Galaxy*, and elsewhere. Her first novel, *Anne*, was published in 1882, and her last, *Horace Chase*, in 1894, the year of her death.

Reprinted from Alexander Cowie, *The Rise of the American Novel* (New York: American Book Co., 1951), 568–78. Sincere and repeated efforts to find a copyright holder have been unsuccessful.

Anne is a long book, presumably autobiographical in the first part and certainly set in a region which the author well knew. Its action, surprisingly enough, is often sentimental, morbid, and melodramatic. The heroine is Anne Douglas, at sixteen a very large girl regarded as a conscientious but somewhat colorless person. Unlike her immediate predecessors in popular fiction, she is not superficially alluring: "This unwritten face, with its direct gaze, so far neutralized the effect of the Diana-like form that the girl missed beauty on both sides."[3] The devoted daughter of a cultivated and amiable but eccentric old gentleman no longer gainfully employed, she does her best to stabilize his shaky personality and to bring up the four somewhat difficult children of his second marriage. Comforts are few and life is slow for Anne Douglas on the remote island (Mackinac) which is her home. Romance crosses her path in the person of a village lad named Rast, who asks her hand in marriage. But Rast must go off to college and, her father dying suddenly, Anne feels that she must accept the offer of a relative in New York who wishes to give her a year of tony schooling to the end that she may later become a teacher. New York itself proves to be a school of experience of more consequence to the story than the fussy little establishment of Mme. Moreau, and Anne is involved with two men, one of them a millionaire who wishes to marry her. The other (Heathcote), to whom Anne is more drawn, is prevented from offering marriage by reason of a commitment to one of Anne's friends, Helen Lorrington. Anne, like a good domestic heroine, runs away. But Heathcote later comes back into her life: he has married Helen but loves Anne! Though now freed from her somewhat tepid engagement to Rast—whose heart has been successfully stormed by one of Anne's step-sisters, the bewitching, ruthless little quarter-breed Tita—Anne resists the entreaties of Heathcote. Ultimately the story broadens into melodrama: Helen is found murdered and it devolves upon Anne to do enough amateur detective work to prove that Heathcote did not perpetrate the deed: the real murderer was left-handed! And Anne gets Heathcote—or vice versa. The story is much too diffuse. It is best in the first part—in the charming description of Anne's circumscribed life on the island. Her queer old father is a more satisfactory character than Heathcote. The portrait of the house-keeper, Lois Hinsdale, is fine: a New England spinster whose severity in the kitchen is balanced by her High Church religious preference. Unconsciously in love with Douglas, she has bitterly resented his (second) marriage to a giddy female of French and Indian blood and of Catholic faith; but she does not weary of caring for his children, and she helps to bind together a story that often threatens to break completely into fragments.

Yet some of the fragments are precious. The opening of the story provides an excellent illustration of Miss Woolson's meticulous impressionistic method. Eschewing the traditional (Victorian) type of beginning—in which the author plainly states what he regards as essential facts for the reader: where the scene is, what sorts of persons are in it, what the time is, what the activity of the moment is, etc.—Miss Woolson, like James, begins at once to communicate an experience *in the present*. She does not wish to tell or relate an action but to present it; not to "introduce" a story but to begin it. Necessary facts will be found as experience is unfolded. Characters are not summarized but will grow out of detailed impressions.[4] The quality of the whole book will be felt from the very beginning: indeed Miss Woolson at her best concretely illustrates James's opinion that

> A novel is a living thing, all one and continuous, like any other organism, and in proportion as it lives will it be found, I think, that in each of the parts there is something of each of the other parts.[5]

Thus Miss Woolson does not begin with a statement of the "inorganic" facts (1) that it was Christmas Eve on Mackinac Island; (2) that a father was conversing affectionately with his daughter while she was decorating a provincial church; (3) that they have different opinions about a valued housekeeper named Lois, etc. etc. Instead, she opens a dialogue which begins to reveal the characters not only of the speakers but of the third person as well. It will be seen that the quality of these paragraphs is precisely that of all other valid parts of the book:

> "Does it look well, father?"
> "What, child?"
> "Does this look well?"
> William Douglas stopped playing for a moment, and turned his head toward the speaker, who, standing on a ladder, bent herself to one side, in order that he might see the wreath of evergreen, studded with cones, which she had hung on the wall over one of the small arched windows.
> "It is too compact, Anne, too heavy. There should be sprays falling from it here and there, like a real vine. The greenery, dear, should be either growing naturally upward or twining; large branches standing in the corners like trees, or climbing vines. Stars, stiff circles, and set shapes should be avoided. That wreath looks as though it had been planed by a carpenter."
> "Miss Lois made it."
> "Ah," said William Douglas, something which made you think of a smile, although no smile was there, passing over his face, "it looks like her work; it will last a long time. And there will be no need to remove it for Ash-Wednesday, Anne; there is nothing joyous about it."
> "I did not notice that it was ugly," said the girl, trying in her bent posture to look at the wreath, and bringing one eye and a portion of anxious forehead to bear upon it.
> "That is because Miss Lois made it," replied William Douglas, returning to his music.[6]

It would be hard to find in fiction of the time an example of more skilful indirect characterization than is here presented. True, the reader must wait for the gradual absorption of these details into the whole body of the work to understand their full relationship to structure. True, also, Miss Woolson falls away, as *Anne* proceeds, from the high technical standard here exemplified, but the same method reappears, more evenly sustained, in her next long narrative, *For the Major* (1883).

For the Major (called by the author a "novelette") is more successful as a whole than *Anne* perhaps because its action is simpler and, except for a few exciting episodes, more suited to her special talent for finely discriminating effects. The situation fundamentally involves two venial deceptions that undoubtedly appealed to Henry James. The first is revealed shortly after Sara Carroll returns from Connecticut to Far Edgerley, a small secluded community presumably set in the mountains of North Carolina. She at first feels queerly frustrated in her attempt to resume the filial relationship with her father which had always been such a joy to her. Jealously she blames Madam Carroll, Major Carroll's second wife. When, however, the latter finally explains that the Major's mind is beginning to fail, Sara promptly co-operates with her in devising every protection for him. This involves coping with an unforeseen crisis that calls for a second deception. The appearance in Far Edgerley of a poverty-stricken, impudently vagabondish musician called Louis Dupont arouses the resentment of Far Edgerley, but Sara's step-mother astonishingly takes him up. Even more incredible to Mr. Owen, the Episcopal clergyman in love with Sara, is the fact that Sara has several clandestine meetings with the gay but sinister Bohemian. As if to end all gossip, Sara stuns the community by announcing her engagement to Dupont. Actually she has no intention of marrying him: he is the son of her step-mother! She has been conspiring with her step-mother to take care of him without revealing to the Major (or to the gossipy village) the true facts concerning Madam Carroll's first marriage. Her husband had been a rotter who had finally killed a man in a duel and fled from the law, taking their boy with him. Both were reported drowned. Left with a ten-year-old girl to support, the mother passed herself off as twenty-three (though she was thirty-five) when the Major courted her, her excuse being that she couldn't bear to destroy the pleasure the Major took in her "youth" and that she needed protection for her daughter who, however, soon died. The stratagem thus begun has to be carried out through the ensuing years by means of dye, rouge, and kindred arts. When the son turned up, the critical condition of the Major forbade an explanation. The son presently dies, but on his deathbed reports that the father had also escaped death by drowning, and was living at the time of his mother's marriage to the Major. This intelligence necessitates a formal marriage with the Major. But the Major happily wakes up one morning with his mind almost completely gone, and it is easy to arrange a ceremony in which he takes part pleasantly with no knowledge of what it signifies. Madam Carroll has had to take Mr. Owen the clergyman into her confidence, of course, but that is now an easy matter, for he will soon himself belong to the family—as the husband of Sara.

Obviously *For the Major* contains plot material which would forbid the author's throwing stones at the artificial structures of the domestic novelists. Yet in this book as in others, it is not finally the exciting plot materials that the author is concerned with, but the motives of the characters.[7] The difference between Miss Woolson and the domestic sisterhood lies in her comparatively condensed treatment of crude plot material and her artful elaboration of ethical problems created in the minds first of Madam Carroll and then of Sara. The impressionistic characterizations of the step-mother pleased Henry James:

> The conception of Madam Carroll is highly ingenious and original, and the small stippled portrait has a real fascination . . . Miss Woolson has done nothing of a neater execution than this fanciful figure of the little ringleted, white-frocked, falsely juvenile lady, who has the toilet-table of an actress and the conscience of a Puritan.[8]

Sara Carroll is almost equally well characterized, though allowed less space. Despite temperamental differences between her and the Major's wife, she willingly shares in the bizarre fiction on which the Major's tenuous happiness rests. Even when her rôle calls for action that seriously damages her in the eyes of her lover, she does not flinch. The key to her character as to that of so many characters in the novels of Henry James is high-minded renunciation.

But quite as fascinating to watch as the raveling of the fantastic fabrication of Madam Carroll is the revelation of the nature of the community in which the story takes place. Far Edgerley, as James has implied, may be a bit too steeped in Anglicanism and provided with more suggested past than a town in the New World can actually be possessed of:

> Miss Woolson likes little country churches that are dedicated to saints not vulgarised by too much notoriety, that are dressed with greenery (and would be with holly if there were any), at Christmas and Easter; that have "rectors," well connected, who are properly garmented, and organists, slightly deformed if possible, and addicted to playing Gregorian chants in the twilight, who are adequately artistic; likes also generations that have a pleasant consciousness of a few warm generations behind them, screening them in from too bleak a past, from vulgar draughts in the rear.[9]

Far Edgerley is brought to life perfectly with brush-strokes that are as faultless as they are gentle. Cranford is not more authentic. Much can be done by patience in a quiet community where the church is the centre of social life and where manners are so conservative that "There were persons in the congregation who considered whist-playing a test of the best churchmanship."[10] Genteel though these mountain folk be, they are so avid of personalia that the rector's every move coins local comment. Without effort Miss Woolson adjusts her tempo to miniature incident which, as in the following example, she often reports with genuine humor:

> Far Edgerley was deprived of its rector. Mr. Owen had gone to the coast to attend the Diocesan Convention. But as he had started more than a week before the time of its opening, and had remained a week after its sessions were ended, Mrs. General Hibbard was of the opinion that he was attending to other things as well. She had, indeed, heard a rumor before he came that there was *some one* (some one in whom he felt an interest) elsewhere. Now it is well known that there is nothing more depressing for a parish than a rector with an interest, large or small, "elsewhere." St. John in the Wilderness was therefore much relieved when its rector returned, with no signs of having left any portion of himself or his interest behind him. And Mrs. General Hibbard lost ground.[11]

The subsequent novels of Miss Woolson do not vary greatly in quality from her first two. Her principal theme continued to be magnanimity expressed in one form or another. In *East Angels* (1886) the main character is a dauntless, an almost incredible, illustration of self-sacrifice. Margaret, the wife of Lansing Harold, has every reason in the conduct of her husband to break with him and marry the affluent and cultivated Evert Winthrop. Instead she willingly shoulders the blame for her unharmonious marriage, resists the agreeable approaches of Winthrop, and when her husband finally returns as an invalid, devotes herself to nursing him. Isabel Archer in James's *The Portrait of a Lady* (1881) is not more heroic, though she is perhaps more real. But the unhappy marriage of the Harolds is only part of the excellent social study of St. Augustine which comprises *East Angels*. The novel also reports the affairs of a giddy group of pleasure-seekers of whom the most conspicuous, Garda Thorne, is a vivacious beauty who manages to get married twice. Her wanton conduct and obvious glamour make her a foil for the resolute Margaret. The book is comprehensive in its dramatis personae, being provided also with (principal) characters from the North, as well as full-blooded Spaniards, and the quarter-Spanish Garda. The characters, though individually well done, have a certain detached or "shipwrecked air"[12] but the Floridan mise-en-scène is firmly established in all its opulence and fascination. Yet by a very fine contrast which is perhaps referable to Miss Woolson's own origin in New England, the author draws one of her most successful characters in the exiled New Englander, Mrs. Thorne, who wholeheartedly hates the entire (Florida) section. Before her death she pours out all her long repressed love of her native region in a finely conceived speech which serves to emphasize the disparities that existed in "American" character in the 1870's. Mrs. Thorne, said James, is the "tragic form of the type of which Mrs. Stowe's Miss Ophelia was the comic."[13] Against these and other characters

Margaret Harold is seen, the utmost symbol of renunciation in personal relationships. *East Angels* is perhaps the fullest, the roundest, the most significant of Miss Woolson's novels.

With what fine integrity Miss Woolson observed her own principles as a writer was amusingly illustrated in a letter written in response to one from a young person who, like a majority of popular readers, would have preferred a happy ending in *East Angels*—a consummation that could easily have been arranged if the author had been willing to decree the death of Lansing Harold. Miss Woolson replies:

> My dear Miss Ethel.
> Your letter made me laugh,—it was so frank! It would indeed have been more agreeable for everyone, if Lansing Harold could have been (as you express it) "taken." But, in real life, such fortunate takings-off seldom occur, & it is real life I was endeavoring to picture. It is seldom indeed that I ask anyone to write to me, as I find it almost impossible to answer the letters I receive. But you are so honest that I propose that, after my next novel, you send a few lines more; what do you say? About "the happy ending" you ask for, we will see![14]

As it happens Miss Woolson's next novel, *Jupiter Lights* (1889), is equipped with a "happy ending" but only after a great quantity of trouble has been seen. The novel is interesting as a local color story "with scenes from each of the three regions with which Miss Woolson is associated: the South, the lake country, and Italy." Miss Woolson is particularly successful in her delineation of the South during Reconstruction.[15] Yet the chief power of *Jupiter Lights* derives from the concentrated study of troubled personal relations, being in this case a study of a woman who interfered disastrously in the affairs of another. A whole train of difficulty is set in motion when Eve Bruce undertakes to meddle in the affairs of Cicely Morrison, formerly the widow of Eve's dead brother, now the wife of a dipsomaniac in a small rundown town on an island off the coast of Georgia during the period of Reconstruction. Results include a shooting, a flight to the Lake Superior region, the death of the degraded husband, a love affair for Eve, her retirement to a convent in Italy, and—the happy ending—her lover's arrival at the convent, where he "batters his way to her and takes her in his arms."[16] Hemingway could have handled this strong plot in its externals much more plausibly than Miss Woolson: he might even have strengthened it by tossing in a few more shootings, stronger drinks, and more general violence. But he would have been puzzled by the ethical problems of Eve who is so troubled about a point of honor (her part in the episode that resulted in Morrison's death) that, like James's high-minded Strether, she wants to have gained nothing for herself "out of the whole affair."[17] "Can have and will not"—

that would be Hemingwayese for the attitude of many of the characters in Woolson. And it is precisely in the mental struggles of persons involved in such cases of casuistry that Miss Woolson, like James, succeeds most notably. In *Jupiter Lights*, however, the problem is largely lost in the frequently improbable action, and the book remains her least valuable novel. Miss Woolson can render setting and she can characterize quiet, well-bred people, but high tensions are likely to induce erratic fluctuations in the delicate instruments of her art.

Horace Chase (1894) marks a return to the narrower scope of action in which Miss Woolson moved with greatest freedom and sureness. Fundamentally it suffers from being too studied, too conscientious. It is unique among her novels in having for its centre of interest a man instead of a woman—in this case a successful businessman of considerable intelligence but of no great refinement. In type he is not far removed from James's Christopher Newman. His language is robust and colloquial. He is frankly interested in making money for the satisfaction of his ego: "For a big pile is something more than a pile; it's a proof that a man's got brains."[18] The time comes when he must prove whether he has fineness of character as well as practical intelligence. His wife becomes infatuated with another man to the point of following him to the house of a friend—only to learn (what except for her blindness she should have known before) that he is interested not in her but in another girl, whom he is about to marry. No simple return to her own hearth is possible, for her husband untimely arrives at the house. A way out of making the embarrassing disclosure of her folly is devised by her sister, but doggedly the wife prefers to face the music, expecting to be sent away by an outraged husband. Instead, Horace Chase magnanimously but quietly indicates that he wishes her to stay: "Have I been so faultless myself that I have any right to judge *you*?"[19] This is a typical situation with Woolson: a character proves his fineness by making a difficult decision when, so far as external pressure is concerned, he is a perfectly free agent. In this case the gesture is one of forbearance rather than of renunciation. To make the scene a mess of sentimentality based upon incredible self-sacrifice would have been easy, but the author prefers to handle the situations with the quiet restraint befitting a realist. The story, she revealed in a letter to the publishers, was based on an instance "from actual life."[20] Her aim in the settings (Asheville, North Carolina, and St. Augustine) is to be utterly faithful to fact. The whole is a good miniature, possessed of much, perhaps too much, well-wrought detail. Yet that subtle process of artistic enlargement by which a work passes out of the specific into the universal is lacking in this book, as well as in most of Miss Woolson's work.

In Miss Woolson's novels the narrative situation is the thing. She carried no banners, religious, political, or sociological. Digressions seldom occur and such social criticism as she indulges in takes a subordinate place on her page. Yet her writing is informed with a realistic spirit that is gradually felt to be characteristic of her nature. Her childhood nickname "And why?" suggests in exaggerated form her critical proclivities. Thus she sees the beauty of the country but she realizes how a rural life limits the opportunities of the individual and intensifies the provincialism of the group, especially on the frontier. When in a minor matter Mlle. Pitre fails to conform to village expectations, there is doubt about her integrity:

> Simple comment swelled into suspicion; the penny-saving old maid was now considered a dark and mysterious person at Lancaster. Opinions varied as to whether she had committed a crime in her youth, or intended to commit one in her age. At any rate, she was not like other people—in the country a heinous crime.[21]

The border Indians of the Great Lakes region were not only part of her story in *Anne* but also a sociological problem. Without sentiment or romance Miss Woolson candidly reports the difficulty experienced by white folk who attempted to civilize them:

> Years before, missionaries had been sent from New England to work among the Indians of this neighborhood, who had obtained their ideas of Christianity, up to that time, solely from the Roman Catholic priests, who had succeeded each other in an unbroken line from that adventurous Jesuit, the first explorer of these inland seas, Father Marquette. The Presbyterians came, established their mission, built a meeting-house, a school-house, and a house for their pastor, the buildings being as solid as their belief. Money was collected for this enterprise from all over New England, that old-time, devout, self-sacrificing community whose sternness and faith were equal; tall spare men came westward to teach the Indians, earnest women with bright steadfast eyes and lath-like forms were their aiders, wives, and companions. . . . The missionaries worked faithfully; but, as the Indians soon moved further westward, the results of their efforts can not be statistically estimated now, or the accounts balanced.
>
> "The only good Indian is a dead Indian," is a remark that crystallizes the floating opinion of the border. But a border population has not a missionary spirit. New England, having long ago chased out, shot down, and exterminated all her own Indians, had become peaceful and pious, and did not agree with these Western carriers of shot-guns. Still, when there were no more Indians to come to this island school, it was of necessity closed, no matter which side was right.[22]

Occasionally she pauses to correct false notions implanted in the popular mind by more sensational writers. When, for example, Anne takes her place in a fashionable school in New York, her fine character does not make her either hated or sanctified. An intermediate reaction on the part of Anne's mates seems more natural to Miss Woolson:

It was soon understood that "the islander" could sing as well as study. Tolerance was therefore accorded to her. But not much more. It is only in "books for the young" that poorly clad girls are found leading whole schools by the mere power of intellectual or moral supremacy. The emotional type of boarding-school, also, is seldom seen in cities; its home is amid the dead lethargy of a winter-bound country village.[23]

Similarly, the common conception of a nurse's romantic rôle during the Civil War is revised when a novice reaches the front:

But during that day, not only did the promised nurse from the Rivertown Aid Society arrive, but with her a volunteer assistant, a young girl, her face flushed with exaltation and excitement over the opportunity afforded her to help and comfort "our poor dear wounded heroes." The wounded heroes were not poetical in appearance; they were simply a row of ordinary sick men, bandaged in various ways, often irritable, sometimes profane; their grammar was defective, and they cared more for tobacco than for texts, or even poetical quotations.[24]

A fine restraint, then, distinguishes the realistic Miss Woolson from those scores of novelists who have erred on the opposite side of prolonged naturalistic descriptions of the horrors of war. Yet she does not lean over backward in this respect; and her sense of balance is shown by the fact that the same novice who found "her romance rudely dispelled" rose adequately to her situation; and since "there was good stuff in her, she would do useful work yet, although shorn of many illusions."[25] This is typical of the author in her better works: she prefers decent proportion to cheap intensity.

On the positive side (for Miss Woolson was not one to spend much time or effort upon correcting others) there was her original and vivid treatment of comparatively new regions; her pioneer studies of the difference between "the Anglo-Saxon and the Latin temperaments" in the South;[26] her faithful recording of Negro speech,[27] and her use of natural if unusually sensitive girls as heroines in place of the pasteboard saints of the popular novelists.[28] It was finally these heroines who inspired most of what was distinguished in the work of Constance Fenimore Woolson. She described their persons with a critical eye, understood the crises of their "private relations" with fine intuition, recorded their self-immolations with a quiet intensity that often lends exaltation to her page. Dynamic action jeopardized her art; larger structural units never quite found their equilibrium. But in the nooks and recesses of human experience she was wholly masterful. In *Anne* there is a church "whose steeple threw a slow-moving shadow across its garden, like a great sundial, all day." In some such sequestered place, where action is natural but unhurried, where light and shadow fulfill each other, belongs the special art of Miss Woolson.

Notes

1. See James's *Partial Portraits*, London, 1888, Chapter VI.

2. For a study of her life and writings see John Dwight Kern, *Constance Fenimore Woolson: Literary Pioneer*, Philadelphia, 1934. For such autobiography as is available in the abridged letters of Miss Woolson, see Clare Benedict (ed.), *Constance Fenimore Woolson*, London [1930]. This latter work is the second part of a three-volume study entitled *Five Generations (1785–1923)*. For a brief biographical and critical study, see Lyon N. Richardson, "Constance Fenimore Woolson, 'Novelist Laureate' of America," *South Atlantic Quarterly* (January, 1940), XXXIX, 18–36.

3. *Anne, A Novel*, New York, 1882, pp. 2, 3.

4. Cf. an observation in one of her notebooks: "Character . . . should . . . grow and develop on the scene; in the book. Not to be introduced completely formed in the beginning." Clare Benedict (ed.), *Constance Fenimore Woolson*, p. 99. Few novelists of the nineteenth century (except Hawthorne and James) have left such copious laboratory or workshop notes—comment on technique, ideas for stories, etc.—as Miss Woolson. These may be found in the work cited, pp. 95–150. At many points her notes distinctly show her kinship with Hawthorne and James. Hawthorne might have been interested by this (*ibid.*, p. 137): "To imagine in an old Italian palace or villa a bell which rang at the top of a very high ceiling, now and then. No one can find any cord or handle to it!" A turn of thought that James might have found interesting (*ibid.*, p. 138): "An American who has lived so long abroad that he is almost de-nationalized, and *conscious of it fully*; which makes him an original figure."

5. "The Art of Fiction," *Partial Portraits*, p. 392.

6. *Anne*, pp. 1, 2.

7. Cf. a comment in her notebook: "I care only for motives; why a man or woman does or has done so and so. Ditto a nation. It is the mental state—the mental problem that interests me." *Constance Fenimore Woolson*, pp. 118–19.

8. *Partial Portraits*, p. 183. As it happens, James achieves this neat antithesis at some slight expense of truth. It was the daughter who was really the Puritan, as Madam makes it clear when she says in discussing her stratagem with Sara: "Under the same circumstances you would never have done it, nor under twenty times the same circumstances. But I am not you; I am not anybody but myself. That lofty kind of vision which sees only the one path, and that the highest, is not mine; I always see . . . the cross-cuts." *For the Major*, New York, 1883, p. 160.

9. *Partial Portraits*, p. 184.

10. *For the Major*, p. 179.

11. *Ibid.*, p. 131.

12. James, *op. cit.*, p. 187.

13. *Ibid.*, p. 191.

14. Kern, *op. cit.*, p. 88.

15. Indeed among Northern writers it was Miss Woolson who had the "surest grip upon a mood of plantation life, the bewildering numbness of that civilization after the full import of the change was realized." Gaines, *The Southern Plantation*, pp. 68–69. The poignant suffering of the South (spiritual and material) after the War is brought out in an almost perfect short story, "Old Gardiston" (published first in *Harper's Magazine* in 1876; collected in *Rodman the Keeper*, 1880).

16. Kern, *op. cit.*, p. 91.

17. Cf. below, p. 723.

18. *Horace Chase, A Novel*, New York, 1894, pp. 269–70.

19. *Ibid.*, p. 419.

20. Kern, *op. cit.*, p. 94.

21.   *Anne*, pp. 185–86.
22.   *Ibid.*, pp. 53–54.
23.   *Ibid.*, p. 156.
24.   *Ibid.*, p. 368.
25.   *Ibid.*
26.   Cf. Kern, *op. cit.*, p. 176.
27.   In this, observed James, Miss Woolson antedated J. C. Harris. *Partial Portraits*, pp. 180–81.
28.   Cf. Miss Vanhorn's comment on another character in *Anne*, a character who reminds her of the "creole" type of beauty: "It is a novelty . . . which has made its appearance lately; a reaction after the narrow-chested type which has so long in America held undisputed sway. We absolutely take a quadroon to get away from the consumptive, blue-eyed saint, of whom we are all desperately tired." *Anne*, p. 196. The Creole was at about the same time making her fascinating appearance, it may be noted, in the works of G. W. Cable. See above, pp. 557–58, 561–62.

[From *Cavalcade of the American Novel*]

EDWARD WAGENKNECHT

James also admired another woman writer in whom posterity does not share his interest: Cooper's grand-niece, Constance Fenimore Woolson (1840–1894). "A born New Englander, reared in Ohio, she has never been surpassed in her interpretation of the wild French *coureur de bois* surviving along the Canadian border; a Northerner, she was the first adequately to interpret the after-the-war South; and, though an American, she has been unsurpassed in her picturings of actual life in the Italy of her day."[1] She had a cosmopolitan mind: she was at home in Mackinac and the Great Lakes country; she wrote of the Great Smokies and the Blue Ridge before Charles Egbert Craddock; and her enchanting pictures of the Florida terrain (then a virgin land in fiction), especially in her finest and most ambitious novel, *East Angels* (1886), can bear comparison with the work of Marjorie Kinnan Rawlings today.

The full force of Professor Pattee's tribute to Miss Woolson cannot be gauged from reading her five novels alone, for much of her best work went into her short stories.[2] She was an artist of absolute integrity and a woman of true nobility of spirit. But she wrote slowly and painfully; she suffered many sorrows during her life; and she died prematurely, apparently under tragic circumstances. High as she stood with her contemporaries, one may still wonder whether she ever quite realized her full potentialities.

As a novelist, she began in 1882 with *Anne*. *Anne* is more "popular" than her other books—*The Wide, Wide World* (one might say) reworked upon a higher intellectual plane. It begins with the heroine's girlhood on Mackinac Island, moves on to her "finishing school" and her rich, eccentric relatives in New York, and ends with a murder mystery and a rather unsatisfying love affair, with the Civil War somewhat incidentally "thrown in." Compared to her other books, it seems naïve, yet not many of them have matched its charm. It was followed by a North Carolina novelette, *For the Major* (1883), which has been much admired by some good judges. But the heroine is a somewhat theatrical figure in girls' dresses and long blonde curls whose cross in life is the necessity of preserving her youth for the delectation of the aged

Excerpted and reprinted from Edward Wagenknecht, *Cavalcade of the American Novel: From the Birth of the Nation to the Middle of the Twentieth Century* (New York: Henry Holt, 1952), 173–77. Copyright 1952 and renewed 1980 by Holt, Rinehart and Winston, Inc., reprinted by permission of the publisher.

and failing husband who believes her still to be a girl and rejoices to think of her in this aspect. Less unusual themes are employed in *East Angels* and in *Jupiter Lights* (1889), both of which contrast the self-sacrificing with the emotionally self-indulgent woman. Constance Woolson carried the devotion of her noble heroines to heights of quixotism where few readers of the present day are able to follow her; among the less admirable women, Garda Thorne, of *East Angels*, is a brilliant study of temperament, a woman so little amenable to ordinary standards that it seems almost beside the mark to call her "selfish." Take, for example, her great grief after the death of Lucian, which is altogether sorrow for her own loneliness: "I had to kill it, you know, or else kill myself. I came very near killing myself." Her last novel, *Horace Chase* (1894), is interesting for her attempt to portray an American business-man, whom she presents as not incapable of ruthlessness, yet able to rise to even greater magnanimity than James's "American."

Constance Woolson's pages are studded with observations which show her wise understanding of human nature. As early as *Anne*, she knows that "It is only in 'books for the young' that poorly clad girls are found leading whole schools by the mere power of intellectual or moral supremacy"; that "whim can be thoroughly developed only in feminine households"; and that the talk of women "over the dressing-room fire at night" is a "delightful mixture of confidence and sudden little bits of hypocrisy." The selfishness of Mrs. Rutherford, the professional invalid who victimizes Margaret Harold, in *East Angels*, is "summed up roughly in the statement that her views upon every subject were purely personal ones." In *Jupiter Lights* we are told that "women have miraculous power of really believing only what they wish to believe; for many women, facts, taken alone, do not exist." For all her seriousness, comedy lay well within Miss Woolson's range, as may be seen by the culture-specialists of *For the Major*:

> Mrs. Rendlesham, who was historical, had made quite a study of the character-istics of Archbishop Laud, and the Misses Farren were greatly interested in Egyptian ceramics. Senator Ashley, among many subjects, had also his favorite; he not infrequently turned his talent for talking loose upon the Crimean War. This was felt to be rather a modern topic.

Such a passage may serve to indicate that Miss Woolson could, when she chose, "do" the eccentrics with whom so much of the pleasure of novel-reading has always been bound up. Mrs. Carew's rambling and senselessly allusive talk, in *East Angels*, is really wonderful, and no reader of *Anne* ever forgets the reticule in which Miss Vanhorn endlessly pursues her ever-elusive search for sugar-coated seeds, a clever use of a theatrical "property," carried far beyond the point at which the stage would be obliged to relinquish it.

It was natural that James should admire Miss Woolson. Both were devoted to Turgenev; both favored impressionism and the dramatic method;

both cultivated the virtues of detachment. Her notebooks are not altogether unlike his. They were alike too in their preoccupation with the nuances of human character and with nice problems of conscience. James would readily have understood the spiritual torture of Eve Bruce, of *Jupiter Lights*, when she falls in love with the brother of the dipsomaniac whom she shot to save his wife and child when they were escaping from him in the South. Here is the "Should she tell him?" problem of shopgirl fiction on a new level. The situation between Owen and Sara, at the close of *For the Major*, is more subtly Jamesian in the girl's implied demand that her lover should preserve his faith in her in spite of the fact that all appearances are against her. "Men are dull," says Madam Carroll. "They have to have everything explained to them."

Miss Woolson's development of the situations in her novels does not, however, equal what James achieved. Her changes of mood are too frequent and not adequately prepared for; her emotional effects are too much "on again, off again." She was too fond of using demented women—and, in one instance at least, a demented man. Perhaps it was because she was essentially a short-story writer that she inclined toward the episodic type of development. I know that the contrast between Margaret and Garda is the very point of *East Angels*, but this fact alone does not seem to me to justify Miss Woolson in shifting the book's center of interest from one woman to the other as she does in the course of her narrative. And this kind of thing is even more troublesome when we come to Eve and Cicely in *Jupiter Lights*.

Notes

1. F. W. Pattee, "CFW and the South," *SAQ*, XXXVIII (1939), 130–141.
2. Some of these have been collected in *Castle Nowhere* (1875), *Rodman the Keeper* (1880), *The Front Yard* (1895), and other volumes; some are still buried in the files of *Harper's*, the *Atlantic*, etc.

[From *The South in American Literature.*
1607–1900]

Jay B. Hubbell

No follower of conventional literary patterns was Constance Fenimore Woolson (1840–1894), the earliest Northern writer of fiction who after the war
treated Southern life with sympathy and knowledge. A grandniece of James
Fenimore Cooper, she was born in New Hampshire and brought up in
Cleveland, Ohio; and her earliest stories dealt with the Lake Country. After
her father's death in 1869 her home in Cleveland was broken up. From 1873
until her departure for Europe in 1879 she lived with her invalid mother,
spending much of each year in Florida, Georgia, Virginia, or the Carolinas.
In her second year in the South she began to write about it in sketches,
poems, and short stories. The shorter pieces which she published in Northern
magazines from 1874 on may well have had something to do with opening
the pages of these magazines, especially *Harper's*, to the Southern writers.
Some of her best sketches deal with Florida, at that time beginning to attract
Northern visitors, but the best of her short stories are about South Carolina
in the Reconstruction period. She was greatly attracted to the well-bred but
almost penniless gentlemen and ladies of Charleston. Until she came South,
she wrote to Paul Hamilton Hayne in July, 1875, she had not understood
the pride of the South Carolinian or the "cause and reason" for that pride.
In the South she discovered that the war was not the "thing of the past"
which it had become in the North. In 1880 she reprinted ten of her Southern
stories in *Rodman the Keeper: Southern Sketches*. These eventually attracted the
attention of Henry James, whose work she admired. In February, 1887,
James wrote of the "high value" he found in these stories, "especially when
regarded in the light of the *voicelessness* of the conquered and reconstructed
South."[1] "She loves the whole region," he said, "and no daughter of the land
could have handled its peculiarities more indulgently, or communicated to
us more of the sense of close observation and intimate knowledge." James,
I may add, had read so little of American fiction that even after a visit to
Richmond in 1904 he could still write in *The American Scene* (1907) of the

Excerpted and reprinted from Jay B. Hubbell, *The South in American Literature, 1607–1900* (Durham,
N.C.: Duke University Press, 1954), 735–37, with permission.

Civil War as "the social revolution the most unrecorded and undepicted, in proportion to its magnitude, that ever was. . . ."

. . . Miss Woolson was conscious of her limitations as an outsider. She showed, for example, no clear understanding of certain mountain types that Mary Noailles Murfree was beginning to portray. In her Preface to *Rodman the Keeper* she made only this modest claim for her Southern stories: "As far as they go they record real impressions; but they can never give the inward charm of that beautiful land which the writer has learned to love, and from which she now severs herself with true regret."

Note

1. *Partial Portraits* (1888), pp. 179–180. The essay first appeared in *Harper's Weekly*, XXXI (12 February 1887), 114–115.

Introduction, For the Major *and Selected Short Stories by Constance Fenimore Woolson*

RAYBURN S. MOORE

Constance Woolson began taking a serious interest in writing in the late 1860's, and her articles and stories appeared in prominent magazines in 1870 and thereafter. These pieces were at first a clumsy combination of fact and fiction, the result of an explorative creative effort to deal with imaginary characters and situations (sometimes thinly disguised treatments of her own experience) in authentic backgrounds and settings. She learned gradually to handle these elements more gracefully and to motivate and analyze her characters on the basis of commonsense experience and a knowledge of psychology. By 1875 when *Castle Nowhere: Lake-Country Sketches* (her first volume of fiction for adults) was published, she had written a number of respectable short stories and sketches. These pieces are set either in the Great Lakes country or in a German Pietist settlement in eastern Ohio; and they reveal a knowledge and appreciation of locale, manners, customs, and people that led many to consider her primarily a local colorist and to compare her work with that of Bret Harte. Few were inclined to disagree with this view when D. Appleton brought out in 1880 her next collection, *Rodman the Keeper: Southern Sketches*. But many were amazed that she, a staunch Unionist and descendant of New England forebears, could treat so dispassionately and sympathetically the land of the recent "rebellion" and its people.

By 1880, when *Rodman* appeared, Miss Woolson had sailed to Europe and had turned to the novel. She continued to write short fiction, but no collections appeared until after her death, though she had agreed to select enough stories for a volume or two for Harper before she died. These books— *The Front Yard and Other Italian Stories* (1895) and *Dorothy and Other Italian Stories* (1896)—contain (with one or two exceptions) the best tales she wrote during her European period and deal mainly with American characters in European settings. They reflect her interest in the contrast between the cultures of the Old World and the New, and especially in the effect the Old World has on Americans who have lived there for some time. In this way Constance Woolson contributed to another important literary current of her

Reprinted from For the Major *and Selected Short Stories by Constance Fenimore Woolson*, ed. Rayburn S. Moore (New Haven: New College and University Press, 1967), 9–20, with permission.

day—the fiction of international incident, a theme that had also fascinated James and Howells.

After her arrival in Europe near the end of 1879, Miss Woolson concentrated chiefly on the novel, a literary development coinciding with the beginning of the serialization of *Anne* in *Harper's* in December, 1880. She had thought about writing a novel as early as 1874 and several years later had expressed her interest in such a project to her friends Edmund Clarence Stedman and Paul Hamilton Hayne. *Anne* was finished by the spring of 1878; but since James R. Osgood, the Boston publisher for whom it was intended, failed to bring it out and since Harper, the New York firm which accepted the manuscript, wanted to begin to serialize the work in the first issue of the English edition of its monthly magazine, the novel did not appear until two and one-half years later.

Anne was well received by all, and Miss Woolson thereafter devoted her creative energies to long fiction, working slowly but steadily and publishing the fruits of her labor first in *Harper's* and then in book form. In this manner she produced *For the Major* (1883); *East Angels* (1886); *Jupiter Lights* (1889); and *Horace Chase* (1894). During this period she did not entirely neglect short fiction, but she found it difficult to write many sketches while working on a novel. In fact, she published only thirteen stories after *Rodman* appeared in 1880.

Her fiction of the 1880's is distinguished chiefly by an interest in local color, in analysis of character, and in relationships between Europe and America. Local color and character analysis manifest themselves principally in the long fiction, and international relationships are most clearly developed in the short stories. In the materials of the present collection, *For the Major* and later pieces such as "The Street of the Hyacinth" and "The Front Yard" amply illustrate these qualities.

During a sojourn of more than fourteen years abroad, Miss Woolson lived in Florence and Venice, in London and Oxford, and spent some time in Switzerland, Germany, and France. She read widely among the nineteenth-century European writers of fiction and admired especially the work of George Eliot and Ivan Turgenev. She became the intimate friend of Henry James, a fellow artist whose principles and craftsmanship appealed to her and whose influence on her later work, along with that of Eliot and Turgenev, was extensive. Her literary tastes and standards were cosmopolitan; but, unlike James, she was no expatriate in either a literary or a political sense. She loved her Uncle Fenimore's novels and Bret Harte's early stories, and throughout her long stay in Europe she constantly wrote to friends and relatives at home of her love for her country and of her ambition to return to it for a leisurely retirement in Florida.

In January, 1894, after a debilitating bout with influenza the previous summer and after completing the galley proofs of *Horace Chase*, Constance Woolson contracted the flu for the second and last time. On January 24 (slightly more than a month before her fifty-fourth birthday) in a state of delirium she either fell or threw herself from her bedroom window while her nurse was momentarily out of the room. She died before daybreak without having regained consciousness.

As a book of local-color sketches *Castle Nowhere* (1875) compares favorably with the first collections of such work in the 1870's by Miss Woolson's contemporaries: Bret Harte, Sarah Orne Jewett, and George W. Cable. The better stories in *Castle Nowhere*—"Peter the Parson," "Solomon," "St. Clair Flats," and "The Lady of Little Fishing"—offer an effective treatment of Lake-country setting, plausible interpretations of human nature in various situations, and a growing mastery of technique and material. "The Lady of Little Fishing" represents the author at her best during this early period.

Published first in the *Atlantic* for September, 1874, and praised by both Howells and Stedman, this tale of the influence of a beautiful woman on the miners and trappers of a camp on an island in Lake Superior reflects Miss Woolson's interest in the work of Harte. The Lady is a Scottish missionary who appears suddenly one night in Little Fishing, and her beneficent reign over the men of the settlement cannot help reminding one of the "Luck's" impact on the roughs of Roaring Camp. The Lady's power declines, however, when the men discover that she has fallen in love with one of their number (ironically, the only man who fails to be bewitched by her spell). But, as both Fred L. Pattee and Claude R. Simpson have pointed out, Constance Woolson went beyond the work of her master. In her sketch the problem of the "unnaturally restrained behavior of the men," as Simpson explains in *The Local Colorists* (1960), is resolved "by the strictly human device of disenchantment, where Harte resorted to chance calamity." Pattee had earlier remarked in his *Development of the American Short Story* (1923) on the keenness of Miss Woolson's insight into human nature in the tale, and he concluded that it "greatly surpassed in short-story art" Harte's "Luck of Roaring Camp."

These comments are valid despite the Lady's failure to become anything more than a shadowy figure and the absence of a necessary robustness in both the narrator and the rough men of this wilderness. The author's purpose, however, lies in another direction: she is concerned with setting, situation, and universal human emotions, and she handles these with assurance and skill. The situation is carefully developed, and the resolution is achieved by a reasonable treatment of the foibles and perversities of human nature. Indeed, in "The Lady of Little Fishing" Miss Woolson has wrought the particular into the universal and produced a work worthy of Harte himself.

In the fall of 1873 Constance Woolson made the first of a number of long seasonal visits to the South, where she spent much of the next six years. In the spring of 1875 she began publishing short fiction with Southern scenes and characters in *Appleton's Journal*, *Harper's*, the *Atlantic*, and other Northern literary magazines. She thus became, along with John W. De Forest, one of the first Northern writers of any significance to deal with such material on a large scale. Ten of these pieces were brought together in *Rodman the Keeper: Southern Sketches* (1880), her best collection in this vein and one which Henry James found "full of interesting artistic work." *Rodman*, like *Castle Nowhere*, clearly exhibits Miss Woolson's interest in local color, analysis of character, and the impingement of one culture upon another; but it also reveals a maturity of insight and a sureness of technique that mark it as an advance over the first volume. Three sketches—"Old Gardiston," "Rodman the Keeper," and "King David"—represent these qualities in the present edition.

"Old Gardiston" first appeared in *Harper's* in April, 1876, before Federal troops were removed from South Carolina and before the flag of reconciliation had been very far advanced in either section. Yet, as Kern and others have suggested, the point of view developed in the sketch is basically sympathetic to the region, which was hardly the case with many of Constance Woolson's Northern contemporaries who were writing about the South during the seventies. Old Gardiston is a home in the rice country not far from Charleston, but it also symbolizes a family whose vitality has reached a low ebb at the time the story begins. The only surviving members—Gardis Duke, a beautiful but proud young belle, and her cousin, Copeland Gardiston, a gentle old dreamer whose primary interest in life is genealogy—seek to maintain some dignity in the midst of the poverty-stricken times of the Yankee occupation. The action revolves around the efforts of Gardis to live according to family custom and tradition despite war's impoverishment and the presence of Federal troops. When, however, Cousin Copeland dies and the old house is destroyed by fire, Gardis accepts the inevitable in the form of a proposal from Captain Newell, the commander of the occupation forces in the locality and a faithful admirer. Thus the work ends on a note of national harmony, but one of larger scope than that found in the mere bonds of matrimony; indeed, this reconciliation results in the union of the pride and courage of the South with the generosity and forbearance of the North.

One of Miss Woolson's contemporaries, Thomas Sergeant Perry, did not like "Old Gardiston." In a review of *Rodman* published in the *Atlantic* in July, 1880, Perry condemned the story chiefly on the grounds of the characterization of Gardis Duke, a "little chit" whose "cantrips . . . read like what one finds oftener in poor novels than in real life." But later critics have found much to praise in this work. Kern remarks on the "understanding and deep sympathy" of the author for the "stricken people" of the area; and Cowie, who touches on the same point, concludes that "Old Gardiston" is "an almost perfect short story." If the heroine's pride has become stereotyped and the reconciliation theme shopworn, one must grant that Miss Woolson was a pioneer in the treatment of these matters in fiction, that she achieved a nice balance between objectivity and sentiment, and that she managed her characters (Northern and Southern) and her material with a comprehension and tolerance worthy of attention today.

"Rodman the Keeper," which appeared about a year later, also deals with reconstruction in the South in a more objective manner than that in "Old Gardiston." It is a tale which depends on character and situation for its effect and, one might add, on the author's knowledge and understanding of both. The central character, a former Federal officer turned keeper of a national cemetery in Georgia after the war, exhibits the aspects of courage and devotion Miss Woolson admired in people in difficult situations, yet he seems altogether plausible without being in the least sentimental. The crux comes when Rodman, though ignored by the community, puts himself in a new relation to it by nursing a wounded ex-Confederate soldier who has returned to his ruined plantation to die. The materials are again available for a symbolic reunion of the states through an understanding established by the two former soldiers. Contrary to the acquiescence eventually achieved in "Old Gardiston," Miss Woolson has no intention of dealing with the theme in this way in "Rodman the Keeper." Rodman and De Rosset never fall on each other's necks and never mention the matter of reconciliation. The former, indeed, may give vent to a modicum of sentiment at the end when he seeks to acquire the piazza greenery from the old De Rosset place, but even this whim is treated ironically when the Maine man who now owns the place offers to sell the vines to him.

The sketch was well received by contemporary critics, and its merits led one publisher (presumably Harper) to offer to take "every line" Constance Woolson wrote and to allow her "to set" her "own price" for her work. Twentieth-century scholars have also thought well of it. Pattee, Richardson, and Hubbell have commented on it favorably; and Quinn has characterized it, along with "Old Gardiston" and "King David," as the best of the author's "post-war stories." More recently, Edel, in the second volume of his biography of James, has cited the piece as "one of her most celebrated sketches," though he has also mentioned its "limitations."

"King David" repeats with some variation the theme of "Old Gardiston" and "Rodman the Keeper," the contrast between Northern and Southern political views of reconstruction in the old Confederacy and the well-meaning efforts of Northern idealists to do something constructive in a land which is quite strange to them and amongst a people whom they do not understand. David King, a "narrow-chested" young man from New Hampshire, feels "called" upon to go south after the war and to teach the "blacks." He settles in a plantation community, establishes a school for the freedmen, and proceeds to try to inculcate both the three R's and morals in his pupils; but he discovers after months of patient labor that his lessons have little effect on his childlike charges of Jubilee Town, that a "glib-tongued" compatriot from the North ("knighted with the initials C. B.") has more influence over them with his demagoguery and liquor, and that a retired planter of the neighborhood (who thinks the blacks an "inferior race by nature") nevertheless understands and appreciates the Negroes and their needs better than either Yankee visitor. Giving up and returning home in the hope that a colored "minister-teacher" will be sent in his place, King David (the Negroes themselves had given him the name) accepts defeat. His mission to the Israelites elicits a final ironic comment from a New England gossip: " 'Didn't find the blacks what he expected, I guess.' " King fails, as the narrative makes quite clear, because he understands neither the region nor the Negro and because he "shrinks from personal contact" with the black man (though he is a staunch believer in equality) and goes about his work from a sense of "duty, not liking."

Again, as in "Rodman," the artist has shown her strong interest in contrast; in each case Miss Woolson examines a character out of his proper element, an idealistic Yankee in the devastated South. Rodman, of course, is made of sterner stuff than King, and he comes closer to success, though he is dealing not with Negroes but with white Southerners; still, he manages to reach only an uneasy armistice with Bettina Ward, De Rosset's cousin and a hearty hater of anything representing the Federal government or the Union cause.

Interestingly enough, though T. S. Perry liked neither "Old Gardiston" nor "Rodman the Keeper," he thought that "King David" was "very good" and that it contained no "exaggeration" and no "inclination toward the use of melodramatic devices, such as are only too apt to make their appearance in the other stories." Kern, Quinn, and Hubbell have also found the sketch to their liking. Certainly, it reveals a knowledge and an understanding rarely manifested in the work of other Northern writers of the day and an objectivity seldom achieved by Southerners in their fictional treatments of the particular problem.

The other stories in the present collection all have European settings. The earliest of these was " 'Miss Grief,' " a tale never reprinted by Miss Woolson though it later appeared in the fourth volume of a Scribner's series entitled *Stories by American Authors* (1884). Published first by *Lippincott's Magazine* in May, 1880, only six months after her arrival in Europe, " 'Miss Grief' " is the author's first effort to deal with Americans abroad (the scene is Rome); and it is interesting to note that the piece appeared shortly before Constance Woolson had either been to Rome or met Henry James, though both these "deficiencies" were speedily remedied. James, for example, came to visit her in Florence at about the same time that the May issue of *Lippincott's* was appearing in America. He was, as she wrote home, "perfectly charming" to her and a "delightful companion" during a month of trips to museums and churches, of walks in the Cascine and on Bellosguardo, and of discussions about art and literature.

Miss Woolson had, of course, long known his work and admired it—a fact which perhaps explains certain aspects of " 'Miss Grief.' " The narrative itself concerns an American woman who goes to Rome to seek literary advice from an expatriated American author who has found financial success in Europe. Aaronna Crief (Moncrief, one learns later) is no longer young, but she has written a drama of great power, something immediately recognized by the expatriate who has only reluctantly undertaken to read the manuscript. The sketch develops as the mentor (who also narrates the proceedings) fails either to improve the play or to get it published. As interesting as the work itself is the resemblance between the narrator and Henry James. Both are men who have inherited money and know the "way of society"; both model their work a "little on Balzac"; both are interested in analysis and motivation in their fiction; and both use the term "the figure in the carpet" in similar ways.

Moreover, " 'Miss Grief' " bears some interesting marks of similarity to "The Street of the Hyacinth" (also set in Rome and brought out after Miss Woolson had not only visited the Holy City several times but had on at least one occasion in the spring of 1881 enjoyed the sights there in the company of James himself). In both stories the chief male character is an American expatriate writer and critic whom an inexperienced and naïve American female seeks out for counsel about work or culture. Both women feel they can get what they need from their advisers, but there are some differences. First, Ettie Macks in "The Street of the Hyacinth" has no artistic talent and Miss Grief has; and, second, Ettie finds her fulfillment in a marriage with her mentor, whereas Miss Grief fulfills herself in her work. Both men remind one of Henry James. They possess Jamesian qualities of aesthetic sophistication and perhaps something akin to his literary position in the early 1880's, and each, indeed, may have been in part modeled on James himself. Also, as both Kern and Richardson have suggested, there is something of the method of James in the telling of these two tales.

Contemporary critics had little to say about either story, but later students of Miss Woolson's fiction have commented on both. Kern, for example, notes that the "central problem" of " 'Miss Grief' " anticipates by eight years James's "Lesson of the Master" and remarks that "the sketch is wholly a study of character and of artistic method in the manner later made famous by James." Richardson describes "The Street of the Hyacinth" and two other late stories as "especially noteworthy." Despite the Jamesian characters and method, however, these pieces are Miss Woolson's own, particularly the later one in which the careful development of character and the treatment of the background reveal the hand of a mature artist at work. Both sketches place characters (chiefly American) in an appropriate Old World setting and allow them to grow within the context of a dramatic contrast between the new and the old, between innocence and experience, between shallowness and depth.

"The Front Yard" also deals with American characters in a European background, but it concerns itself with a social and economic level of life seldom examined by James or Howells. Prudence Wilkin, a plain New England woman of humble class, finds herself stranded in Italy upon the death of her wealthy cousin whom she served as "companion and attendant."

She marries an Italian waiter who offers her the only romance she has ever known and who dies after a year, leaving her to care for his large and demanding family. Accepting with stoicism the duty imposed on her, she struggles for years rearing the numerous progeny of her dead husband and dreaming of replacing the "noisome" cowshed in the front yard with a gate and fence, a "straight path," "currant bushes," and "box-bordered flower beds." The glories of Italy which figure so prominently in fiction by James and Howells (and also in " 'Miss Grief' " and "The Street of the Hyacinth") fail to stir in Prudence the conventional response of the Jamesian "passionate pilgrim." Rather, she is a Pilgrim of another sort: a New Hampshire Prudence whose "idea of Antiquity" is anything that is "old and dirty." This is the way she views Assisi, her present home, and its "picturesque" environs. She never notices the "serene vast Umbrian plain," she never enters the church of St. Francis, and she is of course unaware of Giotto, whose frescoes adorn the walls of that edifice. Yet she has her own notions of beauty, and her dream of establishing a colorful New England front yard on her hill in Italy suggests a different esthetic from that of the cultural antiquity and artistry of the Old World.

Another idea dear to Miss Woolson's heart is developed in "The Front Yard": the theme of "high-minded renunciation" (also typical of Jamesian women), as Cowie characterizes it. Prudence Wilkin spends the best years of her life rearing her dead husband's children and caring for several elderly members of his first wife's family, but she considers this a responsibility incurred by her marriage vows and acts on this obligation until she breaks down after working fourteen hours a day for sixteen years trying to support these largely worthless people. Prudence's notions of honor and duty may appear quixotic to some, but they are basic to her character and so consistently maintained that even the reader who is unwilling to suspend his disbelief is bound to admit that such a nature is possible or, if not, run the risk, as James says in regard to another of Miss Woolson's characters, "of denying that a woman *may* look at life from a high point of view."

At least one contemporary reviewer thought well of this story. Writing in the *Critic* for December 28, 1895, he pointed out that "The Front Yard" was a "brilliant piece of genre-painting executed by an artist who understood her subject to the heart." He was also pleased that its "originality of invention" reflected not "the least straining after effect," and he concluded that its method was "entirely adequate" to its "idea." Many years later Kern cited the piece as one of the best of Miss Woolson's "Italian tales" and described Prudence Wilkin as one of her "finest creations," a view with which Quinn and Richardson have concurred. "The Front Yard" deserves a high place in the canon of the author's short fiction on the basis of a memorable characterization of the protagonist, the effective use of contrast on the levels of both character and culture, and a discriminating treatment of a dominant theme in the whole corpus of her work.

Though "A Transplanted Boy" appeared in *Harper's* several months before Miss Woolson's last published story, it is said by some to have been the last tale she wrote. For this reason and others (it illustrates rather well, for example, its author's capability at the end of her life), it is included in this edition. A bit long for a short story—its almost eighteen thousand words make it longer by about one thousand than "The Street of the Hyacinth" and, therefore, the longest work in the present collection save *For the Major*—its length approximates the *nouvelle* rather than the novelette and its scope gives the author ample opportunity to examine her chief character in terms of the influences on him and to show his native self-reliance in response to a situation that steadily grows worse for him. Maso's predicament, of course, is that he has been "transplanted"; and when he is left to his own devices in Pisa, he discovers that Americans think him Italian and that Italians think him American and that, consequently, neither assistance nor sanctuary is likely. He nevertheless "plays a man's part, without heroics," as Quinn puts it; and the author's restrained treatment of his sturdy courage and perseverance in the face of his plight, despite the sentiment inherent in several aspects of the situation, gives distinction to this poignant tale.

Miss Woolson's readers have liked this story and so have some of the critics. After reading over the letters she received in response to the distribution of her *Five Generations* (the piece is reprinted in the second volume), Clare Benedict reported in her foreword to *Appreciations* (1941) that "A Transplanted Boy," along with "Old Gardiston" and "Rodman the Keeper," were "favourites" with her aunt's public. The critics have been generous in their praise. Writing in the *New York Times Saturday Review* under the pseudonym of Leigh North, Mrs. Elizabeth Stewart Phelps commended the author for a "divine gift of sympathy" which enabled her "to put herself in the place of someone else, to look at life through his lens, for the time being." In 1929 Miss May Harris remarked on Miss Woolson's "magical Italian stories" in the *Saturday Review of Literature* and cited "A Transplanted Boy" as one of five "perfect or finished examples of what a short story should be." Several years later Kern characterized as "notable" the author's "interpretation of the effect of long-continued foreign association upon an American boy," and Quinn observed that the tale was a revelation of a "power that showed no sign of weakening." The sketch of Maso is a memorable one, and the artist's careful use of point of view suggests indeed that her command of technique was as sure as ever.

Cultural Ambivalence in Constance Fenimore Woolson's Italian Tales

Robert L. White

Until recently, Constance Fenimore Woolson, grandniece of Fenimore Cooper and a respected authoress in her own right during the 1870's and '80's, was a figure but dimly remembered by most students of American literature, a figure occupying one of the shadowier niches in the gallery of "local color writers." In the past couple of years, however, her name has been broadcast by two separate scholars. Professor Rayburn Moore has published a book-length study of Miss Woolson which asserts she was a writer of modest but genuine talent who produced, along with a variety of readable short fiction, several novels of merit and substance. And Professor Leon Edel, in his continuing biography of Henry James, has made us aware of the long and pathetic intimacy which existed between the two writers, and of the extent to which James' fiction reverberates with his slow realization of Miss Woolson's would-be love for him.[1]

My concern with Miss Woolson is neither biographical nor strictly literary—although I suppose I should remark my agreement with Mr. Edel's assessment of her as a dispiritingly banal writer. Instead, I should like to discuss the ways in which a distinctive portion of her work lights up one of the most intriguing facets of America's involved relationship with Europe— how a number of her tales are symptomatic of the ambivalent responses of nineteenth-century Americans to Italy: the European land which, simultaneously, United States citizens found the most attractive and most repulsive.[2] (Although Miss Woolson's literary merit is questionable, it is certain that she was a writer whose tales about Italy were popular with magazine editors and, presumably, magazine readers. It seems proper, then, to assume that the attitudes toward Italy to be discerned in her work are symptomatic of the middle-class culture in which she found her audience. Simply because her tales are so mediocre and lacking in individual lustre, they can all the more properly be viewed as an index to the culture which produced and ingested them.[3])

One of a host of nineteenth-century American sojourners abroad, Miss

Reprinted from *Tennessee Studies in Literature* 12 (1967): 121–29. © 1967. Reprinted by permission of the University of Tennessee Press.

Woolson sailed for Europe in 1879 and remained there until her death in Venice fifteen years later. She was never an expatriate, in the twentieth-century sense of the term, but she seems to have enjoyed keenly her succession of *outre-mer* years. She passed most of those years in Italy, and it was Italy, among all the lands of Europe, which most engaged her affections. Once, after a visit to England, she wrote relatives that she was "very fond of the misty, green island" but that she was happy to be returning to Italy; Italy was, she said, "the country I love best of all European ones. It comes next in my heart after Florida."[4]

Miss Woolson's letters home and her published travel sketches constantly descant upon the charms of Italy; several of her short stories, however, reveal an anxious revulsion from Italy. They suggest that the witchery of Italy is not altogether wholesome and that perhaps Americans would be better off if they were not so fascinated by the grace and beauty of Italian life and landscape. These tales, all very unimpressive as fiction, are nevertheless intriguing as documents which reveal the deep-seated distrust with which Americans have always been inclined to regard Europe—and the o'erweening pride with which they flesh out their own inadequacies. Many Americans, of course, have been scornfully leery of Europe; in Miss Woolson's case, what is interesting is not so much the revulsion from Italy discernible in her fiction as the fact that the dark undercurrent of the stories runs counter to her elsewhere expressed affection for Italy. Her letters and travel sketches voice a willed and conscious love; the stories embody doubts, suppressed but nonetheless real, of the worthiness of that love.[5]

Not long after her arrival in the Old World, Miss Woolson announced, in a letter from Florence, that attitude toward Italy she was to maintain outwardly the rest of her life. "Florence is," she wrote, "all that I have dreamed and more. . . . Here I have attained that old-world feeling I used to dream about, a sort of enthusiasm made up of history, mythology, old churches, pictures, statues, vineyards, the Italian sky, dark-eyed peasants, opera music, Raphael and old Michael, 'Childe Harold,' the 'Marble Faun,' 'Romola,' and ever so many more ingredients—the whole having, I think, taken me pretty well off my feet." Miss Woolson's continuing infatuation with Italy found outlets all up and down the peninsula. After one of her first walks in Rome, she wrote: "I come home so excited with it all that I fairly glow! For it *is* so interesting, so wonderful, so beautiful. You see I have 'gone over' body and soul to *Rome!*" In Venice, some years afterward, she exclaimed: "Venice is enchanting. Last night, in the full moon, the canal was dotted with gondolas, and music filled the air. It was beautiful as a dream." And in 1887, after she had taken up residence atop the heights of Bellosguardo, she told one of her friends back in America: "Everywhere . . . I see the most enchanting landscape spread out before me; mountains, hills, river, city, villages, old castles, towns, campaniles, olive groves, almond trees and all the thousand divine 'bits' that make up Italian scenery."[6]

Miss Woolson's persistent love affair with Italy is evident in most of her letters home, but perhaps it is most strikingly revealed in one addressed to an old teacher. She musingly recalls how she had been fascinated by the name of one of her classmates, *"Italia Beatrice,"* and then goes on to remark: "Since then, I have lived much in Italy itself. But it still remains fully as beautiful and romantic as it seemed in imagination, then."[7]

Given the fervor of Miss Woolson's professed enchantment with life in Italy, one might expect her Italian tales to be imbued with a like affection for the land and its people. The short stories do depict a land which is "beautiful and romantic"—but they also project an Italy with imaginative contours strikingly similar to those which coil about the Italy of Hawthorne's *The Marble Faun.* The Italy of both authors is compellingly beautiful, but beneath the mask of beauty lurk violence and evil. Miss Woolson's stories, like Hawthorne's novel, do not deny the charm of Italy; several of the stories, however, suggest that the charm is unwholesome and that, on the moral plane at least, the plain simplicity of America is superior to the beguiling loveliness of Italy.

Altogether, Miss Woolson published, in such major periodicals as *The Century, The Atlantic Monthly,* and *Harper's Magazine,* eleven long tales with Italian settings. Not all display ambivalent attitudes toward Italy; several are merely saccharine love tales set against Florentine and Roman backdrops. Generally, these neutral tales date from the first years of her stay abroad. It was only when her absence from America grew apace, and while she was seemingly growing more fixed in her love for Italy, that her stories begin increasingly to suggest that she was not really convinced of the propriety of her affections. Generally, in these later fictions the note of doubt is expressed in one of two fashions. Several stories intimate that Italians, seemingly the embodiments of charm and grace, are depraved and animalistically vicious beneath the veneer of their picturesque attractiveness. In other stories, the hero or heroine brought forward for our admiration is a person representative of strictly American virtues, one who is unswayed by the spell of Italy and steadfast in his or her upright Americanism.

This second motif is sounded for the first time in a story titled "In Venice." The tale is filled with visits to San Marco, gondola rides, and excursions through the lagoons; but it is centrally concerned with the seeming struggle of a quiet and aging American wife to safeguard her husband's love against the blandishments of a younger and more beautiful woman. The struggle is "seeming" in that the wife knows there is no danger her husband will prove unfaithful; the young girl, however, pathetically thinks it is her destiny to rescue the man, a would-be artist, from what she takes to be the mediocrity and dullness of his wife. Given the straight-laced tone of Miss Woolson's "love" tales with an American setting, it is perhaps noteworthy that something about the atmosphere of Venice prompted her to essay a tale which hints at illicit sex; even more significant, however, is her handling of the differing responses of her two female protagonists, both Americans, to the charms of Italy. Claudia, the young girl, is particularly enamoured of Venice and wishes she could have been a citizen of the Republic during the fifteenth century. The wife, Mrs. Lenox, harbors no such fond desires. She is happy to admit that she and her husband are "very completely of this poor nineteenth century." When Claudia compares the prow of a gondola to "the shining blade of St. Theodore," Mrs. Lenox suggests that "it looks a good deal like the hammer of a sewing-machine." Mrs. Lenox is respectful of the beauty of Venice, but she confesses that she "would give it all for the fresh odor of the fields at home, and the old scent of lilacs."[8]

Claudia is scornful of Mrs. Lenox's response to Venice. She feels that the wife, who spends most of her time caring for a sickly nephew, ought to devote more attention to her husband. During a visit to San Marco, she luxuriates in the warm and magical darkness of the interior and unabashedly observes: "I do believe that if some of our thin, anxious-faced American women could only be induced to come and sit here quietly several hours a day they would soon grow serene and physically opulent, like . . . the women of Veronese." Claudia, convinced of her own Veronesque sumptuousness, feels that Mrs. Lenox's thinness could be modified by a proper diet of Italian art and romance; but the story proceeds toward a dramatization of Mrs. Lenox's heroic New England virtues and toward Claudia's realization that her own enthusiasm for Italy has led her astray. At the end of the tale, after Mrs. Lenox has had singlehandedly to watch the death and burial of her little nephew because Claudia has dispatched the husband on a futile quest after some rumored Titian drawings, Claudia admits the wife's superiority, and the Lenoxes decide to return to America. The stay in Venice has not been harmful to them, but they have no desire to cut themselves off from America. The husband says: "We may return some time . . . but at present I think we want a home."[9] The clear implication is that, for Americans, a *palazzo* in Venice cannot be a home.

Two other stories similarly suggest that Italy is a land of dangerous passions and similarly employ figures of Americans impervious to the spell of Italy to suggest the basic wholesomeness of American values. In "Neptune's Shore," a lurid tale of jealousy, attempted murder, and suicide, Miss Woolson devotes much time to describing the splendors of the Mediterranean landscape, but her chief concern is a sympathetic portrait of the mother of the violent man who, within that landscape, tries to murder a rival in love and then destroys himself. Though older, Azubel Ash is much like the Mrs. Lenox of "In Venice." She is totally oblivious to the heralded charms of Italian scenery and classic architecture. At her hotel in Salerno, she spends most of her time gazing upon the kitchen garden. Indifferent to the view of the sea from the front terrace, she apologetically observes, "I don't know as I care about the sea; it's all water—nothing to look at," and explains that she sits by the back garden because she likes "ter see the things grow." At the end of the story, after a night spent by the side of her dead son, she has moved from a position of obliviousness to the Italian landscape to a lonely domination of that landscape. Her stature is rivalled only by the ancient Greek temples which have long brooded over the countryside—and Miss Woolson consciously couples the grandeur of the temples with the dignity of the American woman who has turned her back on them: "The sun, rising, shed his fresh golden light on the tall lonely figure with its dark hair uncovered. . . . Looking the other way, one could see in the south the beautiful temples of Paestum, that have gazed over that plain for more than two thousand years."[10]

The other story, "A Pink Villa," differs from the general run of Miss Woolson's Italian tales in that it employs a masculine figure to exemplify the peculiar virtues of Americans. David Rod, a young planter from Florida, enters the pink villa on the Sorrentine cliffs to disrupt the plans of an ambitious American mother to marry her daughter to a foppish European nobleman. When Eva, the daughter, meets Rod she immediately falls in love with him—even though his clothes are unfashionable, his hands are brown and hardened, and his mission in Italy is not the pursuit of culture but the recruitment of laborers for his Everglades plantation. The mother struggles against her daughter's love for the young American, but the forthright Rod imbues Eva with his own firmness. The story ends happily with the departure of the wedded lovers for Florida—with Eva's ultimate decision to abandon a life of ease in Italy for a life of striving in America.

Although the young planter is depicted as a man of discrimination and foresight, some of Miss Woolson's other tales might lead readers to think him ill-advised in coming to Italy to seek laborers for his Florida acres. The Italians of these stories are handsome, colorfully picturesque, and seemingly gracious and amenable; beneath their smiling exteriors, however, they are selfish, dishonest, treacherous, animally sensual, and brutally violent. The duplicitous nature of Italian character is explicitly outlined in three of Miss Woolson's tales. In two, "A Christmas Party" and "A Waitress," Americans who have naïvely been taken in by the winning ways of Italian servants suddenly discover that the domestics in whom they have put their trust are capable of horrifyingly passionate criminality.

Modesta, the Tuscan servant in "A Waitress," is a good cook, loyal to her employer, kind to animals and old men, and fervent in her religious devotions; the American tourist who thinks her such a gem learns, however, that she is capable of sensual abandon and insane jealousy. One fiesta night, she attempts to stiletto a Swedish maidservant who is dancing with her betrothed, and the American tourist looks on as the countenance of the good Italian servant is animally transformed: "It was like nothing human; her head was thrust out, the eyes were narrowed and glittering, the nostrils flattened, and the lips drawn up and back from the set, fierce teeth; . . . she was like a wild beast who had made one spring and is about to make another."[11] In

"A Christmas Party," the seemingly perfect Italian servant is not so much transformed as literally undisguised. Carmela is a pert and handsome maid whose only concern seems to be the care and feeding of her American employers. Her real concern, however, is the safety of her son, a thief and murderer, and she coolly deceives the Americans while helping her son escape the police. When her complicity is finally detected, Carmela's façade crumples before the eyes of the police and her employers. She is not young and handsome, but old and withered—and it seems not amiss to infer that Miss Woolson is troubledly suggesting, in the image of the unmasked Carmela, that beneath the shell of Italian loveliness fester decrepitude and ugliness: "What was left was an old, old woman, small and withered, her feeble chest rising and falling in convulsions under her coarse chemise, and the rest of her little person scantily covered with a patched, poverty-stricken underskirt."[12]

"The Front Yard," title story of the first collection of Miss Woolson's Italian tales, doubly calls into question the putative fascination of Italy by coupling sketches of deceitfully charming Italians with an idealized portrait of a simple American heroine unmoved by the supposed wonders of Italian scenery and culture. The heroine of the tale, Prudence Wilkin Guadagni, has received her surname from a handsome Italian waiter who beguiled her into marriage and then soon after left her a widow—with a step-family of seven children by a previous wife, a wastrel nephew, a sonnet-writing uncle, and a querulous grandmother to take care of.

In an exaggerated fashion, the characteristics of the American heroines of "In Venice" and "Neptune's Shore"—a disregard for the attractions of Italy and a homesick longing for the domestic niceties of New England—provide the basis for the narrative action of "The Front Yard." In Prudence's eyes, Italy is primarily a land of "indecent Antiquity," a land where everything is "old and dirty." In picturesque Assisi, where she lives with her new family, she finds these qualities heightened to "a degree that the most profligate imagination of Ledham (New Hampshire) would never have been able to conceive." Her most intense disgust, however, is reserved for a fragment of Antiquity strewn at her very door—a ramshackle stable and pigsty surrounded by heaps of refuse and manure. Her great ambition is to earn enough money to have the eyesore removed and a proper New England front yard laid out. In her dreams she envisions "a nice straight path going down to the front gate, set in a new paling fence; along the sides currant bushes; and in the open spaces to the right and left a big flowerin' shrub—snowballs, or Missouri currant; near the house a clump of matrimony, perhaps; and in the flower beds on each side of the path bachelor's-buttons, chiny-asters, lady's slippers, and pinks; the edges bordered with box."[13]

Prudence's hopes, however, are repeatedly frustrated by the machinations of the Italians whom she toils to support. Working from dawn to dusk to accumulate enough money to fulfill her vision, she sees her savings again and again depleted by the importunities and treacheries of her in-laws.

The grandmother repeatedly demands costly foodstuffs, one son plunders a carefully watched fig crop, another extorts money from her to go off to Florence, the uncle must be rescued from debt, one of the daughters, a shiftless and vain creature, wheedles money from Prudence for a trousseau and then refuses to invite her to the wedding feast. Finally, after several years of constant toil, just when she is on the verge of realizing her goal, another son, a handsome creature upon whom Prudence has lavished a mother's love, steals all the money and flings it away in a bout of dissipation.

Eventually, Prudence Guadagni does get her front yard landscaped after a New England pattern, but only after she has been taken under the care of an American tourist who finds her tottering about Assisi—and only after long years of unceasing labor have brought her to her death bed. When she finally does look upon her renovated front yard, she approvingly sighs, "It's mighty purty." The American lady who has wrought the miracle for Prudence also observes that the view has been much improved since the removal of the pigsty, but her view is that of the "great landscape all about," the landscape which she opines is "the very loveliest view in the whole world." Prudence, however, in spite of her companion's efforts to point out the beauties of the vistas unfolding on every side, will not lift her eyes beyond her new front yard. She will not be taken in by the reputed excellences of the larger view, and the judgment she passes on the Italian countryside may very well echo sentiments deep-rooted within the breast of the maiden American lady who had created her—and who, outwardly at least, was never uncertain of her love for Italy: "The truth is," Prudence says, "I don't care much for these Eyetalian views; it seems to me a poor sort of country, and always did."[14]

Notes

1. Rayburn S. Moore, *Constance Fenimore Woolson* (New York, 1963); Leon Edel, *Henry James*, vols. 2 and 3 (London, 1963).

2. As yet, there is no adequate account of American fascination with Italy during the nineteenth century. Van Wyck Brooks' impressionistic *The Dream of Arcadia* (New York, 1958) and Paul R. Baker's pedestrian *The Fortunate Pilgrims* (Cambridge, 1964) are surpassed in many respects by earlier works by two Italian scholars: Giuseppe Prezzolini's *Come gli Americani scoprirono l'Italia* (Milano, 1933) and Angelina La Piana's *La cultura americana e l'Italia* (Torino, 1938). For a discerning account of the reactions of American novelists to Italy during the early and middle years of the nineteenth century, see Nathalia Wright, *American Novelists in Italy: The Discoverers, Allston to James* (Philadelphia, 1965).

3. For a discussion of the ways in which literary documents may be utilized as indices of cultural assumptions see the stimulating essay by Bernard Bowron, Leo Marx, and Arnold Rose, "Literature and Covert Culture," in *Studies in American Culture*, edited by Joseph Kwiat and Mary Turpie (Minneapolis, 1960), 84–95.

4. Clare Benedict, *Constance Fenimore Woolson* (London, 1930), pp. 292–93. Miss Benedict's memorial volume is mostly a compilation of letters and journal entries. It has obviously been selectively edited, but it seems unlikely that the relevant material about Miss Woolson's responses to Italy has been grossly tampered with.

5.   In a previous article, "Washington Allston: Banditti in Arcadia," *American Quarterly*, XIII (1961), 387–401, I have attempted to demonstrate how a similar pattern of ambivalence is to be discerned in the paintings and fiction of one of the first American travellers to Italy. Although he does not develop the point, Umberto Mariani suggests that Henry James also was torn between his expressed love for Italy and his tendency, in his fiction, always to image Italy as a "ruffled nymph": "The Italian Experience of Henry James," *Nineteenth-Century Fiction*, XIX (1964), 237–54.

6.   Benedict, pp. 184–85, 242, 273, 298.

7.   *Ibid.*, p. 45.

8.   Constance Fenimore Woolson, *The Front Yard and Other Italian Stories* (New York, 1895), pp. 242, 244, 255. Miss Woolson's Italian tales were brought together in two books published shortly after her death in 1894.

9.   *Ibid.*, pp. 252, 266.

10.   *Ibid.*, pp 64, 89–90.

11.   Constance Fenimore Woolson, *Dorothy and Other Italian Stories* (New York, 1896), p. 229.

12.   *The Front Yard*, p. 231.

13.   *Ibid.*, pp. 3, 16.

14.   *Ibid.*, pp. 47–48.

Southern Womanhood in the Novels of Constance Fenimore Woolson

Sybil B. Weir

Constance Fenimore Woolson (1840–1894), a writer belonging to the "realistic" tradition of American literature, was deeply interested in the plight of the South during Reconstruction. Of New England descent, Woolson grew up in Ohio, and her early writings exploit the local color of the Great Lakes region. After the death of her father in 1869, she began to write professionally in order to support her mother and herself. She also took over responsibility for the care of her invalid mother, and the two travelled extensively in the South from 1873 to 1879. Her articles, stories, and novels about the South were well received in the North, where her work appeared in the major magazines and was praised by critics of the stature of Howells and James.[1]

In the twentieth century, Woolson has been commended by scholars for her impartial and sympathetic attitude towards the South.[2] However, a close examination of her Southern novels suggests that she was discriminating rather than impartial, that, in fact, she could not abandon her New England intellectual heritage when judging the South. Although there is ample evidence that Woolson found much to admire about the South,[3] she also criticizes the region for being too provincial and too indolent, for living too much in the past and clinging to old myths.[4] She is deeply suspicious that the seeming Edenic qualities of Southern life allow the South to evade the actualities of Reconstruction and to remain ignorant and immature. In her best work, her revelation of the shortcomings of the Edenic ideal applies not only to Southerners but to all Americans who, in the 1880's, still hoped that a garden state could be established.[5]

Woolson's ambivalence about the South emerges in her portrayal of Southern women in her novels. She believed strongly that a mature person would be willing to renounce personal happiness for the sake of a larger principle, or for the sake of a loved one, or even out of necessity. She does not sentimentalize self-sacrifice, as so many earlier novelists had, by allowing her protagonists to evade the consequences of their renunciatory decision. Her women are complexly characterized; as Alexander Cowie has written,

Reprinted from *Mississippi Quarterly* 29 (1976): 559–68, with permission.

"It was finally these heroines who inspired most of what was distinguished in the work of Constance Fenimore Woolson."[6] What has not been noted before is that in her novels the strong, mature women are all Northern; the self-indulgent, irresponsible women—with the possible exception of Sara Carroll in *For the Major*—are all Southern.

In her first long fiction dealing with the South, Woolson disassociates the principle of self-sacrifice from the sentimental ethic. *For the Major* (1883), the finest of her longer works and still worth reading today, is a penetrating critique of the sentimental heroine and of the South clinging to this outmoded ideal of womanhood during the Reconstruction. In the novelette, as Woolson called it, she demonstrates that women are forced to adopt the disguise of "childlike inexperience"[7] because the men upon whom they depend for survival and love cannot tolerate the revelation of an actual woman. Woolson's analysis suggests that, ultimately, it is the man who is irreparably scarred. Whereas the woman is aware that the sentimental disguise masks her actual self, the man is robbed of self-knowledge by insisting that "the little woman" (p. 300) dedicate herself to building up his ego and preserving his social reputation. Fundamentally, according to Woolson, such a relationship is perverse; its issue, at least in *For the Major*, is a sickly and effeminate child.

Woolson places her protagonist in the pastoral village traditionally associated with the sentimental heroine.[8] She is always called Madam Carroll, though her "mother was plain Mary Foster, from Chester, Vermont" and her father "a Baptist missionary" (p. 347), because she is the squire's wife, the social and moral leader of Far Edgerley. As the novelette proceeds, Far Edgerley loses credence as a seemingly ideal pastoral community. If originally the reader applauds the village's non-commercial nature, we gradually realize that it lacks vitality, its inhabitants preferring to live on memories of the glorious past, refusing to come to terms with the present. The villagers discuss the Mexican war, Tasso, Longfellow, Horace Walpole's letters, Archbishop Laud, and Egyptian ceramics; the Crimean War "was felt to be rather a modern topic" (p. 299). Far Edgerley is sterile; its inhabitants are mainly spinsters and bachelors, widows and widowers. Indeed the village has the same false idyllic quality which envelops another Southern town, Dawson's Landing, in Twain's *Pudd'nhead Wilson*, published eleven years later.

Far Edgerley's refusal to recognize Major Carroll's mental decline becomes emblematic of the South's refusal to abandon the myth of the chivalrous Southern gentleman. Similarly, its quaint pride in the Major's equipage, a relic of pre–Civil War wealth, exemplifies its refusal to come to terms with the present, 1868, the defeated South. Woolson, however, reminds us of present actualities. The Sea Island Carrolls, to whom the carriage belonged before the war, "had not even mules to draw it, and, as they lived all the year round now upon one of their sea islands, whose only road through the waste of old cotton fields was most of the time overflowed, they had nothing to draw it upon" (p. 260). And there are other reminders of 1868 such as

Miss Dalley, forced to take up dyeing after losing her money in the war: " 'You must have noticed her hands. But we always pretend not to notice them, because in all other ways she is so ladylike; when she expects to see anyone, she always, and most delicately, wears gloves' " (p. 286). In *For the Major*, tact, delicacy, gentility—the sentimental heroine's traditional means of ordering anarchic potentialities—become ways of evading the consequences of the war.

Woolson also questions the motives for another of the sentimental heroine's traditional tasks, preserving the established class structure. Nothing is more stilted than Madam Carroll's speech informing her stepdaughter of the social importance of the reception to announce her homecoming after many years' absence: " 'There are, you know, in every society certain little distinctions and—and differences, which should be properly marked; the homecoming of Miss Carroll is one of them. You have, without doubt, an appropriate dress?' " (p. 262). Increasingly, this concern with forms, with appropriate dress, with maintaining class distinctions strikes the reader as a hollow and meaningless charade. Madam Carroll, after all, is primarily motivated by her desire to preserve her husband's status as Far Edgerley's kindly and chivalric squire, and she bravely performs this appointed mission, manipulating village opinion, outrageously flattering her husband, and appearing as a "domestic angel" (p. 271) who evokes reverence in all men.

However, Madam Carroll is a fraud, her actual self imprisoned by the appurtenances of the sentimental heroine: "There was really nothing of the actual woman to be seen save a narrow, curl-shaded portion of the forehead and cheek, two eyes, a little nose and mouth, and the small fingers; that was all" (p. 264). What a relief for Madam when she can discard this sentimental disguise after her husband becomes blind: "Her veil of golden hair, no longer curled, was put plainly back, and fastened in a close knot behind; her eyes . . . looked tired and sunken and dim, with crow's-feet at their corners; all her lovely bloom was gone, and the whole of her little faded face was a network of minute wrinkles" (p. 355).

The bloom has gone from the sentimental heroine, a symbol in earlier American literature of the possibility that the frontier could be transformed into a garden. Woolson suggests that this possibility is dead. The "beautiful rural God's acre" (p. 295) through which Sara Carroll strolls at one point in the novelette is a graveyard, and "beautiful tranquil garden" (p. 297) is used to describe the Major's senility. Further, when the minister wants to protect Far Edgerley from the exotic stranger DuPont, who might "contaminate its sweet, old-fashioned simplicity" (p. 343), it becomes apparent that, in actuality, the pastoral ideal comprises not innocence but ignorance, a willed "fugitive and cloistered virtue," an infantile pretense of prelapsarian status. The community wants to be duped by Madam Carroll and does not want to believe that there is anything wrong with the Major, their symbol of stability.

As Woolson exposes the fraudulent nature of the whole enterprise, the reader becomes aware that by the 1880's the ideal of a pastoral community is no longer viable.

Similarly, the ideal of the sentimental heroine enables men to persist in their immaturity and to evade self-knowledge. In *For the Major*, Woolson repeatedly calls Madam Carroll "the little woman," the "sweet little woman" until the reader wants to gag because of the cloying sentimentality of the adjectives. Gradually, however, it becomes apparent that these adjectives reflect society's mistaken estimate of Madam Carroll, that Woolson is really mocking the men whose ideal woman is an older version of little Eva in *Uncle Tom's Cabin*. Madam Carroll has been forced to become the perfect "little woman" in order to survive. Apparently widowed, unable to support herself and her daughter, Madam Carroll, out of love and out of necessity, pretends to be the Major's ideal woman, "a blue-eyed, golden-haired, girl-mother, unacquainted with the dark side of life, trusting, sweet. It was this very youth and child-like look which had attracted him, man of the world as he was himself, and no longer young" (p. 341). If he knew that "I was the mother of a son," of "a man almost full-grown—would he continue to love me through all this? I was afraid he would not" (p. 342). Although Madam Carroll acknowledges that the Major would have continued to love her even if she had revealed her maturity and experience, the fact remains that she is afraid to discard the disguise until he becomes blind.

Woolson's analysis here is devastating. There is something almost perverse about the Major's love for his "little woman." He seems to feed off her apparent youth; he would be threatened by a mature, experienced woman. The twentieth-century reader might call this perversity the Humbert Humbert syndrome. The Major even invents the "proper" lineage for Madam Carroll. By adding this detail, Woolson not only gently satirizes the South's excessive concern with "pure" blood, but she also anticipates Veblen; the Major's status is greatly enhanced by his possession of such a paragon, who also has the correct antecedents. And indeed Madam Carroll does inspire devotion in the other males, who also seem infected by the Humbert Humbert syndrome. Thus, the junior warden gushes, " 'A little fairy-like girl-mother' " (p. 271).

By repeating the phrase "girl-mother" again and again, Woolson strikes to the heart of the sentimental heroine ideal and reveals the incestuous fantasies which underlie it. If, at the beginning of her relationship with the Major, Madam Carroll was forced to assume the role of daughter, by the end of the relationship, her role is that of mother. These incestuous implications are strengthened by Sara Carroll's excessive attachment to her father, her willingness to sacrifice her own chances for love so that his senile serenity will not be destroyed.[9] Woolson also conveys the fundamental perversity of the relationship by presenting the Carrolls' son as sickly and effeminate. She calls him "little Scar," a fitting nickname for Scarborough which also reflects the scarred relationship of his parents. Appropriately, the novelette ends with the Major murmuring "little Scar" (p. 367).

The triumph of *For the Major* is the characterization of Madam Carroll. Woolson carefully manipulates the reader's attitude toward her. At first we are dismayed by the role of domestic angel which she plays so well. Then, as we see that the heroine is motivated by her love for the Major, we sympathize with the little woman. When her true relationship with DuPont is revealed, we feel deep pity for Madam Carroll, who could not acknowledge her first-born, who risked missing his death, and who was prevented from mourning him publicly. Finally, when she welcomes the chance to take off the sentimental disguise and reveal her actual self, we feel deep respect for her. Indeed, by the end of the novelette, she has attained heroic stature because we realize she knows herself and has consciously chosen her course of action, fully aware of the personal consequences.

What Woolson accomplishes in *For the Major* is to rescue the principle of self-sacrifice from the sentimental ideal; she reaffirms, as James noted long ago, the frequency and beauty of self-renunciation.[10] It may be true, as various critics have suggested, that Woolson's belief in self-sacrifice makes her work seem old-fashioned to modern readers who have been led to believe that self-fulfillment is all. We have lost the religious referent available to Woolson, who, in one of her few authorial intrusions in *East Angels*, calls self-sacrifice "that strange hard bitter right, which, *were this world all*, would be plain wrong."[11] Nevertheless, in Woolson's best work, her treatment of self-sacrifice is sufficiently complex to convince even a contemporary reader.

Woolson saw clearly that it was almost always the woman, either motivated by a principle higher than self-love or forced by necessity, who was called upon to make the sacrifice. Further, she is fully aware of the price the self-sacrificial woman must pay. Her heroines are not like those young women Howells so often satirized, who longed to make grand renunciatory gestures because they had read too many sentimental novels. Woolson's heroines freely choose the renunciatory act, fully aware of the personal consequences. Margaret Harold, the Northern heroine of *East Angels*, Woolson's best full-length work, cries out " 'When have *I* been—permitted myself to be disagreeable? When have *I* ever failed to be kind? I have always repressed myself ' " (p. 497). And later, " 'I have been for years—a slave. Oh, to be somewhere . . . *anywhere* where I can breathe and think as I please—as I really am! Do you want me to die without ever having been myself—my real self—even for one day?' " (p. 498). *East Angels* ends with Lanse Harold's comment: " '[D]o you know that you've grown old, Madge, before your time?' 'Yes, I know it.' 'Well—you're a good woman,' said Lanse" (p. 591).

Although Margaret Harold renounces personal happiness for the sake of a principle we may have difficulty accepting, we should note that Woolson does not, as a sentimental novelist would have, allow her to escape the consequences of her decision. Margaret consciously chooses the hard way, knowing she will be robbed of self-fulfillment, of youth, and of freedom. Most likely Woolson's conception of Margaret Harold is based in part on her own experience, her willingness to sacrifice her own ambitions in order to care for her invalid mother. As Rayburn Moore points out, it was not until she was almost thirty-nine that she "was free to live her own life."[12]

As a counterpoint to Margaret Harold, Woolson presents Mrs. Thorne, who reminds us that women may be forced to sacrifice their principles in order to survive. Like Madam Carroll, Mrs. Thorne must disguise her actual self because she has no way to feed and house her daughter unless she pretends to accept Southern values: " 'I swallowed everything. I even swallowed slavery,—I, a New England girl,—what do you say to that?—a New England girl, abolitionist to the core! It was the most heroic thing I ever did in my life' " (p. 223).

Mrs. Thorne's outburst against Florida, against "the idle, unrealizing, contented life of this tiresome, idle coast" (p. 219) is extraordinary in its intensity, and must, to a certain extent, reflect Woolson's attitude toward the South. Woolson deflates the Edenic ideal which Florida forms in the imagination of the North, reminding the reader that the "real" is not just roses at Christmas or "oranges . . . to be had for the asking" (p. 221), but also slave labor, ridiculous pride, an obsession with past glories and an insular, provincial outlook. Although Woolson is aware that Northern businessmen are about to destroy Florida's exotic beauty, which she renders with great effectiveness in the novel, she cannot wholly discard her Northern, Protestant perspective. Thus, she calls the land speculators "the pioneers of that busy, practical American majority . . . which turns its imagination (for it has imagination) towards objects more veracious than the pious old titles bestowed by an age and race that murdered, and tortured, and reddened these fair waters with blood, for sweet religion's sake" (pp. 54–55).

Although tempted by the Edenic qualities of Southern life, its indolent, leisurely pace and its tropical climate, Woolson also distrusts the effect of all that sunshine, warmth, and leisure. In her novels, although not, one must note, in her short stories, no Southerner appears as a heroic woman, a woman who, like Madam Carroll or Margaret Harold, is capable of self-sacrifice, or a woman who, like Eve Bruce in *Jupiter Lights*, has "a strongly truthful nature," is frank with herself, and "capable of living without illusions."[13] In contrast, Cicely Morrison, the Southern woman in *Jupiter Lights*, is passive, selfish, indulged, sadistic, and degraded by her love for an alcoholic. Similarly, in outlining her conception of the North Carolinian Ruth Chase, Woolson writes that she is neither "brave [n]or high-minded."[14]

Woolson's best realized Southern woman is Garda Thorne, the contrast to Margaret Harold in *East Angels*. Garda embodies the Edenic qualities of Florida; she is indolent, indifferent to that which does not stimulate her, "serenely careless" (p. 105), "singularly natural" (p. 9). Garda is an appealing character, and is presented with great sympathy; indeed, given the many pages of description lavished on her, one could argue that Garda represents some kind of wish-fulfillment for Woolson, whose conception of herself is in marked contrast to the character she creates in Garda.[15]

In *East Angels*, Woolson presents Garda Thorne as a product of Southern culture and climate. Garda's laziness, immaturity, and self-centeredness, as well as her charm and appeal reflect Woolson's ambivalence about the South. In her novels, if not in her short stories, Woolson is critical of the South because of her fundamental allegiance to the Protestant ethic in both its religious and secular dimensions. But Woolson's finest work, *For the Major*, is a criticism not just of the South but of all American society, whose ideal of womanhood forces women to adopt a disguise of eternal adolescence. *For the Major* still speaks to us.*

Notes

1. Unless otherwise cited, all biographical information comes from Clare Benedict, ed., *Constance Fenimore Woolson* (London: Ellis, 1930), John Kern, *Constance Fenimore Woolson: Literary Pioneer* (Philadelphia: Univ. of Penn. Press, 1934), or Rayburn Moore, *Constance Fenimore Woolson* (New Haven: College and Univ. Press, 1963).

2. See, for example, Van Wyck Brooks, *The Times of Melville and Whitman* (New York: Dutton, 1947), pp. 249–270, Jay Hubbell, *The South in American Literature, 1607–1900* (Durham: Duke Univ. Press, 1954), pp. 733–738, and Fred L. Pattee, "Constance Fenimore Woolson and the South," *SAQ*, 38 (April 1939), 130–141.

3. See Moore, pp. 27–30. Moore points out her ambivalence towards the South.

4. For a similar conclusion about Woolson's attitudes towards Italy, see R. L. White, "Cultural Ambivalence in Constance Fenimore Woolson's Italian Tales," *Tenn. Studies in Literature*, 12 (1967), 121–129. Let me add my disagreement with White's estimation of Woolson as a mediocre writer.

5. For an analysis of this ideal, see Leo Marx, *The Machine in the Garden* (New York: Oxford Univ. Press, 1964).

6. Alexander Cowie, *The Rise of the American Novel* (New York: American Book, 1948), p. 578. Quoted in Moore, p. 124.

7. Constance Fenimore Woolson, *For the Major and Selected Short Stories*, ed. Rayburn S. Moore (1883; rpt. New Haven: College and Univ. Press, 1967), p. 341. All further references to this work will appear in the text.

8. See, for example, James Fenimore Cooper's *Home as Found* (1838) or Harriet Beecher Stowe's *The Minister's Wooing* (1859).

9. Woolson does not seem aware of the incestuous implications of Sara's extreme devotion to the Major. Woolson apparently was strongly attached to her father.

10. Henry James, "Miss Woolson," *Partial Portraits* (London and New York: Macmillan, 1888), pp. 190–191.

11. Constance Fenimore Woolson, *East Angels* (New York: Harpers, 1886), p. 556, italics added. All further references to the work will appear in the text.

12 Moore, p. 30.

13 Constance Fenimore Woolson, *Jupiter Lights* (New York: Harpers, 1889), p. 161.

*A grant from the National Endowment for the Humanities enabled me to do the research for this article.

14 Moore, p. 111.

15 Clare Benedict notes that Woolson held "a curiously low opinion of her own personal appearance" (Benedict, p. xv). In a letter to Paul Hayne, Woolson wrote: "To enjoy society a woman must be either personally attractive, gifted with conversational powers, or else must *think* herself one or both, whether she is in reality or not. I do not come under any of those heads. Result; don't care for society at all." (Quoted in Jay Hubbell, "Some New Letters of Constance Fenimore Woolson," *NEQ*, 14 [Dec. 1941], 715–735.) In another letter, Woolson wrote, "Nobody is 'at my feet' at all; don't be satirical. . . . I am as truly out of that kind of thing as a nun" (Kern, p. 51).

Constance Woolson and Southern Local Color

ANNE E. ROWE

The stories published between 1875 and 1880—for the most part written while Woolson was in the South—draw entirely on southern settings and themes. Her novels, which were written later, also treat southern elements. All in all she wrote some fifteen short stories based on various parts of the South, as well as a number of travel sketches, one novelette, and three novels set either entirely or largely in the South.

Most of the short stories involve an assortment of characters, northern and southern, placed in intricately constructed, contrived plots. Although she often protested that she was writing realistically—and her readers frequently criticized the stories for lacking happy endings—most of them are typical of the genteel fiction of the eighties in their inclusion of authorial comments on propriety and in the preponderance of characters who seem isolated from the baser things of life. The realism in her stories, as with other writers of the local color school, derives largely from her careful descriptions of place which create the impression that the author has superimposed the tale upon a very realistic setting.

This delicate etching of details makes her settings much easier to visualize than those of De Forest and Tourgée. Unconcerned with persuading her audience to reform, Woolson concentrated on picturing the South about which she was writing. In contrast to De Forest, who used setting chiefly as a backdrop for his stories and sketches, and Tourgée, in whose works the setting is often sketchy and sometimes conspicuously absent, Woolson painstakingly evokes the uniqueness of each of her locales. . . .

In contrast to her treatment of setting, the development of characterization in Woolson's stories and novels is often superficial and stereotyped. For example, none of her black characters rises above a conventional portrait. The faithful black slave who serves his Confederate soldier master in Woolson's "Rodman the Keeper" retains the devotion exhibited by Peyton Beaumont's valet in De Forest's *Kate Beaumont*. De Forest's novel, however, is set in pre–Civil War times, making the portrait of a servile, docile slave at least palatable to his audience. Woolson presents the very same kind of childlike

Excerpted and reprinted from Anne E. Rowe, *The Enchanted Country: Northern Writers in the South 1865–1910* (Baton Rouge: Louisiana State University Press, 1978), 58–65, with permission. Copyright © 1978 by Louisiana State University Press.

lackey stereotype in a postwar setting. In "Old Gardiston" an old Negro couple remain with their former owners, showing no desire to embark upon a new life. The author even suggests that the blacks' attempts to earn money in order to ward off starvation for the white family is a form of heroism. But here, as in her other stories, the characters are never individualized; they remain merely a charming part of the setting.

Woolson's treatment of blacks in "King David," the story of a young New Englander who fails in his venture to establish a freedom school, reflects an attitude very unlike Tourgée's concerning education of the newly liberated slaves. She rejects the idea of salvation by means of the schoolhouse. The blacks in this story fall into two classes: those who are too dull to learn, and those who have intelligence but use it to seek more immediate gratification such as getting drunk and terrorizing whites. It is a pessimistic story and a convincing argument in support of the growing national sentiment that it was time to let the South again take up the management of its own affairs.

The contrast in this story between David's restless students and the old servant of the southern planter Mars Ammerton makes clear the distance between Woolson's position and that presented by Tourgée in his hopeful portrayals of eager black students. Woolson's blacks could never be educated into equality with whites; and the author implies that for blacks the role of servant is more appropriate than that of student. Even David is forced to acknowledge the contrast between the servant and his master: "There sat the planter, his head crowned with silver hair, his finely chiseled face glowing with the warmth of his indignant words; and there passed the old slave, bent and black, his low forehead and broad animal features seeming to typify scarcely more intelligence than that of the dog that followed him."[1] By the time Woolson came to the South, the northern ardor for black education had been dampened, and, not concerned with provoking social reform, she capitalized on a portrayal of blacks that, perhaps unintentionally, helped to salve the conscience of the nation. In two separate, extended analogies in which blacks are compared with dogs, she implies that letting southerners take control of their government would, in a sense, merely be restoring ever-faithful Old Dog Tray to his much-needed master.

In Woolson's works the treatment of the poor white is also slight, since for her this class was simply not good romantic material.[2] In her few accounts of poor whites she maintains a feeling of great distance between the narrator and these characters, suggesting that she had little opportunity to come in contact with and observe them. When they do appear it is usually as a specialized type of a colorful or exotic nature—the mountain moonshiners or the Minorcans of Florida.

*   *   *

More than anything else these writers who came to the South were intrigued by the very different way of life epitomized by upper-class southern-ers. And Woolson, unlike the earlier "reform" writers, was free to extol every southern virtue available and to capitalize on each unique aspect of a passing way of life; this was, indeed, what her audience expected. In two of her most popular stories, "Old Gardiston" and "Rodman the Keeper," Woolson fulfilled the expectations of her readers by presenting compelling accounts of the passing of a finer way of life. Both stories take place immediately after the Civil War, before the restoration of southern control. In "Rodman the Keeper" the author contrasts a young Union veteran and his Yankee ways with remnants of the old order. Unlike the optimism of Tourgée's fiction, there is in the story little hope of a better future for southerners. Hoping to restore his shattered health, John Rodman returns to the South after the war as keeper of a federal cemetery and encounters a wounded Confederate soldier, tended only by a faithful servant, who has returned home to die in his ancestral mansion. The story is presented from Rodman's point of view and the reader's sympathy is directed toward Rodman's generosity to his former enemies as he takes over the care of the wounded soldier. But the author's greatest preoccupation is with creating a vivid picture of the desolation of a once noble land, and she achieves this effect in an account of the soldier's funeral: "They carried him home to the old house, and from there the funeral started, a few family carriages, dingy and battered, following the hearse, for death revived the neighborhood feeling; that honor at least they could pay— the sonless mothers and the widows who lived shut up in the old houses with everything falling into ruin around them, brooding over the past."[3] At the conclusion of the story Rodman observes a fellow Yankee engaged in tearing down the old mansion. Woolson's point, made clear by showing it through the realization of another Yankee, is that what is going on here is regrettable, and she reiterates this belief in other stories.

In "Old Gardiston" Woolson continues her idealization of the eclipsed order by presenting the plight of an old family immersed in the deepest reaches of poverty and literally subsisting on pride—in its past, and in the few shabby possessions still retained that hearken back to a brighter era. The point of view in the story is that of Gardis Duke, a young girl who lives with her ancient Cousin Copeland in the old Gardiston mansion with only two loyal servants to help her manage the estate. When soldiers from a Union regiment encamped on their property protect them from an uprising of blacks, Gardis is faced with the problems of repaying them in the face of two obstacles—her well-developed hatred of Yankees and poverty so obvious that it will require all her ingenuity to provide a decent dinner for the two commanding officers of the regiment.

Gardis wishes to emulate her late aunt, who in the midst of ruin had valiantly invited two other "ancient dames" to make a visit of several days according to the old ways. She had admired "the state the three kept together in the old drawing room under the family portraits, the sweep of their narrow-skirted, old-fashioned silk gowns on the inlaid staircase when they went down to dinner, the supreme unconsciousness of the breakneck condition of the marble flooring and the mold-streaked walls, the airy way in which they drank their tea out of the crocodile cups, and told little stories of fifty years before."[4]

She gathers together all her forces for the dinner she feels compelled to give the officers out of a sense of "noblesse oblige," and it is a success in spite of the fact that the only dinner dress she has to wear is one that belonged to her great-grandmother and that there are not enough silver forks and spoons left to be used in company. She is able to present at least a semblance of the old order. Dinner is served in the lofty dining room, and the guests take coffee from the crocodile cups in the drawing room while Gardis sings for them. Having fulfilled her obligation according to southern customs, Gardis burns the dress she has worn to entertain Yankees.

As in "Rodman the Keeper" Woolson suggests that the old order is indeed passing, and, more importantly, that it can never really be possessed by the Yankees who speculate in purchases in the South. For when Gardis realizes that there is no longer enough money on which to live, she sells the house to a northern contractor's wife. Before the woman can take possession, however, it burns, "as though it knew a contractor's wife was waiting for it. 'I see our Gardis is provided for,' said the old house. 'She never was a real Gardiston—only a Duke; so it is just as well. As for that contractor's wife, she shall have nothing; not a Chinese image, not a spindle-legged chair, not one crocodile cup—no, not even one stone upon another."[5] Woolson's work projects a terrible sense of loss; the destruction of the past is regrettable, she implies, especially because no one can ever have it again. Southerners here are not getting their just deserts, as is sometimes implied by De Forest and Tourgée; their losses, in Woolson's picture, are tragic.

Notes

1. Constance Fenimore Woolson, "King David," *Scribner's*, XV (April, 1878), reprinted in *For the Major and Selected Short Stories*, ed. Rayburn S. Moore (New Haven: New College and University Press, 1967), 112.

2. *Ibid.* Woolson was obviously repelled by the poor whites of the Piedmont and the coastal areas of the Carolinas and Georgia. She refers to King David as being "spared the sight of their long, clay-colored faces, lank yellow hair, and half-open mouths; he was not brought into contact with the ignorance and dense self-conceit of this singular class" (110).

3. Constance Fenimore Woolson, *Rodman the Keeper: Southern Sketches* (New York: D. Appleton, 1880), reprinted in *For the Major*, ed. Moore, 101.

4. Constance Fenimore Woolson, "Old Gardiston," *Harper's*, LII (April, 1876), reprinted in *For the Major*, ed. Moore, 50.

5. *Ibid.*, 75–76.

The Traditions of Gender: Constance Fenimore Woolson and Henry James

CHERYL B. TORSNEY

Couched in the diction of other women's writing of the day, Margaret E. Sangster's obituary for Constance Fenimore Woolson, which appeared in *Harper's Bazar* a week after her death in Venice on 24 January 1894, uses conventional imagery: "Now that the pen has fallen from the nerveless hand, that the busy brain is quiet in the last sleep, that on the roll-call of our women of genius another name must hereafter be printed with the star that signifies decease, we are sorry, *sorry*. We have lost more than we can tell in cold type. But her beautiful books remain, and in their pages, she lives and breathes."[1] Or at least they did, and she did.

As the *Harper's Bazar* notice suggests, Woolson was not always dismissed as a minor writer of local-color fiction. Henry James wrote in 1884 that Woolson (whom he called Fenimore, though her family called her Connie) was the only English-language novelist he read besides William Dean Howells,[2] and he included a sketch of her along with those of de Maupassant, Turgenev, Emerson, George Eliot, Trollope, Daudet, and Stevenson in *Partial Portraits* (1888). Woolson's writing continued to be admired and anthologized through the 1920s. Fred Lewis Pattee declared that "during the seventies undoubtedly she was the most 'unconventional' feminine writer that had yet appeared in America."[3] He offers, however, an unusual assessment of her limitations: "Not in many ways was she significant: in some important details she was actually a retrogressive force. She never wholly outgrew, for instance, the earlier lessons she learned from her first enthusiasm, Charlotte Brontë."[4] In 1936 Arthur Hobson Quinn suggested that "James' judgment [of Woolson's writing] was sounder than that which had apparently forgotten her" and that when she died, she was known as "one of the most consummate artists in that great epoch of the novel."[5] By 1948, although Woolson's achievement was still reviewed favorably, her reputation had diminished. Alexander Cowie called her a "superior minor writer who is periodically 'rediscovered' by a sensitive critic or a zealous historian."[6] Two

Reprinted from *Patrons and Protégées: Gender, Friendship, and Writing in Nineteenth-Century America*, ed. Shirley Marchalonis (New Brunswick: Rutgers University Press, 1988), 161–83, with permission of Rutgers University Press. © 1988 by Rutgers, the State University.

critical biographies of Woolson attempt to reclaim her, but she is normally treated only in passing in studies of regional fiction.[7] No work to date has effectively resuscitated her reputation.

One reason that Woolson and her work have been consigned to oblivion has been the decidedly male critical bias we see in the scholarship as early as Pattee, who attributes Woolson's insignificance to her unbridled love for Charlotte Brontë. Lyon Richardson apologizes for Woolson in a similar way:

> Her memories of girlhood were sensitive, but only from girlhood's point of view, and one is left with the distinct impression that the daughter-father relationship was more adequately realized in her fiction than that of the daughter-mother. She was careful to choose heroines who were not beautiful, but who possessed some distinction of personality. There is sorrow and abnegation on occasion, but her wives are frequently self-centered and purposeless, whom the men would have done well to avoid. Briefly, nobility is lacking in a number of her characters for the very reason that the basic ambitions, interest, functions, and fruitions of life are lacking.[8]

Richardson faults Woolson, it appears, for her gender and her characters because they are not men with plenty of ambition that gets rewarded in the course of the fiction. It comes as no surprise that Woolson disappears from the anthologies of American short stories just about the time that the canon of American literature comes into being.

Although one expects these sorts of evaluations of Woolson from those unsympathetic with one feminist critical assumption—that women's fiction derives from gender-specific experience—we find Evelyn Thomas Helmick's recent judgment of Woolson harder to swallow, especially since it appears in a collection entitled *Feminist Criticism: Essays on Theory, Poetry, and Prose*: "Such unattractive, if not improbable, martyrs are perhaps part of the reason Miss Woolson's work is seldom read today. . . . Her characters, in exercising a restraint admirable to the Victorian mind, seem wooden and unreal; the endless feminine analysis of emotions and motivations becomes too circumstantial to bear."[9]

Thus it appears that Richardson dislikes Woolson's prose because, to his mind, she writes like a woman, and Helmick's distaste results from the same flavor spicing Woolson's work: "the endless feminine analysis." While Helmick finds redeeming qualities in Woolson, however, she nonetheless rejects the fiction for the same reasons the male establishment does: Woolson's traditional, passive woman's response to experience.

Although a male- (or male-identified) critical bias is one possible explanation for the disappearance of Woolson's works from our literary histories, most likely her name has disappeared because she was born into a lost generation of American women writers. No longer at home in their mother's domestic spheres but not ready for suffrage, Woolson and others like her, labeled regionalists or local colorists, suffered an identity crisis that manifested itself in diminished fictional forms, like the short story and the domestic sketch. Their work has been perceived as a short, secret passage between the great, echoing halls of romance and realism. And because the passage is secret and few use it, no one else misses it.

Alice Hall Petry offers still another theory to explain the strange disappearance of the once-famous Constance Fenimore Woolson from literary consciousness. "Part of Woolson's decline is due," she reasons, "to the simple fact that she 'existed,' as it were, only in her writings rather than as a distinct personality. She did not explore her inner life, as did Adams in his education; nor has she been granted an exhaustive psychobiography, as has James in Leon Edel's multi-volume analysis."[10] Thus, the reasoning goes, she remains forgotten either because she did nothing to memorialize herself or because no critics devoted their lives to retelling hers.

Edel's biography of James provides, in fact, the most accessible of the available Woolson biographies, and most readers who recognize her name do so because of Edel's valuable research. His recognition of Woolson's role in Henry James's life is, however, a mixed blessing. For although he is to be commended for raising the issue of the writers' relationship, he is primarily responsible for perpetrating the legend of the lonely spinster who carries a torch for the icy James all over Europe. Despondent over her rejected attentions—James paid her visits only out of kindness, so the story goes—Woolson threw herself out of her second-story window on that winter morning in Venice. A guilty James resurrected her in the character of May Bartram in "The Beast in the Jungle."

Such is the fiction penned by Edel, who asks point-blank, "Had her act been a partial consequence of frustration—of frustrated love for Henry?"[11] Edel writes that in the four extant letters from Woolson to James "she plays the woman scorned and the woman pleading; full of self-pity at her footloose state. . . . Their tone, above all else, however, is one of despair and of a touching loneliness—a middle-aged woman reaching out to a man younger than herself."[12] (Edel leads his reader here: Woolson was, in fact, only three years older than James.) Throughout their correspondence, Edel claims, Woolson casts herself in the role of the "rejected woman."[13] The picture he draws is of a desperate, lovesick writer, no longer a cub, nipping at the heels and thereby embarrassing the exalted lion. In relying on the stock figure of the rejected woman, Edel betrays his bias.[14]

James and his contemporaries would not have assented to Edel's portrait of Woolson as "on the whole rather prosy and banal, a journey-woman of letters. Without style, and with an extreme literalness. . . . Her work is minute and cluttered."[15] Edel wrongly assumes that James's praise of Woolson's writing in his *Partial Portraits* is disingenuous, motivated by "loyalty and friendship" rather than by sincere and simple admiration for her achievement: "The final impression can only be that he is honoring Fenimore's dedication to letters less than her devotion to himself."[16] Given James's opinion of the high responsibility of the critic, however, it is unlikely that he would praise Woolson unless he meant it. As he declares in his review of Rebecca Harding Davis's novel *Dallas Galbraith*, the critic "must be before all things clear and empathic. If he has properly mastered his profession, he will care only in a minor degree whether his relation to a particular work is one of praise or censure."[17] Moreover, if James's purpose were to feign for the public, why would the private man write to William Dean Howells that Woolson was the only American novelist he read besides his friend? Why would James, in a letter to his brother William three years after his correspondence with Howells, call Woolson "the gifted authoress"?[18] For James, Woolson exemplifies woman writing in the late nineteenth century, and in her portrait he speaks of her in the same breath as he speaks of Sévigné, de Staël, and Sand. She is to be admired.[19]

Not only James himself but also his sister Alice valued Woolson's fiction. In fact, Katherine Loring, Alice's close friend, was reading Woolson's story "Dorothy" to Alice as James's sister died. James's sister and Woolson were longtime friends, Woolson visiting frequently and corresponding "about everything from recipes for baked beans to Ruskin" to medical school education for women.[20] Alice offers the negative of Edel's snapshot of the James-Woolson relationship, presenting her brother as an attached admirer. To her brother William she writes that "Henry is somewhere on the continent flirting with Constance," and later to her Aunt Kate that "Henry has been galavanting on the continent with a she-novelist; when I remonstrated he told me that he thought it a 'mild excess.' "[21]

James's frequent references to Woolson in letters to friends contradict Edel's assertion that James rarely mentioned his "virtuous attachment" to others.[22] In a note to John Hay at Christmas 1886, James reports that their "amiable and distinguished friend Miss Woolson . . . dwells at five minutes' distance" and that they meet every few days, frequently dining together.[23] A few months later he describes Woolson to Grace Norton as "an excellent woman of whom I am very fond, though she is impractically deaf."[24] Woolson and James also shared their friendship with fellow expatriate Francis Boott and his daughter Lizzie, their neighbors in Florence. In nearly every letter to Boott, whose song Woolson quotes in "Dorothy," James mentions their mutual friend. In fact, just before Woolson died, James wrote to Boott that he was preparing to "pay a visit to our excellent friend Fenimore." He continues to say that she is exhausted by her revision of her last novel: "She is to have, I trust, a winter of bookless peace."[25] Upon her death, James, horrified and despondent, wrote of the tragedy to at least six different people: Dr. W. W. Baldwin, Rhoda Broughton, John Hay, Francis Boott, Katherine De Kay Bronson, and William James. This is not the response of a man hounded by a woman, but rather of a friend who has lost a companion with whom he shared both professional and personal interests.

The legend of the spinster chasing the lion over a continent is further dismantled by an examination of Woolson's other correspondence, for the tone Edel catches in Woolson's letters to James—paradoxically assertive and simultaneously self-effacing but always effusive concerning her correspondent's latest work—is the same tone she employs in her letters to others whose work she admires: E. C. Stedman, John Hay, and Paul Hamilton Hayne.

To clear things up, or at least to bring them into better focus, given the distorting glasses of history and literary criticism, much of what Edel reports is verifiable. Constance Fenimore Woolson, holding a letter of introduction from Minny Temple's sister, Henrietta Pell-Clark, met Henry James in April 1880. (Edel embellishes the truth when he writes that she came to Europe "half in love with James.")[26] The two writers got along swimmingly, corresponded religiously (Woolson tells James that she writes him mostly to entertain herself), and visited each other frequently. During these visits they walked, toured galleries, and dined. In 1887, in fact, James and Woolson inhabited neighboring apartments of the Villa Brichieri in Florence. As his letters detail, they met in several European capitals in the year following, once discreetly lodged in hotels on opposite banks of Lake Geneva. Certainly James must have admired Constance Woolson and enjoyed her intelligent humor enough to have been distraught over her death.

The documented details of her probable suicide are few. Early in the morning of 24 January 1894, Woolson rang for one of her servants at the Casa Semitecolo to fetch her some warm milk. Upon returning, the servant found Woolson in a crumpled heap on the pavement below her second-story window. Her favorite gondolier carried her unconscious body back to her bedroom, where she soon died. John Hay handled the funeral arrangements, and Woolson, like Daisy Miller, was buried in the Protestant cemetery in Rome. Reasoning the death a suicide, James, Edel presumes, refused to attend the funeral of his companion. Several months later, however, James volunteered to accompany Woolson's niece to the writer's sealed rooms to wrap up her aunt's affairs, and, Edel says, to see that Woolson had kept her vow to burn his letters upon reading them. Once granted access to her things, James could also destroy any other papers that could be interpreted as incriminating.

Edel's text of James's reading of Woolson's death is a convention-laden male fantasy. In that patriarchal romance the dependent woman prefers not to live at all if she cannot possess the man completely. While there is reason to believe that Woolson threw herself rather than fell to her death in an influenza-induced delirium as others have speculated, it seems unlikely that she was prompted by unrequited love for Henry James.[27] Rather, evidence of a philosophical consideration of suicide, coupled with hereditary and perhaps postpartumlike depression (she had just finished her novel *Horace*

Chase) and financial worries, suggest that issues more immediate than Henry James may have driven her to take her own life.

Woolson's books and letters suggest why she may have committed suicide. First, in her personal copy of *The Teaching of Epictetus* she has both bent down page corners and marked with pencil lines the sections justifying suicide.[28] A particularly significant paragraph in the chapter, "On Solitude," is marked in the inside as well as the outside margin with a double line. It reads: "And when, it may be, that the necessary things are no longer supplied, that is the signal for retreat: the door is opened, and God saith to thee, *Depart.*"[29]

The chapter note to this passage is also marked with a double line and is especially pertinent since it condones self-annihilation in the face of one's being unable to await "God's time": "But the Stoics taught that the arrival of this time might be indicated by some disaster or affliction which rendered a natural and wholesome life impossible. Self-destruction was in such cases permissible, and is recorded to have been adopted by several leaders of the Stoics, generally when old age had begun to render them a burden to their friends."[30]

Woolson's letters to all of her regular correspondents—E. C. Stedman, her nephew Samuel Mather, and John Hay—are shot through with references to illnesses and attending depression, their onslaughts and retreats. She is ill for months, even entire seasons at a time, with influenza, inner-ear problems (which her doctor diagnoses as neurotic), and "a succession of ailments and difficulties."[31] In one letter, dated 10 December 1888, she considers her health at that time of year newsworthy for its stability: "I am quite scandalously well this winter. Haven't had an ill moment; and am as stout as can be. I am so much better—my health so much *firmer* than it used to be that it is really quite remarkable. (I was ill last winter; but that was owing to mental depression.)"[32]

Depression, characterized by her as a male monster, is Woolson's nemesis. In a letter to her girlhood friend Arabella Carter Washburn, she acknowledges that she suffers the same fits of depression her father had: "Don't fancy I am sad all the time. . . . But at times, in spite of all I do, this deadly enemy of mine creeps in, and once in, he is master. I think it is inconstitutional, and I know it is inherited."[33] Her recurring malaise becomes even more pronounced whenever she finishes a project, resembling postpartum depression. In a letter to her niece Katherine Mather she writes that the effort of writing a novel "takes such entire possession of me that when, at last, a book is done, I am pretty nearly done myself."[34] When we now read the letter James wrote to Boott only weeks before Woolson's death, in which he wishes her a quiet winter recuperating from the completion of her last novel, we can only smile at the irony.

In tracing the fluctuation of Woolson's moods and health, I have found her depressions to be most severe in midwinter, when daylight hours are short. This pattern suggests that the writer was suffering from Seasonal Affective Disorder, what Jack Fincher describes as "a baffling depression whose cyclic onset appeared to be curiously governed by the changing length of the day."[35] In fact, Woolson's references to illness and depression increase considerably during the autumn and winter months. January seems to be the cruelest month for her, while May brings relief. In the last months of 1893 this strange disease may have convinced her that her life was nearing its end, and her thoughts of suicide may have been a self-fulfilling prophecy. In letters preceding her death, we see her dwelling more and more on what she considers her advanced age. Just a month before her death she writes to her nephew Samuel: "But one must do, from day to day, the best one can. And my infirmities are upon me now: they will not grow worse. (This last sentence means that your aunt is already pretty old!) I hope you will not be shocked if I add that for a long time my daily prayer has been that I may not live to be old; I mean really old."[36] Three days later, in a short note, she admits that she feels "old, & tired, & indifferent."[37]

Woolson's sense of helplessness and hopelessness had been accelerated, undoubtedly, by her feeling that she was running out of both time and money. Throughout her years in Europe, Samuel Mather had her power of attorney in America and oversaw his aunt's finances; thus, many of her letters to him concerned the drawing of bank drafts and the sale of property. During the last three years of her life, however, her worry about money grew, and her letters reflect increasing desperation as she felt her lifetime dream of retiring to a quiet Florida cottage slip away. In a letter posted from Cairo and dated 17 April 1890, Woolson writes that although she is enamored of the Holy Land, she cannot allow herself to stay the summer: "No; if I am to get my finances into shape, I *must* give myself to steady work, in the most quiet & unexciting place I can find."[38] Two years later, on 8 February 1892, she composes another letter in the same key. I quote from it extensively, as much to make available that "distinctive personality," which Alice Hall Petry thinks missing from our literary histories, as to demonstrate Woolson's growing nervousness over the constraints of time:

> To have done with the blue part first, let me say that I am still suffering from the pain which attacked me a month ago. But it is now much less severe, so that I bear it better. (I have not much fortitude about pain, you know!) The English doctor here, a clever young man, thought the whole affair was neuralgia. "Neurotic" was his word; that is, a malady of the nerves of the head. I did not, in my heart, agree with him. And I think it *now* pretty well decided that it has been a slow gathering in the inner ear, first on the right side; & now on the left. I say "inner," because there has been no sign of anything *visible* any where. . . . The loss of time preys upon me most of all. I try not to think of it. I read & read. And when I can no longer do that, I even play solitaire! If you & Flora could have peeped in half an hour ago, and seen me

seated on the rug, with the kettle on a trivet attached to the grate behind me, & all the materials for the linseed poultices assembled on a tray at one side, while I, with tear-stained face, was drearily playing solitaire on an atlas propped on my knees, you would have laughed, I am sure. I never play games you know; so when I play solitaire, it is desperation indeed.

Later in the letter Woolson responds to her nephew's request that she spend the summer with him and his family at Newport:

I can't come this summer simply because every well moment *must* be given to finishing the novel which begins in a serial in Harper's Magazine next December. I have already postponed it a whole year, owing to the tiresome condition of my health; never really ill, I may say, sadly enough with truth, that for a year I have not been really well. Unless I wish to make Harper's lose all patience with me, I must keep my engagement fully & promptly this time.[39]

Finally, on 20 November 1893, she asks Sam to sell one of her bonds and send her a thousand dollars to cover the expenses of setting up housekeeping at the Casa Semitecolo. "I have made the necessary first purchases; and now having settled myself for a while, I find I am beginning to be haunted by the fear that my reserve fund at the Bank here is not large enough to leave me free from immediate care."[40]

Personal philosophy, depression, illness, age, and financial worries all probably combined to lead Constance Fenimore Woolson to commit suicide. Early in her career, in a letter of 23 July 1876, she had written to E. C. Stedman asking, "Why do literary women break down so. . . . It almost seems as though only the unhappy women took to writing. The happiest women I have known belonged to two classes; the devoted wives and mothers, and the successful flirts, whether married or single; such women never write."[41] Elaine Showalter has cited "an increase in psychosomatic illnesses and stress diseases" in women writers of Woolson's era resulting from tension over their identities. This generation, Showalter observes, is the first in which female suicide becomes a trend.[42] Woolson's depression and probable suicide, then, suggests that she is an American sister of the British writers Showalter studies in *A Literature of Their Own*. Like them, Woolson is a woman for whom stress and illness became a way of life and drastic means the way of death. Although her death was devastating for Henry James, Edel's suggestion that this sorrow was actually guilt probably resulted from Edel's own fantasy of the literary lion and the spinster.

The standard reading of Woolson's death, now unraveled, begins to suggest how her life and her writing have always been marginalized, have always been read as ancillary to James's. Her life, for example, has been seen as the inspiration for much of James's fiction after her death, following the traditional master-disciple pattern. Edel, for instance, cites Woolson as the real-life May Bartram and suggests that James's sense that Woolson had betrayed him inspired "The Altar of the Dead."[43] Although she aspired to "the style, the manner, the mastery of Henry James," she could only pretend to the Jamesian literary laurel, he asserts.[44]

Woolson's works have been read, even by her champions, as the ash from which the Jamesian phoenix rises.[45] My purpose here is not to create more anxiety by arguing influence, however. Rather, it is more important to recognize how James's and Woolson's differing genders led the two writers to experience the world according to variant patterns as well as to suffer such different historical fates. James, the male, has gone down in history as the master, the patron, with all of the authority those titles imply. Woolson, however, has been remembered as the journeywoman, the protégée, who relied on James for guidance. An examination of *The Portrait of a Lady* and *Anne* demonstrates that literary history has simplified not only the personal relationship but the literary relationship as well.

Both Henry James's and Constance Fenimore Woolson's first important novels were published serially, his in the *Atlantic* (from November 1880 to December 1881) and hers in *Harper's Monthly* (from December 1880 to May 1882). Both are novels of love and marriage, a theme as old as the genre itself. Both *The Portrait of a Lady* and *Anne* present female protagonists akin to the prototypical women's heroine whose characteristics, "intelligence, will, resourcefulness, and courage," have been outlined by Nina Baym.[46] Isabel Archer and Anne Douglas are provincial orphans who are adopted by eccentric aunts following the deaths of parents with whom the aunts had argued. Both young women make a successful entry into society after being taken in by their relations, and both marry men of questionable virtue. In each character's case another man, Ralph Touchett and Gregory Dexter respectively, at some point provides for the heroine's material well-being. Although the novels share structural similarities and a relation to the Ur-plot of trial and triumph as elucidated by Baym, they are based on different gender assumptions, traditions, and development.

Carren Kaston has defended James against the charges of some hostile feminist criticism by noting that "James wrote regularly with a profound sensitivity to what it was and very often still is like to be a woman."[47] Although, as Alfred Habegger asserts, James was "in sympathy with the best feminine values," he was nonetheless male, still on the outside.[48] Still, his effort to understand is genuine, his understanding as certain as possible. From his own hegemonic position, he presents a woman of imagination who, because of the constraints of the male world in which she lives, cannot realize the triumph of that imagination. As Kaston puts it, "such independence to which Isabel at first aspires is unattainable not only because of the existence of others, who constitute society and exert pressure on her, but because of conditions within Isabel herself."[49] It is Isabel's tragedy that she cannot really act independently. She can only be managed. As James writes, "Madame

Merle had married her."[50] Even grammatically Isabel is an object, not a subject. She is passive, not active, as a woman in her place was expected to be by a male culture.

Keys to Isabel's failure lie in her own habits of mind, habits born of her reading two classes of literature: romances by and about women and texts from the transcendentalist tradition. These two sources of Isabel's ideas suggest what Kaston calls her "conflicting attitudes toward power: her desire for self-origination on the one hand and, on the other, her attraction to dependency."[51] Isabel (and James, of course) is not at fault; rather, as Kaston puts it, "given the powerlessness women frequently feel, the challenge of self-origination could not easily be met by any woman, even one as generously conceived as Isabel is by James.[52]"

From the beginning Isabel understands her world in textual terms. Upon her arrival at Gardencourt, she is thrilled to meet Lord Warburton: "Oh, I hoped there would be a lord; it's just like a novel!" she gushes (27). Indeed, in the following flashback to Lydia Touchett's visit to Albany to fetch her niece, Isabel is ensconced in the library, where she reads indiscriminately, "guided in the selection chiefly by the frontispiece" (33). Her reading includes "the London *Spectator*" and "the latest publications" (41–42), both of which would have treated women's issues. Other evidence demonstrates, however, that Isabel has been reading romantic women's novels as well. These unnamed novels help to set up her expectations only to have reality decimate the tenderly held images.

Mr. Touchett, sensing Isabel's impending disaster, raises the issue of the discrepancy between fantasy and reality in women's fiction, but Isabel either does not hear or does not heed the warning. Their discussion begins with Isabel's wondering whether English character confirms what she has read in books. Her uncle replies that he is unfamiliar with what appears in novels, that he believes only what he has learned from firsthand experience. But Isabel continues to push the question of novelistic representations of reality by asking how she will be treated in society. "I don't believe they're [the English] very nice to girls; they're not nice to them in novels" (58). Daniel Touchett's response might have served to warn Isabel, but finding herself in a situation usually reserved for novels, her ears are deaf to her uncle's warnings.

> "I didn't know about the novels," said Mr. Touchett. "I believe the novels have a great deal of ability, but I don't suppose they're very accurate. We once had a lady who wrote novels staying here; she was a friend of Ralph's and he asked her down. She was very positive, quite up to everything; but she was not the sort of person you could depend on for evidence. Too free a fancy—I suppose that was it. She afterwards published a work of fiction in which she was understood to have given a representation . . . of my unworthy self. . . . Well, it was not at all accurate; she couldn't have listened very

attentively. . . . I don't talk like the old gentleman in that lady's novel. . . .
I just mention that fact to show you that they're not always accurate."

(58–59)

Isabel might have taken to heart James's ironic joke about people who
think that novels faithfully record experience, but she does not. Throughout
the early sections of the novel, she reads real-life situations according to
women's writing conventions: she sees Warburton "as a hero of romance"
rather than as a troubled man caught in a changing political order, and his
home as "a castle in a legend"; she has read that the English are "at bottom
the most romantic of races"; she identifies herself as a young woman being
made love to by a nobleman in a "deeply romantic" situation (66, 75,
77, 96). When Henrietta Stackpole tries to penetrate Isabel's novelistically
clouded vision by asking her, "Don't you know where you're drifting?" Isabel
replies, "No, I haven't the least idea, and I find it very pleasant not to know.
A swift carriage, of a dark night, rattling with four horses over roads that
one can't see—that's my idea of happiness." Henrietta responds that her
language sounds like that of "the heroine of an immoral novel" (146).

That Isabel uses such language should come as no surprise since she
understands her world in part through the filter of the romance tradition of
women's novels. As William Veeder observes, Isabel talks a conventional
line, using the extravagant language of women's fiction. Like women's heroines, she relies on "pretty set-speeches conventional with pretty heroines."[53]
Her own naive reading deceives her and tricks her into marriage with a man
whose name, Gilbert, suggests the heroes of romances written both by Sir
Walter Scott and by Susan Dudley Warner.[54] Following the literary convention of her romance novels, at the end Isabel is left with only one way out—
self-sacrifice. Ironically, it has been another women's fiction convention, the
sickly, feminized Ralph Touchett, himself a writer (and reader) of the genre,
who prepared Isabel for her downfall when he convinced his father to provide
for the requirements of his cousin's imagination, thus authoring the pretext
of her disaster.

But the romance tradition is not the only literary tradition that fails
Isabel. When Mrs. Touchett first meets Isabel in the family library in Albany,
the girl has been "trudging over the sandy plains of a history of German
Thought" (34). She takes to heart the superiority of the male virtues of logic,
reason, and mind over the female ones of emotion, sensitivity, and heart.
Had she been conscious enough to note that her reading was indicting her
own character, she might have become a resisting reader, recognizing that
the texts she was reading made her own gender into the enemy.[55] Isabel's
transcendentalist reading tricks her into believing in the possibilities of her
own independence, possibilities reserved, according to the American tradition of idealism, for men. Emerson, one of Isabel's heroes, for instance, as
Joyce Warren notes, was "unable to see women as individuals like him-

self. . . . It is clear that his philosophy [of self-reliance and insistence upon high goals] was not intended to apply to women."[56] In the beginning of the novel Isabel is the embodiment of the Emersonian idealist: she believes in the world "as a place of brightness, of free expansion, of irresistible action" (54); she believes in "the continuity between the movements of her own soul and the agitations of the world" (41). But Isabel is a woman, as James well knows (as Kaston comments, "Isabel Archer is more than incidentally female").[57] Her reading of a male intellectual philosophy does not serve her; "she had desired a large acquaintance with human life, and in spite of her having flattered herself that she cultivated it with some success this elementary privilege had been denied her" (431). The "privilege" is denied her because of her sex and of her goodness, and both the reader and James mourn her lost opportunity.

Thus, Isabel's naiveté fails her on two levels. First, she thinks the world of the romance novel real, allowing it to dictate experience to her, revealing her dependency; second, she thinks male transcendentalism and idealism written for her, thus revealing her paradoxical desire to write her own text of self. James does not condemn the romance vision itself; however, he thinks that the tradition of German-Concord transcendentalism was responsible for Isabel's naive perception of reality and for her failure to allow her imagination free rein. But finally, Isabel, as a woman in a man's world, a woman written by a man (sympathetic though he be), can only respond as she does: as a mostly passive participant whose glorious imagination will never experience free reign though it may triumph over some of the obstacles it confronts.

Nearly three-quarters of a very long letter from Woolson to James, dated 12 February 1882, is taken up with her criticism of *Portrait*. By far the most telling of Woolson's responses to the novel is the whole of her last paragraph:

> How did you ever dare write a portrait of a lady: Fancy any woman's attempting a portrait of a gentleman! Wouldn't there be a storm of ridicule! . . . For my own part, in my small writings, I never dare put down what men are thinking, but confine myself simply to what they do and say. For, long experience has taught me that whatever I suppose them to be thinking at any special time, that is sure to be exactly what they are *not* thinking.[58]

Woolson, of course, is making a mild joke, and, in fact, she does attempt several portraits of gentlemen, both in her last novel, *Horace Chase*, and in "Miss Grief," a narrative told from a male first-person perspective. Yet, just as James's *Portrait*, though about a woman, presents a heroine from a male tradition where women, even admirable, imaginative ones, are in a sense forcedly passive, Woolson's narratives featuring male characters evolve from the women's writing tradition described in Nina Baym's *Woman's Fiction* and Mary Kelley's *Private Woman, Public Stage*, among others.[59] In this tradition the female character is active, not passive; the protagonist, the writer's alter ego rather than a female character for whom he has a large degree of sympathy. In a letter dated 30 August 1882, Woolson compares her work to James's:

> All the money that I have received, and shall receive, from my long novel, does not equal probably the half of the sum you received for your first, or shortest. It is quite right that it should be so. And, even if a story of mine should have a large "popular" sale (which I do not expect), that could not alter the fact that the utmost best of my work cannot touch the hem of your first or poorest. My work is coarse beside yours. Of entirely another grade. The two should not be mentioned on the same day. Do pray believe how acutely I know this. If I feel anything in the world with earnestness it is the beauty of your writings, and any little thing I may say about my own comes from entirely another stratum; and is said because I live so alone, as regards my writing, that sometimes when writing to you, or speaking to you—out it comes before I know it. You see,—I like so few people! Though I pass for a constantly smiling, ever-pleased person! My smile is the basest hypocrisy.[60]

That her writing "comes from entirely another stratum" is undeniable: hers is the writing of a woman, as the passage abundantly demonstrates. It is cautious, modest, self-effacing, yet the turn at the end, the suggestion of wearing a mask, is reminiscent of a familiar strategy used in American women's writing since the time of Woolson's sister New Englander, Anne Bradstreet. Like her letter to James, Woolson's writing employs women's writing traditions, such as the writer's identification with her heroine and the widespread use of feminine archetypal patterns and images; like the domestic writings from the earlier part of the century, Woolson's works empower women in many ways rather than lament their powerlessness in the outer world while compensating them with an imaginative inner life.[61]

Anne, the novel about which Woolson wrote to James, is the first of her strong-women narratives. It was printed in several editions during her life, again following her death, and just recently with a new introduction.[62] Although past critics have praised *Anne* primarily for its local-color descriptions of Mackinac Island, Michigan, many agree that because the novel is replete with issues of self-identity, it deserves renewed attention. The issue of identity is the same one James treats in *Portrait*, yet since male and female definitions of *identity* and *power* differ, the thread is spun out with differing tension by male and female writers.

One of the ways that male and female texts differ is in the identification of the writer with the protagonist. Isabel is not James, nor was she meant to be, and Woolson teases James about his attempt to paint the portrait of a woman. Anne, however, is in many ways Woolson herself, substantiating Judith Kegan Gardiner's hypothesis that a woman writer "uses her text, particularly one centering on a female hero, as part of a confirming process involving her own self-definition and her empathetic identification with her character. Thus, the text and its female hero begin as narcissistic extensions of the author."[63]

Anne Douglas and Constance Fenimore Woolson share interests and background, not the least of which is the name Anne, which Woolson adopted as a pseudonym for her first publication, *The Old Stone House* (1873), a children's book. Both Anne and Woolson were New Hampshire natives, and as children lived for periods on the Upper Peninsula of Michigan, where a memorial to Woolson with the name "Anne" at the head of the tablet was erected in 1916. Both young women, though accomplished in the liberal and fine arts, protest that they are ugly. Woolson's portraits and her descriptions of Anne, however, belie such evaluation. Perhaps as a reaction against her sense that she falls short of the American ideal of beauty, Woolson develops a love of letter writing, the art of communicating without being seen. Anne shares that love. Just as Woolson tells James that she writes to him for her own amusement, Anne, in writing to her fiancé, Rast Pronando, finds that through the use of language she may assert a control over her life. (It is, on the other hand, the workings of language in literature that stand for Isabel's inability to control her life.)

Both Woolson and her textual daughter also assert power and identity in physical activity and exertion. Throughout her life Woolson rowed to release energy as well as to pass a pleasant Saturday afternoon. Near the end of *Anne*, the heroine uses rowing as a release and as a means of coming to terms with her identity. In addition to rowing, Woolson loved any sort of physical activity, especially walking, and her letters are filled with references to hour-long morning walks and afternoon treks of six to eight miles. The place of physical exercise in Anne's and Woolson's lives is reflected in Ellen Moers's reading of walking as a recurring pattern in women's writing, signaling feminist independence and drive.[64]

Woolson's use of archetypal patterns and images in women's writing further identifies her (and *Anne*) with the women's writing tradition, gaining for Woolson depth and power. Among the archetypes Woolson's novel uses in some fashion are those of the green world epiphany (the coming to self in nature) and the green world lover (the coming to passion in nature), both elements of the archetypal feminine *Bildungsroman* as discussed by Annis Pratt. As she explains, nature, the stage for growth, activity, and confirmation of self-identity, is where women find "solace, companionship, and independence."[65] An important distinction is to be made here: for the transcendentalists (and for Isabel) nature is intellectualized, as evidenced by the analytic presentation of the subject in Emerson's famous "Nature" essay. Nature is a representative force rather than a fundamentally real part of our lives. In women's writing, however, nature is a personified friend. In the female *Bildungsroman* the girl takes possession of herself in taking possession of nature. Anne loves the trees so much that she talks to them. Like her heroine, Woolson feels most independent and powerful—most herself—out in nature.[66]

The green world is the most important setting in Woolson's novel. In a culminating scene, Anne recognizes her friend's killer and is thus empowered to exonerate her lover through knowledge gained while rowing on a lake. In another of her green world epiphanies "among the arbor vitae, where there was an opening like a green window overlooking the harbor," Anne agrees to marry young Rast Pronando after believing he has been drowned.[67] But Rast is not Anne's green world lover. That figure, associated with the mythic dying god, appears in the person of Ward Heathcote, whose surname is Woolson's adaptation of another famous woman's green world lover. She retailors a rather wild, uncivilized Heathcliff into a more civilized, well-bred Heathcote. A Union captain in the Civil War, he is wounded in West Virginia, and, nearly dead, is restored to life by Anne.

In the archetype, the restorer is a goddess: Aphrodite, Ishtar, or Isis. Anne, in fact, is endowed with similar mythic resonance tying her to the power of the archetypes. From the second page of the narrative, Anne is described as "a young Diana," an allusion that reverberates throughout the novel. Both James and Woolson play on the allusion with their respective heroines; however, James's use is disguised in Isabel's last name while Woolson's use is overt, appealing directly to the women's literary tradition of using goddess archetypes. James uses it from a male perspective to suggest Isabel Archer's female virtue, an abstract idea, while Woolson uses it to suggest Anne's physical "vigor" and "elasticity," a concrete description. Their use of the references to Diana echoes their differing versions of transcendental nature: for James and Isabel it is intellectual; for Woolson and Anne it is sensate.

Anne, posed braiding her hair, is also called Ariadne, a figure as familiar as Diana in the women's literary tradition. Indeed, she is both: in her guise as Diana, she is the huntress who dwells alone in the woods and mountains; as Ariadne, she is abandoned by Rast Pronando. But Anne (Woolson) is also Ariadne, a weaver, a domestic maker of fictions, who grows in that capacity over the course of the novel. Early in her recognition that she enjoys writing, we are told that "she never put down any of her own thoughts, opinions, or feelings: her letters were curious examples of purely impersonal objective writing":

Egotism, the under-current of most long letters as of most long conversations also, the telling of how this or that was due to us, affected us, was regarded by us, was prophesied, was commended, was objected to, was feared, was thoroughly understood, was held in restraint, was despised or scorned by us, and all our opinions on the subject, which, however, important in itself, we present always surrounded by a large indefinite aureola of our personality—this was entirely wanting in Anne Douglas's letters and conversation.[68]

Throughout the course of *Anne* the heroine's narrative talents grow until, at the climax of the novel, Anne demonstrates her new mastery of narrative form by weaving on the witness stand the fabric of truth, designed to acquit her lover. When the jury cannot arrive at a verdict, Anne rereads the text of the murder herself, discovering the killer. Finally, in the last pages of the novel, the passive voice of her early reflection of writing is rewritten in the active, identifying herself as the star of the show: "I, Anne, take thee, Ward, to my wedded husband, to have and to hold, from this day forward."[69] Unlike Isabel, Anne can assert her identity in the real world as suggested by her new command of language. To the end, Isabel, given her circumstances, cannot vigorously and independently pursue her dream. She remains, in the last words she utters in the novel, an object, as she begs Casper Goodwood, "As you love me, as you pity me, leave me alone!" (489).

Writing her own text of self and arriving at her own identity has not been easy for Anne. At every turn in the novel someone is looking to appropriate her by stripping her of her linguistic being. Rast calls her Diana; Mrs. Vanhorn calls her Phyllis; Helen calls her Crystal (a particularly suggestive nickname since it implies a reflective relationship between Anne and Helen, as a singularly complex inner composition and transparency); and Miss Lois calls her Ruth Young. Her egotistical assertion at the end, "I, Anne," both defines her powerful new statement of identity and marks an assertion of Woolson's fictional power. Tied into archetypal patterns, that power strengthens the weave.

Woolson's power, in *Anne* as well as in other fictions, derives from traditions of women's writing as well as from her own unique talent. The tradition is the most important element that differentiates her from Henry James, a man who chose (aside from George Eliot, a curious case given her choice of pseudonym) mostly male writers as his models. We realize that Emerson spoke to him, not women like Woolson, when he wrote: "The Poet is representative. He stands among partial men for the complete man." One of Isabel Archer's mistakes is in thinking that Emerson wrote to her. Women, as Ellen Moers suggests by her rewriting of Emerson in her headnote to chapter one of *Literary Women*, are themselves forced to rewrite Emerson because they belong to a variant tradition.[70] Constance Fenimore Woolson found her representative poets in that tradition, in the works of Elizabeth Barrett Browning, George Sand, George Eliot, and the Brontës. Her individual talent is remarkable, too, not simply for her vivid local-color descriptions of Michigan, Ohio, North Carolina, Florida, and Europe (those landscapes which form the boundaries of her career) but also for her energetic struggle with issues of identity, language, and art. Her relationship with Henry James was not that of a love-starved stereotypical spinster to one of the greatest literary talents of that or any age. It was one of personal, private friendship.

In her fine article "Archimedes and the Paradox of Feminist Criticism," Myra Jehlen proposes a method of radical comparison to demonstrate "the contingency of the dominant male tradition."[71] Using this method we can project a border between Woolson and James and explore the frontier. Such a technique, akin to Woolson's "way of looking at photographs (likenesses) upside down, [to bring] out undiscovered characteristics,"[72] reveals the inaccuracy of the myth of the lonely spinster who falls first in love with the suave lion and then to her death. To view their relationship upside down—to see James and Woolson as compatriots sharing the literary life of the age rather than as ill-fated lovers—encourages a rereading of *The Portrait of a Lady* and *Anne*, their contemporaneous novels about a woman's struggle for independence and identity. To see James in terms of Woolson and Woolson in terms of James is not to assert the strength of one and the shortcomings of the other, thus organizing their relationship into a hierarchy; rather it is to recognize the divergent gender-inflected qualities, which work to create variously tinted literary artifacts, artifacts colored, after their first meeting in 1880, by the strong friendship between these two writers.

Notes

I would like to thank the Western Reserve Historical Society (WRHS), Cleveland, Ohio, for permission to quote from Woolson's letters collected in the Mather Family Papers; and the Butler Library, Columbia University, New York, for permission to quote from Woolson's letters in the Stedman Manuscript Collection. I am also grateful to Rollins College, Winter Park, Florida, for allowing me access to the Woolson Collection of memorabilia.

1. Margaret E. Sangster, "Constance Fenimore Woolson," *Harper's Bazar* 27 (3 February, 1894):93–94.

2. Henry James, *Henry James Letters*, ed. Leon Edel, 4 vols. (Cambridge: Harvard University Press, Belknap Press, 1980), 3:29 (hereafter cited as *Letters*).

3. Fred Lewis Pattee, *The Development of the American Short Story: An Historical Survey* (New York: Harper and Brothers, 1923), 250.

4. Ibid., 254.

5. Arthur Hobson Quinn, *American Fiction: An Historical and Critical Survey* (New York: D. Appleton-Century, 1936), 342.

6. Alexander Cowie, *The Rise of the American Novel* (New York: American Book, 1948), 568.

7. See John Dwight Kern, *Constance Fenimore Woolson: Literary Pioneer* (Philadelphia: University of Pennsylvania Press, 1934); and Rayburn S. Moore, *Constance Fenimore Woolson* (New York: Twayne, 1963).

8. Lyon N. Richardson, "Constance Fenimore Woolson: 'Novelist Laureate' of America," *South Atlantic Quarterly* 39 (1940):34.

9. Evelyn Thomas Helmick, "Constance Fenimore Woolson: First Novelist of Florida," in *Feminist Criticism: Essays on Theory, Poetry, and Prose*, ed. Cheryl L. Brown and Karen Olson (Metuchen, N.J.: Scarecrow, 1978), 238.

10.   Alice Hall Petry, " 'Always, Your Attached Friend': The Unpublished Letters of Constance Fenimore Woolson to John and Clara Hay," *Books at Brown* 29–30 (1982–1983):12.

11.   Leon Edel, *Henry James*, 5 vols. (1962; reprint, New York: Avon Books, 1978), vol. 3, *The Middle Years, 1882–1895*, 363.

12.   Ibid., 87.

13.   Ibid., 88.

14.   Edel further reveals his patriarchal perspective in his choice of names for his subjects. Although he will occasionally pair their first names, Henry and Constance, his other pairings, "James and Miss Woolson" and "James and Fenimore," are conspicuous from a feminist standpoint. I am indebted to Susan Allen Ford for bringing this to my attention.

15.   Edel, *Middle Years*, 203.

16.   Ibid., 204.

17.   Henry James, *Literary Criticism: Essays on Literature, American Writers, English Writers* (New York: Library of America, 1984), 223.

18.   *Letters*, 3:150.

19.   James, *Essays*, 639.

20.   Jean Strouse, *Alice James: A Biography* (New York: Houghton Mifflin, 1980), 260.

21.   Strouse, *Alice James*, 259.

22.   Edel, *Middle Years*, 215.

23.   *Letters*, 3:153.

24.   *Letters*, 3:176. After the mid-1870s Woolson became increasingly deaf and was finally forced to rely on an ear trumpet.

25.   *Letters*, 3:436–437.

26.   Ibid., 3:xvi.

27.   Woolson's few critics have hesitated to believe, as James apparently did, that her death was a suicide. Most think the circumstances surrounding her death too vague to be certain about.

28.   I found Woolson's personal copy of this text in the Woolson House on the Rollins College campus in Winter Park, Florida.

29.   Epictetus, *The Teaching of Epictetus*, trans. T. W. Rolleston (London: Walter Scott; New York: Thomas Whittaker; Toronto: W. J. Gage, 1888), 135.

30.   Ibid., 200.

31.   Woolson to Samuel Mather, 16 January 1884, WRHS. In quoting from Woolson's letters I have retained her idiosyncratic spellings and punctuation.

32.   Woolson to Samuel Mather, 10 December 1888, WRHS.

33.   Constance Benedict, ed., *Five Generations (1785–1923)* (London: Ellis, 1930), vol. 1, *Voices Out of the Past*, 224 n.

34.   Benedict, *Five Generations*, vol. 2, *Constance Fenimore Woolson*, 52.

35.   Jack Fincher, "Notice: Sunlight May Be Necessary for Your Health," *Smithsonian* 16 (1985):72.

36.   Woolson to Samuel Mather, 20 November 1893, WRHS.

37.   Woolson to Samuel Mather, 23 November 1893, WRHS.

38.   Woolson to Samuel Mather, 17 April 1890, WRHS.

39.   Woolson to Samuel Mather, 8 February 1892, WRHS.

40.   Woolson to Samuel Mather, 20 November 1893, WRHS.

41.   Woolson to E. C. Stedman, 23 July 1876, Butler Library.

42.   Elaine Showalter, *A Literature of Their Own: British Women Novelists from Brontë to Lessing* (Princeton: Princeton University Press, 1977), 194.

43.   Edel, *Middle Years*, 377, 385.

44.   Leon Edel, *Henry James*, 5 vols. (1962; reprint, New York: Avon Books, 1978), vol. 2, *The Conquest of London, 1870–1881*, 417.

45.   See especially Sharon Dean, "Constance Fenimore Woolson and Henry James: The Literary Relationship," *Massachusetts Studies in English* 7 (1980):1–9. She astutely notes that "The Beast in the Jungle" springs from an entry in Woolson's notebook; "Old Gardiston," a Woolson story, which predates by twenty-one years *The Spoils of Poynton* (written close on the heels of Woolson's death), features a climactic conflagration; "The Figure in the Carpet," the title of the James story, is a phrase from Woolson's notebooks; Woolson's "Transplanted Boy" tells of a child's rejection by adults, much like James's "Pupil"; and Tita, the sister of Anne in Woolson's first successful novel, is the original name of Tina in "The Aspern Papers."

46.   Nina Baym, *Woman's Fiction: A Guide to Novels by and about Women in America, 1820–1870* (Ithaca: Cornell University Press, 1978), 22.

47.   Carren Kaston, *Imagination and Desire in the Novels of Henry James* (New Brunswick, N.J.: Rutgers University Press, 1984), 40.

48.   Alfred Habegger, *Gender, Fantasy, and Realism in American Literature* (New York: Columbia University Press, 1982), 56.

49.   Kaston, *Imagination and Desire*, 41.

50.   Henry James, *The Portrait of a Lady*, ed. Robert D. Bamberg (New York: W. W. Norton, 1975), 430 (hereafter page numbers are cited parenthetically within the text). For the purpose of this essay I have chosen to use the Norton Critical Edition since it offers a list of textual variants from the first edition of 1881 in addition to the text of the New York edition. Because the 1908 edition differs from the original, written while Woolson was at work on *Anne*, the reader should consult the 1881 first edition variants, as I have done.

51.   Kaston, *Imagination and Desire*, 41.

52.   Ibid.

53.   William Veeder, *Henry James—The Lessons of the Master: Popular Fiction and Personal Style in the Nineteenth Century* (Chicago: University of Chicago Press, 1975), 71.

54.   Ibid., 120

55.   For the idea of the resisting reader, I am indebted to Judith Fetterley, *The Resisting Reader: A Feminist Approach to American Fiction* (Bloomington: Indiana University Press, 1978).

56.   Joyce Warren, *The American Narcissus: Individualism and Women in Nineteenth-Century Fiction* (New Brunswick, N.J.: Rutgers University Press, 1984), 43, 49.

57.   Kaston, *Imagination and Desire*, 40.

58.   *Letters*, 3:535.

59.   See Baym, *Woman's Fiction*; and Mary Kelley, *Private Woman, Public Stage* (New York: Oxford University Press, 1984).

60.   *Letters*, 3:544–545.

61.   For extensive discussions of how women's writing empowers its female readers, see for example, Baym, *Woman's Fiction*, and Kelley, *Private Woman, Public Stage*.

62.   *Anne* was published by Harper and Brothers in 1882, 1903, and 1910, and by Sampson and Low (London) in 1883. The Arno Press has reprinted the Harper's text with a new introduction by Elizabeth Hardwick.

63.   Judith Kegan Gardiner, "On Female Identity and Writing by Women," in *Writing and Sexual Difference*, ed. Elizabeth Abel (Chicago: University of Chicago Press, 1982), 187.

64.   Ellen Moers, *Literary Women* (1976; reprint, New York: Oxford University Press, 1985), 130.

65.   Annis Pratt, *Archetypal Patterns in Women's Fiction* (Bloomington: Indiana University Press, 1981), 21.

66.   I located a list of wildflowers Woolson had seen, written in the back cover of a wildflower text in the holdings of the Olin Library at Rollins College, where I also found two unpublished Woolson poems, "Ferns" and "Fern Fragments," tucked in the back of a book.

67.   Constance Fenimore Woolson, *Anne* (1882; reprint, New York: Harper and Brothers, 1903), 132.

68.   Ibid., 98.

69.   Ibid., 539.

70.   Moers, *Literary Women*, 1.

71.   Myra Jehlen, "Archimedes and the Paradox of Feminist Criticism," in *The Signs Reader: Women, Gender, and Scholarship*, ed. Elizabeth Abel and Emily K. Abel (Chicago: University of Chicago Press, 1983), 79.

72.   Benedict, *Five Generations*, vol. 2, *Constance Fenimore Woolson*, 117.

Island Fortresses: The Landscape of the Imagination in the Great Lakes Fiction of Constance Fenimore Woolson

Victoria Brehm

Henry James noted only two "defects" in Constance Fenimore Woolson's 1889 novel *Jupiter Lights*: "One is that the group on which she has bent her lens strikes us as too detached, too isolated, too much a desert island. . . . The other fault is that the famous 'tender sentiment' usurps among them a place even greater perhaps than that which it holds in real life. . . ."[1] Although James rightly spotted two unresolved problems in Woolson's work, he did not understand that there was a connection between them, nor could he have perceived how they were an attempt to resolve a personal conflict. *Jupiter Lights* was only the most recent manifestation of a theme Woolson had repeated obsessively in more than twenty Great Lakes stories, where she tried to solve the problem of being a single, self-supporting woman as well as a serious artist in the two decades after the Civil War. Her solution, perhaps unconscious, was to encode her painful struggle in stories with conventional romantic patterns, using idiosyncratic motifs of character and landscape to undercut the promised marriage her readers expected.

Unfortunately, Woolson left little record of this early struggle except her stories. Her career spanned several decades—she was the first woman to write maritime fiction about the Great Lakes, the first writer to chronicle the Reconstruction South, and one of the first to describe American expatriate life in Europe—before she died suddenly at age 54, perhaps a suicide, in Venice in 1894. Because she did not live to write an autobiography and always requested that her correspondents destroy her letters, we seldom know how close she was to the themes in her work. The biography compiled by her niece is a potpourri of fragments of Woolson's work and undated excerpts from surviving letters, thus compounding the difficulties of scholarly investigation of this reticent, retiring woman.[2] Nevertheless, there is enough evidence to suggest that she contended all her life with the dilemma of wanting to be part of her nineteenth-century world and yet needing to remain aloof

Reprinted from *American Literary Realism* 22 (1990):51–66, with permission. © 1990 McFarland & Company, Inc., Publishers, Jefferson, N.C.

from it. If she fulfilled the expectations of her society to marry and have children, her freedom, both personal and professional, would be severely restricted. To ignore those social expectations was to condemn herself to loneliness, to become, as she wrote late in her life, a "very quiet person whose circle constantly narrows around her."[3] Yet she had early revealed a reluctance toward the conventional feminine role; in her twenties she wrote to a friend who had recently married, "Although I am willing to settle down after thirty years are told, I do not care to be forced into quiescence yet awhile."[4] As her many travel articles attest, she never stayed anywhere long, even in places she loved. She gave up her prized apartment in the Villa Brichieri in Florence, where she had settled after seventeen years of wandering Europe and the Middle East, to take lodgings in England because

> I have come here to do a long job of literary work. I could do almost nothing in Florence; there were such endless numbers of people to receive & to go and see. . . . I hated to give up the beautiful Bellosguardo View; it tore me to pieces to do it. But after a struggle to write & attend to social duties at the same time through three long years, I at last recognized that it was impossible. At least impossible for *me*.[5]

At this time (1890), Woolson was artistically and financially successful, yet the societal world still seemed threatening. And when she first began to write, she could not have had the bulwark of success. Her struggle shows in her first stories, where she approached her problem by creating characters who did what she was trying to do, who served as the examples she lacked in life. She projected her conflict into her characters and onto the landscape of her imagination, creating singular, isolated individuals who find an island refuge. In her fiction she found the freedom to envision another life, one that anticipated what her own would become.

Her personal conflict of longing for complete independence, but fearing its price, was compounded by her public relations. She despised the predictable, romantic fiction that appealed to what she witheringly referred to as "the public," once relating how she had flung a popular novel across the room.[6] Elsewhere she wrote, "I have such a horror of 'pretty,' 'sweet' writing that I should almost prefer a style that was ugly and bitter, provided it was also *strong*."[7] But many of her early stories are constructed with a conventional romantic plot that ends in marriage, and her first novel, *Anne* (1882), was a best-selling model in the genre, reminiscent of the domestic novels already popular for three decades. This paradox can be explained only partly by the demands of the marketplace. When she did risk "going back to nature and exact reality"[8] in stories like "Castle Nowhere" (1875) and "Peter the Parson" (1874) her readers complained:

> At least twenty awful letters have I received because I made Old Fog ("Castle Nowhere") say he did not believe in eternal punishment. Is it possible that I

am to be held personally responsible for the morality of my characters? I want you to think of me not as your old friend, when you read my writings, but as a "writer," like anyone else. . . . The truth is . . . whatever one does must be done with one's might and I would rather be strong than beautiful, or even good, provided the "good" must be dull.

And, under the abuse which has been showered upon me for my "brutal killing of Peter the Parson," I have steadily maintained to myself that both in an artistic and truthful-to-life point of view, my ending of the story was better than the conversion of the miners, "the plenty to eat and the happy marriage" proposed by my critics.[9]

The second comment suggests that Woolson's first readers disliked not only her refusal to write saccharin stories, but her use of isolato figures as a contrast to the romance, characters who chose not to conform and often felt no need to justify themselves. Set down amidst the trappings of romance, their examples flash like buoys marking the hidden rocks in a placid channel, warning readers that below the surface prettiness of wedding plans lies another, more disturbing, reality.

Despite her questioning of fictional conventions, Woolson has been shunned by many recent feminist critics in favor of other nineteenth-century women writers whose work falls into the patterns of "women's fiction" currently in fashion. If they judge her at all, it is as a "serious" writer whose use of a love plot undercuts her intentions.[10] Thus to them she is either a failed realist or a failed sentimentalist, and her ability to use both conventions equally well is considered a fault rather than a virtue. Other critics have categorized her as a local colorist,[11] or as straddling "the border between local color and realism."[12] These conclusions are based on the inference that since she wrote about the Great Lakes and then the South and then Europe and described each setting with fidelity of detail, realistic evocation of place was her major talent. But the many differences in her work and her life that distinguish her from women local colorists should by now have made such categorization fallacious.[13] Some critics have noted that she always wrote about characters who sacrifice what they love so that others can be happy.[14] Few have considered how her use of this familiar renunciation theme differs from the ordinary, and none how inseparable it is from her use of landscape. She did write one story over and over, and it was about the cost and gains to women who refused to go along with the obligatory domestic femininity of their time. Few American women had written it before.

I

The landscapes of the Great Lakes stories are remote, as those who class Woolson with the local colorists commonly point out, settings more common to that mode than to the "inner spaces" of the domestic fiction of the 1840s and 1850s. But remoteness of place or the use of curious characters does not necessarily make a local color story. Woolson uses dialects sparingly; she shows little or no nostalgia for a vanished way of life. Unlike the work of Rose Terry Cooke, Mary Wilkins Freeman, Sarah Orne Jewett, or Mary Murfree, Woolson's stories are as likely to be narrated by men as by women and to have both male and female protagonists. Moreover, Woolson's stories of women seldom depict them retreating to their native villages, a common theme in feminine local color writing; rather, especially in the early stories, they trace the fates of those who do not follow husbands into the wilderness but go alone, a different pattern from what Annette Kolodny describes[15] or from what Margaret Fuller had noticed when she was traveling in Great Lakes country in 1843.[16]

Raised in Cleveland, Woolson never wrote about her native city because, she said, "there was no 'background' there but the lights from the blast-furnaces at Newburgh on a dark night."[17] Woolson's territory, her imaginative landscape, is the Michigan wilderness, what might more properly be called the Old Northwest Territory. To her it seemed not a sparsely settled frontier but often a true wilderness, a place "where man himself is a visitor and does not remain."[18] What Woolson does not admit is that this wilderness had not existed since she was a child, and hardly then. Even before the Civil War Michigan was being lumbered, mined, settled, and rapidly transformed into a tourist mecca. Caroline Kirkland's *A New Home—Who'll Follow?*[19] had described the Michigan frontier a year before Woolson was born in 1840. When Woolson began to write, Kirkland's frontier was comfortably settled and Michigan had been a state for over thirty years. A recent historian half-humorously describes the Great Lakes shortly after Woolson's birth this way:

> In 1845 . . . approximately 200,000 passengers crossed the upper Lakes bound for Chicago, Milwaukee, and other western ports. Tourist excursions by steamboat to Green Bay and other points of interest in the near North had become fashionable: wealthy New Yorkers engaged in Great Circle tours— up the Mississippi by steamboat, a short rail or stage transfer to the Lakes at Chicago, down the Lakes by luxury liner to Buffalo, and thence by train or Erie Canal packet boat to the Hudson and home. It had been just twenty-five years since the Cass expedition had found most of the Lakes a howling wilderness. Now they were seeing women in evening gowns and men in tails on promenade decks lined with plush cushions. Henry Schoolcraft, now the Indian Agent at Mackinac, quit his post and went home in disgust to write his memoirs. Civilization, he thought, had taken over far too completely.[20]

Woolson wrote several travel pieces about the Lakes, one a humorous debunking of just such luxury excursions. Yet with few exceptions, the majority of her fictional settings are not only wild, but beyond history. Her descriptions of nature may be beautiful, evocative of a rapidly disappearing paradise that Champlain had called *la Mer douce*, the sweet sea. But her land is a land of imagination, not experience. From her childhood memories of the Lakes, she created a landscape to serve as the stage for her actions, a wilderness that is frequently an island where social expectations need not be honored, where those who have fled society make their refuges.

"Ballast Island" (1873), an early piece, begins, like many of these stories, with a storm on the Lakes and a lover's quarrel. Elizabeth, fleeing from her betrothed, Frederick, is caught in a storm on Lake Erie and her boat is blown ashore on Ballast Island. Frederick pursues her and they are both taken care of by Miss Jonah, the solitary middle-aged woman who has kept the light there for many years. The lovers' quarrel resolved and the wedding date set, Miss Jonah's tale is then revealed at the center of the story. After a long engagement she had discovered that her betrothed loved her younger sister, so Miss Jonah faked her own drowning and stole away, leaving her farm to the lovers, and wandered until she came to the island. Determined not to be found and brought back into the family circle where she would either marry a man she knew did not love her or be forced to watch him marry someone else, she changed her name, taking that of a mountain near her home, "Yonah." But the people of Lake Erie mispronounced it and she became "Miss Jonah," a mistake she never corrected. Although Elizabeth and Frederick plead with her to come with them to the city, she refuses: "Here I'm going to stay. I like it. It's lonely, but I'm best alone. . . . I have a fancy I shall not live long, and I want to be buried here on Ballast. There mustn't be any stone or even a mound, for I want to be clean forgotten; and this is what I ask you two to do for me."[21]

Superficially, this story appears to resemble the Shell Heap Island episodes in Sarah Orne Jewett's *The Country of the Pointed Firs*, but there are significant differences. "Poor Joanna" is rejected by her lover, whereas Miss Jonah sacrifices herself for his happiness. Joanna isolates herself on an island, but Shell Heap is within sight and sound of her former home and people frequently sail their boats near or stop and leave packages for her. She remains emotionally, if not physically, within her former society. But Woolson's Miss Jonah changes her name and flees north. When she dies only three people bury her, not the whole town. More important, while Jewett constantly refers to Joanna as "poor Joanna," Woolson does not pity Miss Jonah any more than Miss Jonah pities herself. She is described as strong and competent as a man, capable of handling any emergency, but also still feminine, a good cook and a lover of flowers. She chides Elizabeth's dainty femininity with "What's the good of your hands?" and her one culinary accomplishment, cream pies, with "Cream pies! . . . Will *they* save the nation?"

At first glance "Ballast Island" may seem only a love story with a spinster figure for contrast, a common type before the Civil War. But Miss Jonah is much more than simply a Wise Aunt. Woolson is careful to make her life an alternative to marriage, an example of how a woman can thrive without love. In earlier women's fiction, the so-called "handbooks of feminine revolt"[22] and stories of the "philosophy of the fortunate fall,"[23] the heroine often renounced love, only to have it restored to her when the plot threads were neatly tied. But Woolson is concerned with what happens to women who renounce and then discover there is no restoration. The women local colorists explored this theme repeatedly, but their women wither away in dark, decaying houses or, like Poor Joanna, immolate themselves in sight of the community.[24] Miss Jonah does neither. Like so many of Woolson's heroines who sacrifice themselves for another's happiness, she leaves without good-byes and begins life over in another place, becoming stronger for her struggle.

She does not, however, necessarily become happier in a conventional sense. True to her Biblical namesake, Miss Jonah has sacrificed her own joy for a greater good, but her renunciation was not without pain and she still weeps when she considers all that she lost. At the same time, her hard-won strength and wisdom overshadow Elizabeth's naive romantic posturings with an example of how fragile romantic happiness truly is, how quickly a young woman can be forced to create another life for herself. Yet Miss Jonah has not become bitter, nor does she begrudge the young lovers their happiness. As they leave, she "climbed upon a rock and stood gazing after the sloop, her tall form outlined against the gloomy sky," becoming like the mountain whose name she had chosen, rather than the grim prophet whose name society had given her.

The metaphor of Miss Jonah as mountain is interesting because it prefigures the last entry in Woolson's journal before she died in 1894:

> Upon seeing the sharp peaks of the Dolomites and the great snow masses of the Alps from the point of the Lido on Christmas Eve, 1893, the thought came to me that they are riding along through immeasurable space, they are the outer edge of our star, they cut the air as they fly. They are the rim of the world. I should like to turn into a peak when I die: to be a beautiful purple mountain, which would please the tired, sad eyes of thousands of human beings for the ages.[25]

Woolson wrote that passage twenty years after "Ballast Island," but the metaphors in question had not changed. By 1893 she too had become isolated, and while that isolation often made her weary, as it did Miss Jonah, she had made for herself an artist's life, distinct from conventional married lives.[26]

In *The Experience of Landscape*, Jay Appleton suggests that like most animals we prefer landscapes where we feel secure. Landscapes which offer protection—high hills, the edges of forests, or islands—which allow us to detect strangers long before they arrive, are more attractive than other landforms. He suggests that this atavistic instinct for "prospect and refuge" explains many configurations in landscape paintings we find pleasing, and that this instinct operates even more powerfully in the symbolic language of literature. The act of reading forces the reader to produce a landscape from the cues of the writer's imagination and thus to participate in the experience of place more intimately than he may when presented with the accomplished facts of pictorial representations.[27] If Appleton is right, it seems reasonable to believe that a writer who creates fictional landscapes also completes such an inferential process. And so Woolson's late journal entry seems a residual form of such operations she had conducted when writing her fiction, where an isolato on an island, often an island with a high escarpment, appears in almost every Great Lakes story after "Ballast Island." Through her landscapes she gains symbolic power and control outdoors and far away, rather than in what Henry Nash Smith has called "the middle landscape" of small towns and gentle spaces.[28] Woolson's response is more like that of her grand-uncle James Fenimore Cooper, what Richard Slotkin has described as "the characteristic American gesture in the face of adversity . . . immersion in the native element, the wilderness, as the solution to all problems, the balm to all wounds of the soul, the restorative for failing fortunes."[29] For a woman writer who felt the conventional feminine role as a restriction on her freedom—"I do not care to be forced into quiescence"—the usual female, domestic, fictional setting with its garden was an anathema.

Edith Cobb claims that resort to a landscape known earlier is common among persons of genius, where it takes the form of an imaginative return to a "middle age of childhood, approximately from five or six to eleven to twelve . . . when the natural world is experienced in some highly evocative way, producing in the child a sense of some profound continuity with natural processes . . . when what a child wanted to do most of all was to make a world in which to find a place to discover a self." The recreation of this landscape in later life is an attempt to renew at its source the impulse and power to create.[30] For Woolson, this meant a return to the Great Lakes islands she had visited as a child, particularly the Wine Islands of Lake Erie (of which Ballast Island is one) and Mackinac Island at the Straights. During the next five years before she wrote her first novel, *Anne* (partly set on Mackinac Island), Woolson would write nine more stories set on Great Lakes islands, moving the settings generally north and west farther into the wilderness until she reached the Apostle Islands in western Lake Superior. With "Ballast Island" the group is:

"Ballast Island"	1873	Wine Islands	Lake Erie
"St. Clair Flats"	1873	Lake St. Clair	Lake Huron
"A Flower of the Snow"	1874	Mackinac	Lake Huron
"Jeannette"	1874	Mackinac	Lake Huron
"The Old Agency"	1874	Mackinac	Lake Huron

"Misery Landing"	1874 Apostles	Lake Superior
"The Lady of Little Fishing"	1874 Apostles	Lake Superior
"Mission Endeavor"	1874 Apostles	Lake Superior
"Castle Nowhere"	1876 Hog Island?	Lake Michigan
"Raspberry Island"	1877 Bois Blanche?	Lake Huron

Many of these islands rise like cliffs from the water, particularly Mackinac, which was a military garrison chosen for the impregnability of its ramparts when Indians had attacked Fort Michilimackinac on the mainland across the Straits, and the Apostles in Lake Superior. The protagonist of "Misery Landing" (1874), John Jay, builds an eyrie on one of the Apostles, "fortified by a high stockade across the land side; the other three sides were cliffs rising from the deep water,"[31] a setting more convenient for eagles than for a man.

Those islands not described as cliff-like are fortresses hidden in labyrinths. Waiting Samuel, a crazed religious prophet, and his long-suffering wife Roxanna of "St. Clair Flats" (1873) live in the great marsh on Lake St. Clair, surrounded by channels so confusing that only by trailing string behind can outsiders find their way back to the island house.[32] Old Fog of "Castle Nowhere" (1875) has so cleverly camouflaged his inland house with floating sedge that one can approach it only by knowing just which piece of sedge to move.[33] All these island isolatos have been unhappy, sometimes persecuted wanderers in the world, until they find their islands where they are free and safe. Even the members of the garrison at Mackinac, secure in a military society, mourn when they must leave for other posts; in "Jeannette" (1874) a mixed-race island girl gives up a chance to marry the garrison doctor who will educate her and take her traveling with him to stay at Mackinac and marry a local boy who is as wild and free as she.[34]

In contrast, those characters in stories not set on islands but in wilderness clearings, isolated by the lake on one side and impenetrable timber on the other, are quite different. The setting of Pine City in "Hepzibah's Story," an early, unpublished manuscript, is typical:

> [It was] a small settlement gathered around the sawmills; back on the ridge there was a row of white houses, a long dock ran out into the lake, and on all sides stood the woods, the great trees so close together that I could not see between them, stretching down to the water's edge and closing around the clearing like a well.[35]

Significantly, the characters in these "clearing" stories do not fare so well as Miss Jonah or Old Fog. Hepzibah returns to New England when she finds her betrothed loves another, the only one of Woolson's heroines to retreat. Peter, the ascetic Episcopal priest of "Peter the Parson" (1874), is mocked by the rough miners of his congregation, even as he gives his life to save a thief who once maimed him. Peter's sacrifice is neither appreciated nor avenged, and the young girl who loved him promptly marries his replacement. Unlike Miss Jonah, he reaps no satisfaction from his sacrifice: "I have failed in my work, I have failed in myself, I am of all men the most miserable!"[36]

Even Woolson's infrequent pastoral landscape of small towns and settled fields is not a good place, particularly for women. Her two stories of the Zoar Community of Ohio, "Solomon" (1873) and "Wilhelmina" (1875), are set in the archetypal middle landscape, yet both describe the lives of doomed and suffering characters. Solomon, a talented but untutored artist, paints the same picture repeatedly, trying to create what he sees only in his imagination. Once given a lesson, he realizes his vision on canvas, only to die the next day in a mining accident. His wife, who understood neither his genius nor his desire, pities only herself.[37] Wilhelmina waits steadfastly for her lover to return from the Civil War so they may marry, but when he marches home, he abandons her. Forced to marry a man she doesn't love, she dies soon after.[38] For Woolson, society, and often love or marriage, equalled loss of power and loss of self. There is no "prospect" or "refuge" where one who falls outside the social norm can feel confident; the forest or the fields suffocate, "closing around [like] a well."[39]

II

Like Miss Jonah, however, none of Woolson's island isolatos, man or woman, is happy in a conventional sense. At best they are aware that their lives, cut off from society, can make truce with loneliness only by strength and resignation. Even though their social isolation is not always pleasant, however, it does give them independence, and this is the key to Woolson's obsession with her theme. To define herself as an artist took courage in a time when most women defined themselves as daughters, wives, and mothers, particularly when, as in Woolson's case, there was no nurturing group of other writers around her. James and Howells, who faced the same difficulty in becoming serious artists during a period awash in conventional fiction, lived in urban centers. Woolson had no such support. That she missed it is evident from letters even late in her life: "I am terribly alone in my literary work. There seems to be no one for me to turn to. It is true that there are only two or three to whom I wd. turn!"[40]

And so Woolson respectfully projects her strong, singular, independent men and women, particularly women, who are proud, willing to settle for less than their due and yet able to take the consequences. Whereas John Jay gives up his Misery Landing to return to the city and marry a woman he loves but whom he knows wants only his money, Woolson's women seldom capitulate, even if it means permanent isolation or death. When Miriam, the heroine of "Mission Endeavor" (1876), abandons a man she has saved from execution by agreeing to marry him, she leaves him to a lesser woman in an explanatory letter. Like many other Woolson heroines, Miriam has sailed off into a lake without saying good-bye, but she gives a parting shot:

> I hate hypocrisy. Therefore I wish to say that it was not religious enthusiasm or self-sacrifice that made me try to save you when Ruth failed. (For she did fail; you can never alter that.) I *was* religious—once. I had deep religious enthusiasms—once. I was capable of making just such a sacrifice for a doomed criminal—once. But that was long ago—before I loved you!
>
> Yes, Richard Herndon, I loved you, I love you now. But through all the complications and temptations of my fate I am coming out right; I am leaving you forever.
>
> Go back to Ruth if you like; I do not care, nor shall I know. For I can not marry you if I would, being a wife, at least in name already; and I would not if I could, being very proud. For you did not love me first, Richard; therefore you shall not love me last.[41]

Richard's reaction to this unexpected feminine independence is that he has had a "happy escape; she would have been very inconvenient." To which Woolson as narrator adds her last line, like an ironic smile, "And so she would I fear."

It is intriguing to compare "Mission Endeavor" with an earlier tale considered among Woolson's best, "The Lady of Little Fishing" (1874). This story, which she patterned after Bret Harte's "The Luck of Roaring Camp," was far more appealing to nineteenth-century readers than "Mission Endeavor," for obvious reasons. Yet Woolson seems to have felt compelled to reconsider the Bret Harte materials in the later story, to restructure the sentimental plot in a less romantic manner more aligned with her own philosophy. Nowhere else in her work does she create two stories with characters and situations so similar but with such different endings. The Lady of Little Fishing, a missionary to a camp of trappers, falls in love with the only man who does not love her. When he rejects her, she weakens and dies, murmuring that although she had "held herself above her kind," God had shown her that she was "the weakest of them all."[42] In both stories the group of men who rule are initially afraid of the woman missionary because of her strength and saintly demeanor. But both the Lady and Miriam "fall," experiencing unrequited love and showing that they are human after all. The significant difference in "Mission Endeavor" is that Miriam does not die from loss of love; she sails off into the lake, presumably to become an isolato, and leaves her erstwhile lover to walk along the beach for twelve hours to reach a settlement. Woolson's message is again that love is capricious and that the best way for a woman to cope, particularly if her love is unreturned, is to gather strength and make another life. To refuse to do that, to continue expecting that somehow fate will restore happiness, is death.

As Ann Douglas has pointed out, in the post–Civil War years many women faced just such a possibility, for there were relatively few available men. She suggests that local colorists recognized a statistical probability in cataloguing lonely women left at home with no alternatives except death or a mouldering, witch-like insanity.[43] But Woolson creates an alternative: sane women, secure in what they know they must do to survive, realistic about their chances for happiness. In so doing she also shows that by freeing herself from the constraints of self-destructive love, a woman can avail herself of men's personal freedom to travel, to explore, to become competent at taking care of herself. Woolson's strong women may be uppity and unpredictable, like Miriam; they may have their moments of deep regret, like Miss Jonah; but they endure in a hostile world. Margaret Morris survives after a shipwreck on Lake Michigan through sheer anger at a fellow survivor's condescension: "The pride and high temper of Margaret Morris, lashed into vigor by the sharp questions of the stranger, saved the life of her exhausted body, and the two were still talking when the cold dawn rose slowly into sight, revealing the gray surface of the stormy lake and the blue line of distant shore."[44] Contrary to convention, moreover, Margaret does not marry her raftmate, but soon boards another steamer and continues to Chicago. Flower Moran, of "A Flower of the Snow" (1874), is another strong woman willing to be alone. Believing the man she loves does not love her, she sets off into a blizzard. Her guide gives up, the dog train is close to exhaustion, but Flower trudges on. "I am not a coward," she replies to a seductive voice in her head, which urges her to lie down in the snow and sleep into certain death. " 'What have *you* to live for?' pursued the voice. 'To conquer myself. . . . Do I not know that I am unloved and unlovable? Am I not trying to do right? Have I not left all that is dear to me in life to follow my wretched, lonely way through the world?' " After continuing to walk, despite the pain of cold and exhaustion, Flower suddenly remembers a Bible verse, "As if written in letters of fire in the air. . . . He that overcometh shall inherit all things."[45] Much has been written about the covert feminism of the women's literature of the 1840s and 1850s, but recent critics have suggested that after the Civil War, when feminism moved out of books and into the streets, literature became regressive.[46] Woolson's stories prove this is not completely accurate. Moreover, Woolson's feminism is of a different character than that of the Sentimentalists, who were intent on giving women power within the home.

III

But Woolson's pattern of story—a character who begins in a love, loses the love, creates another self in nature in response to loss, but then is alone—can become an imaginative dead-end. Woolson's "Natalie Bumppos" have only a single story, and its repetitions can pall. As Kolodny writes of Leatherstocking, the price for returning to the womb of the wilderness is "adult sexuality and much of what we know of civilized norms. Natty can never experience adult human relations within the social community."[47] Woolson's growing recognition of the limitations in her early theme becomes apparent in one of her last Great Lakes isolato portraits, the title story to her collection of Lake Country sketches, *Castle Nowhere*.[48] Old Fog has left civilization for the fog-shrouded northern reaches of Lake Michigan, where for many years he secretly wrecks ships to obtain food and clothing for his beloved foundling child, Silver. When a wealthy stranger from the city happens on Fog's "castle," Silver is grown, but she is still a joyful child who knows nothing of death or evil because of Fog's protection. As Silver comes to know and love the stranger, her naiveté vanishes. "Frightened, shy, bewildered, she fled away from all her dearest joys, and stayed by herself in the flower-room with the bar across the door, only emerging timidly at meal-times and stealing into the long room like a little wraith; a rosy wraith now, for at last she had learned to blush." When they marry and prepare to leave the island, Fog dies, and on her wedding day Silver learns her first lesson of death. Although her husband dutifully teaches her the Christian doctrine of the resurrection, the reader is left wondering if marriage and religion, however laudatory, compensate for Silver's losses. She has learned of evil, and in Woolson's island paradise, evil comes from civilization to take away childlike joy and replace it with a controlling husband who suggests to Fog that, "Of course it is a great thing for you to have the child off your hands and placed in a home so high above your expectations."

At the same time, Woolson clearly portrays the danger Fog courted by remaining isolated in his castle, for if no stranger had ever come for Silver, when Fog died of old age she would have starved to death. In this paradox of strength and naiveté inevitably forced to face death or return to society, Woolson admits that to remain an isolato on an island is to refuse to acknowledge reality. Painful as that reality may be, the person, or the artist, who shuns it will forever remain a child, trapped in a dream of landscape that will one day destroy by psychic starvation.

By the time Woolson came to write *Anne* she had been living in the South for nearly ten years and setting fiction there for five. Thus it was logical that she should try to use both island and Southern settings as she did later in *Jupiter Lights*. The combination is not satisfactory, however, as nearly every critic notes.[49] The first section of *Anne*, set on Mackinac, is universally praised, but once the heroine leaves the Strait, the novel becomes episodic, unfocused, and traditionally sentimental. The large middle section of *Jupiter Lights*, set on Lake Superior, lies incongruously between the southern beginning and close. In both books Woolson seems caught in transition between two different metaphors of landscape, a North of escape and retreat, and a South of closeness and familial tradition.

The North remains, in both novels, a place of safety and power. Anne, like Silver before her, is forced by circumstances from her island paradise at Mackinac, and the rest of the novel traces her attempt to make her way in the world alone. When finally she succeeds, she returns to the island to be married, high within the ramparts of the fort that crowns the escarpment overlooking the water. The whole cast of *Jupiter Lights* flees north to escape danger; most of the resolution of the plot takes place near the Lake, and the return to the South at the end is only a return to a stable family situation. But in neither novel does Woolson achieve the dramatic power of Great Lakes landscape and character as she had in her stories. There is no isolato on an island at the center, no conflict between remaining within a social world and rejecting it. These novels are apprentice-pieces for Woolson's later work as a novelist of manners and they reveal her growing recognition that the metaphorical structure she had imposed on her childhood country was no longer sufficient for her imagination. The magic that had come from a seamless blending of character and place was gone; she had grown beyond it.

Rather than boredom with her local color materials, as most critics have suggested, this is the major reason why Woolson stopped writing about the Great Lakes country. In the post-Reconstruction South she could explore the isolato's position within an established society; like Henry James, she would create a complex investigation of the outsider in a social setting. In her Southern stories, and her later European stories as well, this outsider is often a northerner or a Yankee set down in a foreign culture. Although she still wrote of isolated houses by the water, they were filled with family life. She still described mountains, but they provided comfort and shelter for the towns set down among them; they had no escarpments to keep away the world. Throughout her life, she created characters who sacrifice themselves for another's happiness, but in her later stories, they do not run away after having done so; they remain in their society, tied by bonds of kinship and affection.

Woolson had created her singular Great Lakes island wilderness as a projection of and solution for her dilemma as woman and artist, using landscape to help her escape the mores and tropes of sentimental fiction while she drew inspiration from her childhood memories of place. Once she had explored the implications of the isolato on an island, she could leave her island fortresses behind; she had internalized their strength. Like Miss Jonah, Woolson had become a mountain and she could reside in the world on her own terms: a woman who had chosen to become an artist and succeeded in publishing frequently and well. She was then ready to learn to create characters who could defy convention without denying social relationships. When she wrote the closing line of "Castle Nowhere," she anticipated her farewell to the Great Lakes landscape she would soon abandon: "The fogs still steal across the lake, and wave their gray draperies up into the northern curve; but the sedge-gate is gone, and the castle is indeed nowhere."

Notes

1. Henry James, "Miss Woolson," in *Partial Portraits* (London: Macmillan & Co., 1988), pp. 177–192.

2. Claire Benedict, *Constance Fenimore Woolson* (London: Ellis, 1929–1930). The most recent, and by far the best, critical biography of Woolson is *Constance Fenimore Woolson: the Grief of Artistry* by Cheryl B. Torsney (Athens: Univ. of Georgia Press, 1989).

3. Alice Hall Petry, " 'Always, Your Attached Friend': The Unpublished Letters of Constance Fenimore Woolson to John and Clara Hay," *Books at Brown*, 29–30 (1982–1983), 74.

4. Benedict, p. 19.

5. Petry, p. 104. Woolson's italics.

6. Rayburn S. Moore, *Constance Fenimore Woolson* (New York: Twayne, 1963), p. 130.

7. Bendict, pp. 21–22. Woolson's italics.

8. Benedict, p. 21.

9. Benedict, p. 23.

10. Elizabeth Hardwick, "Introduction," *Anne* (New York: Arno Press, 1977), pp. i–ii.

11. There are three significant studies of Woolson as a local colorist: Fred Lewis Pattee, *The Development of the American Short Story* (New York: Harper & Brothers, 1923); John Kern, *Constance Fenimore Woolson: Literary Pioneer*, dissertation, Univ. of Pennsylvania, 1934; Ann Douglas [Wood], "The Literature of Impoverishment: The Women Local Colorists in America 1865–1914," *Women's Studies*, 1 (1972), 2–40.

12. Alfred Habegger, *Gender, Fantasy and Realism in American Literature* (New York: Columbia Univ. Press, 1982), p. 105.

13. Ann Douglas (see note 11) groups Woolson with the local colorists, often women, who retreated to remote parts of the country, often failed to make a financial success of their writing, and lacked any sustained productivity, none of which applies to Woolson. Douglas also notes the "conspicuous absence of male romantic leads" in the local colorists' settings of backward towns and villages, again a point that fits Woolson's work haphazardly.

14. Moore, p. 127.

15. Annette Kolodny, *The Land Before Her* (Chapel Hill: Univ. of North Carolina Press, 1984), Chapters 6 and 7.

16. S.M. Fuller [Margaret Fuller], *Summer on the Lakes, in 1843* (New York: Charles S. Francis and Co., 1844).

17. Petry, p. 51.

18. Roderick Nash, *Wilderness and the American Mind* (New Haven: Yale Univ. Press, 1967), p. 5.

19. [Caroline Kirkland], *A New Home—Who'll Follow? Or, Glimpses of Western Life. By Mrs. Mary Clavers. An Actual Settler* (1839; rpt. New York: Garrett Press, 1969).

20. William Ashworth, *The Late Great Lakes: An Environmental History* (New York: Knopf, 1986), p. 97.

21. *Appleton's Journal*, 9 (28 June 1873), 833–839.

22. Helen Waite Papishvily, *All the Happy Endings* (New York: Harper and Brothers, 1952), Chapter 1.

23. Nina Baym, *Woman's Fiction* (New York: Cornell Univ. Press, 1978), p. 20.

24. Douglas, pp. 18–19.

25. Benedict, p. 411.

26. Woolson's history of depression and her probable suicide suggest that, as she grew older, her personal metaphors of strength became less efficacious. Other American writers have relied on paradigms of character they created while young, only to find themselves

without materials for fiction as they aged. Woolson won her struggle for independence, but undoubtedly discovered that strength seldom suffices past youth.

27.   Jay Appleton, *The Experience of Landscape* (London: Wiley & Sons, 1975), Chapters 4 and 7.

28.   Henry Nash Smith, *Virgin Land: The American West as Symbol and Myth* (Cambridge, Massachusetts: Harvard Univ. Press, 1950), Chapters 11 and 12.

29.   Richard Slotkin, *Regeneration Through Violence: The Mythology of the American Frontier 1600–1860* (Middletown, Connecticut: Wesleyan Univ. Press, 1973), p. 267.

30.   Edith Cobb, "The Ecology of Imagination in Childhood," *Daedalus* 88 (1959), 537–548. For another discussion of this concept see Judith Fryer, *Felicitous Space: The Imaginative Structures of Edith Wharton and Willa Cather* (Chapel Hill and London: Univ. of North Carolina Press, 1986), Chapter 1.

31.   *Harper's New Monthly Magazine*, 48 (May 1874), 864–870.

32.   *Appleton's Journal*, 10 (4 October 1873), 419–426.

33.   *Castle Nowhere* (Boston: J.R. Osgood & Company, 1875), pp. 7–98.

34.   *Scribner's Monthly*, 9 (December 1874), 232–243.

35.   Robert Gingras, " 'Hepzibah's Story': An Unpublished Work by Constance Fenimore Woolson," *Resources for American Literary Study*, 10 (1980), 33–46.

36.   *Scribner's Monthly*, 8 (September 1874), 293–305.

37.   *Atlantic Monthly*, 32 (October 1873), 413–424.

38.   *Castle Nowhere*, pp. 270–303.

39.   Gingras, p. 35.

40.   Petry, p. 65.

41.   *Harper's New Monthly Magazine*, 53 (November 1876), 886–893.

42.   *Atlantic Monthly*, 34 (September 1874), 293–305.

43.   Douglas, pp. 28–30.

44.   *Appleton's Journal*, 7 (13 April 1872), 394–399.

45.   *Galaxy*, 17 (January 1874), 76–85.

46.   For example, see Douglas, p. 13.

47.   Annette Kolodny, *The Lay of the Land* (Chapel Hill: Univ. of North Carolina Press, 1975), p. 114.

48.   *Castle Nowhere*, p. 98.

49.   For example, see the Henry James review cited above.

NEW ESSAYS

◆

Women as Daughters; Women as Mothers in the Fiction of Constance Woolson

SHARON L. DEAN

In *Woman's Fiction: A Guide to Novels by and about Women in America, 1820–1870,* Nina Baym has located an overplot that reveals women trying to overcome "recurrent injustices occasioned by [their] status as female and child." Within this overplot, "there are very few intact families . . . , and those that are intact are unstable or locked into routines of misery." Nineteenth-century writers of popular fiction, says Baym, seek an end to injustice not through female isolation but by a redefinition of family: "men as well as women find greatest happiness and fulfillment in domestic relations, by which are meant not simply spouse and parent, but the whole network of human attachments based on love, support, and mutual responsibility."[1] Mary Kelley has argued that this attention to domestic relations enabled women to choose writing as a career without really entering the public sphere, a place open to them only at the expense of their more highly valued domestic roles.[2] Neither Baym nor Kelley discusses Constance Woolson, probably because she wrote after the peak of the popular domestic genre and because her fiction is more consciously literary than that genre.[3] But an examination of Woolson's life and work reveals a writer keenly aware of the implications of valuing domestic roles and one whose observations of women's roles as daughters and as mothers are remarkably consistent with modern sociological and psychological theory.

Unlike the women Baym describes in her fictional overplot, Woolson had been raised in a traditional family. But her family had also been deeply scarred, first by the deaths of three sisters shortly after her birth, and later by the deaths of an infant sister, of a sister from tuberculosis, and of another sister in childbirth. Even her remaining sister, Clara, became a single parent when her husband was killed in a railroad accident, and her only brother, Charly, may have died a suicide. The information on Charly, the youngest of the Woolson children, is still available only in unpublished documents, but Joan Weimer provides some background in her introduction to *Women Artists, Women Exiles: "Miss Grief" and Other Stories,* quoting in particular a

This essay was written especially for this volume and is published here for the first time with the permission of the author.

letter Woolson wrote to her nephew Sam Mather about how her mother's "whole happiness, even her life I might almost say, depends, and has always depended upon how Charly is and how he feels."[4]

Despite his preferential treatment, Charly clearly represents Nancy Chodorow's and Carol Gilligan's theories that male children tend to break from the family.[5] Chodorow believes that males identify themselves as masculine by using negative differentiation; that is, by identifying themselves as not like the mother. This differentiation undercuts their capacity to relate to others and causes them to emphasize separateness rather than connectedness. Charly's differentiation from the mother into male identification may have been exaggerated because even from birth he was valued as other, as the only male child. In fact, he broke so totally from the family that he became a profligate son, eventually dying alone in California, a victim of the hereditary depression that affected Woolson and her grandfather and father. While Charly replicates the breaking from the family, Woolson herself became increasingly connected to her family. Her development represents the tendency Gilligan finds in women to preserve relationships rather than subordinate them to the process of independent achievement, a tendency not surprisingly reflected in the overplot of women's fiction that Baym has described. Thus Woolson defined her value as a daughter by how much she remained connected to her parents, faulting herself for being on a pleasure trip when her father died[6] and giving up much of her personal life to care for her mother until the mother's death when Woolson was nearly forty years old.

Not only does Woolson's life support Chodorow's and Gilligan's theories, but the pattern that emerges in her fiction further illustrates them. Woolson moves from exploring how the female child defines herself in relationship to the father, able to break from him only when he dies, to exploring how male children abandon mothers and female children remain connected to them. Her parent-child relationships fall into three categories: the relationship between father and daughter, between mother and son, and between mother and daughter. Lyon Richardson believes that Woolson's father-daughter relationships are more fully realized than her mother-daughter relationships,[7] but if one takes all of the fiction into account it becomes apparent that Woolson focuses on fathers and daughters more often in her early fiction written shortly after the death of her father and that the notion of mothering becomes predominant in the fiction written in Europe after her mother's death. Furthermore, Woolson examines mother-child relationships with both younger and grown children, distinguishing here between male independence and female connectedness. Any father–younger child relationships are usually between fathers and sons and exist more as asides in the fiction than as developed relationships. In *Anne*,[8] for example, the twice-widowed father has three young sons and a thirteen-year-old daughter by his second marriage, but the central relationship is between him and the sixteen-year-old daughter from his first marriage. In *For the Major*,[9] the father, who is approaching senility, educates his son into a game-like code of honor that suggests a childhood friendship more than a father-son relationship.

In Woolson's fiction concerning fathers and grown daughters, the connectedness the daughter brings to the relationship is so strong that at least two commentators have suggested incest themes, Sybil Weir in her discussion of *For the Major*[10] and Joan Weimer in her introduction to *Women Artists, Women Exiles*.[11] But these relationships suggest less the sexual or incestuous than Chodorow's and Gilligan's theories about female development. Most often, the relationships depend on the daughter's caring for an ailing or inept father. As if she realized that too much caretaking could inhibit women's growth, Woolson typically has the father die, freeing the daughter to abandon her role as nurse-wife and to marry more independently, according to her own wishes. Yet Woolson does not seem to have felt that her own father hindered her possibility for marriage. Despite a brief infatuation, she seems never to have planned marriage, having begun to think of herself as a "desolate spinster" even before her father's death.[12] A letter she wrote to her longtime friend Col. John Hay after her father's death indicates that the relationship had been extremely close: "I have never recovered from the sense of desolation I felt when I lost my father; the world has never been the same to me since, for he made a pet of me."[13] In making a pet of her, perhaps he also hindered her ability to find her own identity, for it is only after his death that she began to write.

As Woolson sought her identity, she may, through writing the early fiction, also have been confronting the loss of her father. The theme of the death of the father first appears in "Castle Nowhere."[14] Here, the father figure is an adoptive one who has rescued an orphan and raised her in order to expiate a crime he once committed. The father and daughter live an isolated, Edenic existence, hidden in a Lake Michigan cove on an ark reminiscent of the one in Cooper's *The Deerslayer*. Joan Weimer reads this as a commentary on the patriarchal systems that mate "men with grown-up children" and that keep women innocent by keeping them ignorant,[15] a theme Woolson is even more explicit about in *East Angels* when the heroine's husband explains to a friend that he married a girl fourteen years his junior because he "always had a fancy for young girls," though he despairs because they all seem to grow up."[16] In "Castle Nowhere" when an outsider finds the girl, Silver, and her "father," Fog, and falls in love with Silver, Silver cannot establish a marriage away from the ark. Failing in her attempt to leave Fog by marrying, she returns immediately to find him dying. Only his death in her arms frees her to live as a wife, but whether this will also allow her to establish her own space, in Weimer's terms her own "Somewhere," remains doubtful. The death of the father motif occurs again in several stories in *Rodman the Keeper*,[17] most fully in "Old Gardiston," where the father figure is an old uncle who tries to keep the southern tradition alive by writing a meticulous genealogy and where the female protagonist would rather starve than marry a northerner. With the death of her uncle and the burning of the genealogy and their dilapidated home, the young woman is freed from her southern pride and does marry the northerner. And again the motif occurs in *For the Major*, where the subplot necessitates that the father figuratively die—by becoming senile—before the daughter plans marriage.

We see Woolson confronting her ambivalence about the love and confinement generated in father-daughter relationships most clearly in her first novel, *Anne*. Anne's father, William Douglas, shares Woolson's father's tendency to be clinically depressed. This, the loss of two wives, and an artistic temperament combine to make Douglas a loving but dependent father who uses Anne to care for the younger children and to tend to the domestic chores. Woolson captures Anne's dilemma when the father is in the last stages of a depression that ends with his death: "For strange patience have loving women ever had with dreamers like William Douglas—men who, viewed by the eyes of the world, are useless and incompetent. For personally there is a sweetness and gentleness in their natures which make them very dear to the women who love them. The successful man, perhaps, would not care for such love, which is half devotion, half protection; the successful man wished to domineer" (91). The problem with this, as Woolson sees, is that the non-domineering, dependent father has the same impact on the daughter who cares for him as a more domineering man would have. For as long as she must care for her father, Anne can "never [live] for herself or in herself" (91). Still, Anne's service to her father has its compensations. Although she lives in a shabby and financially insecure home, she can dream of the time when she will be able to decorate each of the rooms according to her taste. She has a sense of place, she is loved and loves, and she has an important role in caring for the younger children.

But this is not enough for Anne to grow. Woolson begins to follow her pattern of having the father die and the daughter marry when she has Anne accept a proposal from her childhood friend Erastus Pronando. Poverty necessitates that Anne, despite her engagement, go east to school to become a self-supporting teacher; she, like Pronando, who attends a western college, will grow by becoming educated. While his fiancée is gone, however, Pronando elopes with Anne's younger stepsister, Tita. Interestingly, Tita has also been hindered by her father, whose preference for Anne she senses and envies. Tita rebels in many subtle ways, especially by devoting herself excessively to the Catholicism that was her mother's religion but is anathema to the local Protestant community. Although we do not see her elopement, we surmise that this too is an act of rebellion directed toward a sister who never recognized her as more than a child and a father who preferred that sister. In fact, while he lived, Douglas looked at Tita as a personification of his error in marrying her mother; she represented for him "his own mistakes" (12) and was someone he cautioned Anne to "stand by" but not to "expect too much of" because of "her Indian blood" (20). By having Tita and Pronando elope, Woolson provides Tita with space away from a home that has discriminated against her heritage and, at the same time, opens numerous avenues for Anne, who has fallen in love with someone else and is relieved to be free of Pronando, to awaken to her own nature. The novel contains many complications before Anne finally marries the man she loves. The point is not that she marries but that her long period of independence allows her to awaken to herself and her own potential, a potential she could never have achieved had she remained the daughter of a loving but needy father.

In the later fiction written in Europe, Woolson's patterns change to emphasize mothers' relationships with their children rather than fathers' with their daughters. Where the early fiction suggests that Woolson was confronting the loss of her father, the sense that families are always doomed to suffer losses, and the question of independence from care-giving roles, the later fiction suggests that with the death of her mother, she was now confronting questions about mother-child relationships. Although Woolson had approached the nature of mothering to young children in her early fiction, she did so only peripherally, using children to intensify the sense of loss she associates with mothering. In the early fiction, the loss usually centers on young male children, the gender that separates more than relates. She uses the death of a young male child as background to "St. Clair Flats" in the *Castle Nowhere* volume and the death of a genderless child in "Sister St. Luke" in *Rodman the Keeper*. Even the latter volume's strongest mother-child story, "In the Cotton Country," distances the process of mothering by using a narrative method that reports the loss of a young son to a northern guardian rather than shows the relationship between the child and the mother figure. Later in her novella *For the Major*, Woolson uses mothering as the impetus behind her protagonist's duplicitous marriage, again associating mothering with loss. Madame Carroll marries her second husband pretending to be someone younger and believing that her first husband is dead. She does not acknowledge the existence of an older male child, whom she presumed drowned, so that she can find a home for her younger female child and protect that child from the knowledge that her father was a murderer. Because the female child's health is poor, Madame Carroll also needs the Major's money to care for the child. After the marriage, the child dies, and *For the Major*, like many of the mother–young child stories in *Castle Nowhere* and *Rodman the Keeper*, associates mothering with a child's death or metaphorical death, a fact Woolson experienced so often in her own family.

In her later pieces, Woolson looks more closely at mother–young son relationships, which center on exclusion rather than connectedness, as if women's desire for affiliation goes awry when the relationship involves sons. *Jupiter Lights*[18] explores not just the relationship between a mother and young son but also how this relationship excludes the child's aunt, Eve Bruce. The child, a victim of abuse by his stepfather, is the son of Eve's dead brother.

Even when she is unaware of the abuse, Eve wants to make the child her ward so that she can find a sense of family through him. Eventually she rescues both the boy and his mother from the abusive stepfather, but ultimately she loses the child to his natural mother. Again, there are no intact family units and the idea of mothering is associated with loss. An interesting scene encapsulates the theme. The young boy is stranded in a storm in a canoe, and Eve saves him just as she saved him from his stepfather. The rescue allows the boy to live, but for Eve the boy really dies in this scene because despite her heroic efforts, the natural mother will not relinquish him. Just as Anne Douglas in Woolson's first novel cannot become the natural mother of her stepbrothers and her stepsister, Eve cannot take the place of her nephew's natural mother. Nor can the process of mothering be fully realized through the natural mother because, like Woolson's mother, she has been traumatized by death, in this case not of other children but of her second husband. Although the novel examines how much a mother—or an aunt— may love a child, it dramatizes a weak relationship between mother and child. So fraught with pain or so biologically impossible is mothering that Woolson, despite the love for children expressed in her letters, finds it difficult to suspend the idea of pain or exclusion to look at the daily interaction between mother and child.[19]

Woolson continues to focus on the separation between mothers and young sons in her Italian stories, "In Venice"[20] and "A Transplanted Boy,"[21] even though here she shows more interaction between mothers and sons than in her early stories. The boy in "In Venice" is being parented by an aunt and uncle. A rather obnoxious child, like Randolph Miller in Henry James's *Daisy Miller*, he is carted around Europe and uses the excuse of illness to pester and to whine. The aunt caters to him so much that she nearly loses her husband to an infatuation for a younger woman. In fact, the marriage remains intact only because the boy dies, once again underscoring Woolson's inability to find a model for dual parenting: to parent seems to negate marriage; marriage, to negate parenting.

The child Maso in "A Transplanted Boy" illustrates dramatically how the interaction between mother and child too easily becomes a process of neglect. While the boy in "In Venice" lacks a real home, Maso lacks not only this but also anything else that would give him a sense of identity. He does not know anything about his country or his heritage; he does not even recognize his real name. An exile from all that might develop his sense of self, he also becomes exiled from his mother, who leaves him with an incompetent tutor while she, at Maso's insistence, goes on a recuperative journey. The tutor leaves and the boy fends for himself, eventually becoming ill and, we surmise, dying. In this story, the only one Woolson wrote primarily from the child's point of view, the child is the one who endures pain and loss for the sake of a mother who loves him but who is too selfish to mother adequately. The reader but not the child perceives how inadequate some women can be as mothers, and the irony creates one of the most negative portrayals of mothering in the Woolson canon.

Only one of Woolson's stories, "Felipa" in the *Rodman* volume, centers on mothering a young female child, with provocative gender implications. Felipa's parents are dead, and, in addition to the child's grandparents, the story contains two mother figures and a father figure. Dressing always in a dead boy's clothing, Felipa is so isolated that she has seen only three women before the arrival of the female artist-narrator and her friend Christine: her old grandmother, a Seminole Indian woman, and the "wife of Miguel, who seemingly had no name of her own" (205). The narrator's wording here is apt, for Felipa's behavior in the course of the story points up Woolson's sense of the invisibility of women. Felipa becomes fascinated with the two women, particularly with Christine after her fiancé, Edward Bowne, arrives. Unable to differentiate between them, she tries to win their love by copying Christine and dressing in a white dress that she thinks will make her pretty. The narrator helps her to sew a more appropriate dress for herself, one that complements rather than wars against her Minorcan blood and that reflects some of the racial issues of the story.[22] When Edward calls her pretty, she assumes this means that Christine also admires her beauty and loves her. But Christine cannot bear that Felipa loves her and Edward equally and so rejects the child. When Felipa learns that Edward and Christine will marry and leave her, she tries to commit suicide by poisoning herself and to stab Edward before she dies. Felipa survives her attempted suicide, and the story ends with her grandfather saying, "It was two loves, and the stronger thrust the knife" (220), an ambiguous comment that may refer to Felipa's love being stronger than the love between Christine and Edward. With the male-female Felipa and the Christine-Edward unity, it is tempting to read the story as one about androgyny. More likely, though, it is one where femaleness gets lost without beauty and without male approval. What matters is not that Felipa seems male but that she does not know what it means to be female. She rejects the possibilities of connectedness offered by the mother figure embodied in the narrator. Instead, she looks for a model of parenting that makes mother-father-child an inextricable unit rather than one based on negotiated relationships, so that she can only feel rejected when the male-female love sometimes excludes her.

If we look at Woolson's fictional relationships between mothers and adult sons, we get a similarly bleak view. A pattern strikingly consistent with Chodorow's and Gilligan's theories involves only adult male children and emerges as predominant in the fiction written in Europe, a pattern in which the adult male disappoints the mother figure. We see the pattern first in "Miss Elisabetha" in *Rodman the Keeper*, where the mother figure, a northern spinster, has come south to care for her orphaned nephew, who ultimately disappoints his industrious aunt by marrying a Minorcan girl with whom he leads an indolent life. This pattern becomes a prodigal son motif in *For the*

Major and *East Angels*: in *For the Major* the mother nurses her adult son, who had been raised by his father, a murderer, and who lead a mysterious foreign life until, impoverished, he returns to his mother in his dying hours; in *East Angels* the mother figure, an aunt, makes her home with her nephew's wife while the nephew has an affair in Europe. Four of the Italian stories collected in *The Front Yard* develop the prodigal flaw into a more serious defect in the grown male: one is a character only mentioned, a "ne'er-do-well, a rolling stone," a son who is not "dutiful" but whom the mother loves more than the daughter ("The Street of the Hyacinth," 186); one is a stepson, again the most loved child even though he gambles away the stepmother's carefully saved money ("The Front Yard"); one is a murderer and a robber whom the mother protects ("A Christmas Party"); and one suffers from an hereditary disposition toward uncontrollable anger that results in a near-murder and his own suicide ("Neptune's Shore").

Only the last of these stories focuses on the son closely, for Woolson is less interested in characterizing a defect than in documenting her belief that heredity can account for some kinds of behavior. As much a prodigal as her brother, Charly, may have been, Woolson saw that the family tendency toward depression had taken root in him. In an unpublished letter written to Sam Mather,[23] she mentions, as she frequently did in her letters, her own tendency to depression. This letter is particularly interesting because she attributes an illness of several months to the shock of learning of Charly's death, lamenting the great suffering he revealed in a diary that she had destroyed. Feeling a personal connection to a prodigal brother but also feeling limited in her ability to write from the male perspective,[24] Woolson develops the archetype from the mother's rather than the prodigal's point of view. She focuses on the pain the son causes the mother and on the mother's inability to betray the child who does not deserve her love. As in the stories featuring mothers and young children, in her stories of mothers with grown sons, Woolson expresses her dis-ease with the idea that mothering can be fulfilling as well as painful.

Woolson's vision of mothers and grown daughters shows as much dis-ease as her portraits of mothers and grown sons. Perhaps because her connectedness to her own mother inhibited her freedom, she seemed unable to confront the issues facing mothers and grown daughters in her early fiction. She does not address these issues at all in the stories written before her mother's death, and even in the novels she subordinates them to other kinds of relationships. *Anne*, written shortly after the death of Woolson's mother, centers on a motherless protagonist; *For the Major* is primarily a father-daughter, mother-son story and although the stepmother and daughter do have a strong relationship, the daughter has been living away from home and sees her stepmother more as a friend than a mother; *Jupiter Lights* has no mother-daughter units. In *East Angels* and *Horace Chase*,[25] the mother-daughter relationships cease when the mothers in both novels die. The pattern is particularly interesting in *East Angels* because the mother wants her daughter to marry someone the daughter sees as a surrogate father. The daughter escapes this fate, however, when the woman whom her dying mother appointed as guardian does not force the issue. As a result, the guardian mother figure, unhampered by the need to control the daughter's, and therefore her own, future, becomes the ideal mother, able to let the daughter choose her future. This future, however, is rather limited because while the mother lived, she spoiled the daughter so much that she is fit only to become a child-wife. The same kind of spoiling occurs in *Horace Chase*, where the mother defines herself so much in terms of her male child that she dies when the son dies. Daughters in these works are either literally motherless or are mothered in a way that denies them full autonomy.

Woolson addresses the mother–grown daughter relationship most intensely in "The Street of the Hyacinth" (*The Front Yard*), where the daughter at first refuses marriage to Raymond Noel, a man she believes willing to accept her mother with her but unwilling to respect the mother. The daughter, Ethelinda (Ettie) Faith Macks, is one of Woolson's artist figures who abandons her art when Noel and other male artists convince her she has no talent.[26] Perhaps she has none—or perhaps she is easily convinced of this because she has never developed autonomy from her mother. In fact, she seems to define her relationships according to how people treat her mother. Another admirer, a famous painter whose proposal she refuses because she does not love him, she judges as having an "unbounded" goodness because "if he had lived, he would have remained always a faithful, kind, and respectful son to my dear mother. That, of course, would have been everything to me" (173). This admirer stands in marked contrast to Ettie's brother, whom the narrative calls "the dearest child of the two, as the prodigal always is" (187). When Ettie goes to America to bury her brother, Noel attends to her mother so much that, on her return, Ettie listens to her praise him " 'most as if he was my real son' " (188). Ettie's loyalty has, she suggested earlier, kept her from suicide when she began to believe herself an artist of no talent: " 'I had my mother to think of,' " she tells Noel in explanation of how she has survived her belief in her lack of talent, " 'my—good sense might not have been so faithful otherwise' " (175). When the home she and her mother have inhabited in The Street of the Hyacinth is about to be torn down, Ettie, despite her resolve not to marry Noel, breaks down, thus making the final sacrifice of marrying someone whom we have come to see as lacking both depth and integrity. Woolson, though, has a final revenge by ending her story with a view of the mother shedding her mourning black for the kind of outrageous clothing that has defined her as such an embarrassment to Noel in the first place: "She wears black, but is now beginning to vary it with purple and lavender" (193).

If we read "The Street of the Hyacinth" alongside "A Transplanted

Boy," where the young son serves his mother at his own expense, we see Woolson at the end of her career questioning the value of devotion when the giver loses so much for an undeserving person. Mothers serve their adult sons no matter what their defect, while more typically adult daughters serve their mothers no matter what the cost to themselves. The adult male breaks away from the mother, either by disappointing her or by dying; the adult female supports her mother, ultimately having to define herself by connectedness rather than independence. The displacement of this motif onto the young male child in "A Transplanted Boy" may suggest that to define oneself as connected keeps the female a child if connectedness requires sacrifice on behalf of a mother who needs mothering herself. But even in "A Transplanted Boy," Maso's devotion to his mother gives him an independence that none of the adult daughters find, an independence that Woolson herself seems to have found only after the death of her mother, when she began to learn that independence also meant loneliness.

As noted, Woolson's observations about connectedness and disconnectedness to the mother are remarkably consistent with Chodorow's and Gilligan's theories about mother-child relationships. Her relationship to her mother also seems consistent with the fiction. The biographical connection is most predominant in "The Street of the Hyacinth," but Sybil Weir also sees Woolson's devotion to her mother reflected in *East Angels* where the protagonist gives up love to remain married and, thus, to continue her allegiance to her husband's aunt, the novel's mother figure. Weir believes that Woolson was willing "to sacrifice her own ambition to care for her invalid mother."[27] Rayburn Moore may concur when, as Weir points out, he sees Woolson at her mother's death as being at last "free to live her own life."[28] At the end of her career, however, Woolson may have begun to ask what might have been for her had she not been such a devoted daughter. Such speculation might, of course, add fuel to the question of a thwarted relationship with Henry James. Regardless of her feelings toward James, the question of what might have been was likely a topic they discussed in connection with their work, and a topic that Woolson documents in her own journal prior to James's treatment of it in "The Beast in the Jungle."[29]

Woolson's ambivalence over mother-daughter relationships might also have been intensified by her relationship to her niece Clare Benedict, thus explaining why the mother figures in her fiction are so often aunts. After her aunt's death, Benedict spent a great deal of time promoting her fiction, even sending complimentary copies of her own books on Woolson to hundreds of libraries. Benedict's *Appreciations*[30] is an extraordinarily curious book, one that consists entirely of notices "appreciating" the work Benedict had done in *Five Generations* on her family and on Woolson in particular. A majority of the book appreciates Woolson's more than Benedict's work and the tone is distinctly lionizing. If, before her death, Woolson had begun to brood on what might have been for her had she not devoted herself to her mother, she might well have been prompted by a sense of her niece's devotion at a time when her niece could have been developing attachments apart from her mother and aunt.

While one may speculate that Woolson was ambivalent about her devotion to her mother, she does not seem to have regretted these years or have admitted a wish that she had chosen a different path. As grieved as she was by her father's death, she was even more devastated by her mother's. She expresses this grief in a letter to her friend Jane Averell Carter, saying she is haunted by the question of whether she could have done something more to prolong her mother's life but feeling comforted by Carter's assurance that her efforts actually did prolong that life.[31] In a letter to Paul Hamilton Hayne, she writes about her "effort . . . to break up the depression which took possession of [her] after the death of [her] dearest Mother in Florida, just one year ago."[32] The late story "A Pink Villa," collected in *The Front Yard*, illustrates well the ambivalence she may have felt. The story's mother figure expects her daughter to marry someone who would enable both to live comfortably in Europe. Instead the daughter chooses her freedom, in effect leaving the mother stranded. The story ends with a question: "And the mother?" (136). Whether or not this is the kind of question Woolson would have asked herself had she not shaped her travels to care for her mother, she does show only two patterns in her fiction for the relationship between mother and child: mothers who demand, however subtly, service from their children, thus causing the children to lose their freedom; or children who die or in some other way renege on their filial responsibilities, thus betraying their mothers. Both paths are unattractive, and Woolson examines them more closely as she ages. Given her often expressed loneliness in her European years, she may have wondered if she might have been less lonely had she become a mother. As she confronts the nature of mothering in her fiction, she seems to have felt that mothering would replace loneliness only with loss of freedom. While she seems to have felt that others criticized her free life of traveling for its lack of "*duties*," she also was quick to defend her choice, asking in her notebooks why people without families shouldn't be allowed the pleasures of travel: "They did not marry and have children; then let them have the pleasures of such a life, since they have not those of the family. Family people appear to think that unmarried people are very self-indulgent because they want to amuse themselves. It does not occur to them that they (the married) gave themselves the pleasures which *they* preferred."[33]

In studying the patterns of parent-child relationships in fiction, it is wise to remember that writers tend to confront those parts of life that they brood on, that they try to come to grips with. Happy families have never been the subject of much literature or have been the subject of literature relegated to the category of juvenile literature. The part of life that Woolson broods on in her fiction centers over and over again on the painful choices women must make. For Woolson's female characters, unlike for her male characters, life consists of negative either/or propositions: one can choose family and loss or solitude and exile. Woolson had exile chosen for her when her mother died. Freed from obligation to her mother, her wandering became her strength, for it gave her the freedom she needed to write and, despite her worries about financial insecurity, the financial means she needed to live. But in her bouts of depression, she did lament her lack of connectedness. Having been close to a family that shaped her and left her, she never engendered a family so that she could reproduce herself as mother to young children.

In Woolson's day, women had few models for both freedom and family, making it inevitable that this model would not be central in their literature. The belief that writing and childrearing are incompatible, as if childrearing saps a woman's creative juices, has been so long engrained in our culture that only in 1989 did Ursula Le Guin pose the obvious possibility that childrearing, as much as it may slow the quantity of writing, may be the catalyst to some women's creativity.[34] In Woolson's day, it was certainly difficult to maintain a writing career and a family, but many women did so: E.D.E.N. Southworth raised two children after her husband deserted her. Helen Hunt Jackson had two sons, Kate Chopin had five children, and Harriet Beecher Stowe raised six. Still, even today, we mythologize the separateness of the female creative and procreative spheres, remembering more than mother-writers, women like Emily Dickinson, Sarah Orne Jewett, Mary Wilkins Freeman, Louisa May Alcott,[35] Charlotte Perkins Gilman, who was ostracized by society for not raising her child the way society demanded,[36] and Edith Wharton, whose experience with children was so minimal she once asked for help in understanding how they talked.[37] Although Woolson fits this model, she also observed fully its implications. She saw that family relationships involve more than the way parents raise young children, but that whether the children are young or old and the parents mothers or fathers, the burden for the relationship falls on women. The depth of this vision allows us to see Woolson not just as a model of someone who successfully pursued a career that has been open to women longer than the canon suggests, but also as an example of a woman who observed closely the impact of limited choices on women and who examined parent-child relationships in a way that anticipates current theories about women's commitment to attachment and responsibility.

Notes

1.   Nina Baym, *Woman's Fiction: A Guide to Novels by and about Women in America 1820–1870* (Ithaca, N.Y.: Cornell University Press, 1978), 17, 27.

2.   Mary Kelley, *Private Woman, Public Stage: Literary Domesticity in Nineteenth-Century*

America (New York: Oxford University Press, 1984). Recently, Nina Baym has used the public career of Lydia Sigourney to challenge us to reconsider the assumption that women avoided the public sphere. See "Reinventing Lydia Sigourney," *American Literature* 62 (1990): 385–404.

3. Cheryl B. Torsney in *Constance Fenimore Woolson: The Grief of Artistry* (Athens: University of Georgia Press, 1989) discusses various reasons for critics' neglect of Woolson, locating this neglect largely in Woolson's position as a woman born after the flowering of domestic fiction and before the advent of fiction about the New Woman.

4. Joan Weimer, *Women Artists, Women Exiles: "Miss Grief" and Other Stories* (New Brunswick, N.J.: Rutgers University Press, 1988), xii. Rayburn Moore omitted any reference to Charly in his study *Constance F. Woolson* (New York: Twayne, 1963), as did Clare Benedict in *Five Generations (1785–1923)*, 3 vols. (London: Ellis, 1929–30).

5. Nancy Chodorow, *The Reproduction of Mothering: Psychoanalysis and the Sociology of Gender* (Berkeley: University of California Press, 1978); and Carol Gilligan, *In a Different Voice: Psychological Theory and Women's Development* (Cambridge: Harvard University Press, 1982).

6. Alice Hall Petry, " 'Always, Your Attached Friend': The Unpublished Letters of Constance Fenimore Woolson to John and Clara Hay," *Books at Brown* 29–30 (1982–83): 11–107.

7. Lyon N. Richardson, "Constance Fenimore Woolson: 'Novelist Laureate' of America," *South Atlantic Quarterly* 39 (1940):18–36.

8. Constance Fenimore Woolson, *Anne*, 1882 (Rpt. New York: Ayer, 1977); further page references in text.

9. Constance Fenimore Woolson, *For the Major*, in *For the Major and Selected Short Stories*, ed. Rayburn S. Moore (New Haven: New College and University Press, 1967); further page references in text.

10. Sybil B. Weir, "Southern Womanhood in the Novels of Constance Fenimore Woolson," *Mississippi Quarterly* 29 (1976):564.

11. Weimer, xi, xxix.

12. *Five Generations*, ii, 19.

13. Petry, 81.

14. Constance Fenimore Woolson, *Castle Nowhere: Lake Country Sketches*, 1875 (Rpt. New York: Garrett, 1969); further page references in text.

15. Weimer, xxviii–xxix.

16. Constance Fenimore Woolson, *East Angels* (New York: Harper, 1886); further page references in text.

17. Constance Fenimore Woolson, *Rodman the Keeper: Southern Sketches*, 1880 (Rpt. New York: Garrett, 1969); further page references in text.

18. Constance Fenimore Woolson, *Jupiter Lights*, 1889 (Rpt. New York: AMSP, 1971); further page references in text.

19. Woolson frequently asked about children in her letters, and her love for them is clear. In a letter to Sam Mather concerning her brother Charly's death, for example, she spends several pages asking about the new Mather child whose picture she has been showing off to friends. Her letters to Col. and Mrs. John Hay often ask that they kiss the children for her, and in one she speaks admiringly of Henry James, who "cares more for a child than for a grown person, any day! When there is a child (a nice one) in the room, he can't keep up a conversation." See Petry, 42.

20. Constance Fenimore Woolson, *The Front Yard and Other Italian Stories* 1895 (Rpt. Freeport, New York: Books for Libraries, 1969); further page references in text.

21. Constance Fenimore Woolson, *Dorothy and Other Italian Stories* (New York: Harper, 1896); further page references in text.

22. To some extent, Felipa is the southern version of the northern Tita in *Anne*. Felipa's Minorcan blood parallels Tita's Indian blood and, in both, Woolson stereotypically attributes their passion to race.

23. Mather Family Papers, Western Reserve Historical Society, Cleveland, Ohio.

24. While writing *Horace Chase*, Woolson wrote to Henry Mills Alden that the male character "is intended to be more important than the woman," but that she found it difficult as a woman to describe the "masculine mind." See Moore, 111.

25. Constance Fenimore Woolson, *Horace Chase*, 1894 (Rpt. Upper Saddle River: Literature House, 1970); further page references in text.

26. See Torsney for a full discussion of Woolson's artist figures.

27. Weir, 566.

28. Moore, 30; Weir, 566.

29. *Five Generations*, ii, 144–45.

30. Clare Benedict, ed., *Appreciations* (London: Ellis, 1941).

31. *Five Generations*, ii., 24–25.

32. Jay B. Hubbell, "Some New Letters of Constance Fenimore Woolson," *New England Quarterly* 14 (1941):715–35.

33. *Five Generations*, ii, 11–12.

34. Ursula Le Guin, "The Hand That Rocks the Cradle Writes the Book," *New York Times Book Review*, 22 January 1989, 1, 35–37.

35. In her late story "In Sloane Street" (*Harper's Bazar*, 11 June 1892, 473–78), Woolson has a character marvel that Alcott "worked all her life as hard as she possibly could, turning her hand to anything that offered no matter what, and her sole motive was to assist her parents and her family, those dear to her; of herself she never thought at all" (475). The irony here is that the character admires Alcott for sacrificing for her family but is appalled when a male writer in the story does the same.

36. Ann J. Lane, "Introduction," *The Charlotte Perkins Gilman Reader: "The Yellow Wallpaper" and Other Fiction*, ed. Ann J. Lane (New York: Pantheon, 1980).

37. R. W. B. Lewis, *Edith Wharton: A Biography* (New York: Oxford University Press, 1985).

The "Admiring Aunt" and the "Proud Salmon of the Pond": Constance Fenimore Woolson's Struggle with Henry James

Joan Myers Weimer

Henry James admitted that he could offer little help to other writers, except to tell them how *he* would have treated their material.[1] Still, his fiction, his criticism, and his personality had an enormous impact on many contemporary writers. While his influence on such male artists as Joseph Conrad was benign, for women writers it was highly problematic. Edith Wharton, for instance, paid him critical tribute by alluding to his fiction in hers and by trying to get him the Nobel Prize for literature, but she ignored his advice to tether herself in her New York backyard and claimed she couldn't read his late works. Violet Paget ("Vernon Lee") solicited James's endorsement of her first novel, then satirized him savagely in her story "Lady Tal."[2]

Constance Fenimore Woolson was more intimate with James than either Wharton or Paget, and more susceptible to his personal and literary influence. Shortly before she met James in 1880, she twice reviewed his novel *The Europeans*, and at the height of their friendship, revised it in her best novel, *East Angels* (1886). Like James's brilliant Baroness Eugenia, Woolson's heroine is a repudiated wife, but while James left Eugenia's motives mysterious, Woolson analyzes both the conscious and unconscious motives of her heroine. While James's novel works brilliantly with the conventions of comedy, Woolson's novel moves from a comedy of manners into an exploration of the tragic implications for women of the comic genre. James's uneasy response to this novel, to Woolson herself, and to women writers generally appears in a highly revealing essay, "Miss Woolson," which he included in his 1888 *Partial Portraits* with studies of Turgenev and George Eliot.[3] This cluster of related texts reveals a great deal about the conflicted personal and literary relations of nineteenth-century women writers with their male mentors.

These relations were often productive. Woolson and James frequently adapted images and situations from each other's work, built characters around one another's personal traits, and considered writing a play together.[4] But

This essay was written especially for this volume and is published here for the first time with the permission of the author.

the relationship was also stressful and threatening to both of them. Shortly after they met in 1880, each of them began writing stories in which artists of their own sex are seriously menaced by the other sex. Woolson wrote three tales about women artists thwarted by male critics and writers who strongly resemble James, and James wrote four tales in which women destroy the work or lives of male artists.[5] Woolson clearly recognized and tried to evade James's dislike of women writers and fear of entanglement with women: she told him that "I do not come in as a literary woman at all, but as a sort of— admiring aunt. I think that expresses it."[6] But hers was a costly strategy. To avoid rejection as a literary competitor or as a threatening woman, she had to deny both her literary and her sexual identities.

It was Woolson's fate to be closely connected to two male writers of towering influence, if very different talents. Although the fame of her mother's uncle James Fenimore Cooper both encouraged and coerced her,[7] she easily surpassed him as a stylist. Woolson's relationship with James, however, made her aware to the point of "despair" of the distance between her own skill and James's, and led her to belittle her own success. When Harper's rewarded her for the extraordinary popularity of her first novel, *Anne* (1880), she wrote James that even this success "could not alter the fact that the utmost best of my work cannot touch the hem of your first or poorest. My work is coarse beside yours. Of entirely another grade. The two should not be mentioned on the same day."[8]

Although she grovels before his genius, she also tells him with astounding frankness how she hates him for it: "I do'nt think you appreciated . . . the laudation your books received in America, as they came out one by one. We little fish did! We little fish became worn to skeletons owing to the constant admonitions we received to regard the beauty, the grace, the incomparable perfections of all sorts and kinds of the proud salmon of the pond: we ended by hating that salmon."[9] When he read her journal after her death, James found this hostility dramatized. Just after an entry about a James-like man who "avoids women forever" after they tell him he "has no heart," Woolson imagines this scenario: "the grave of an author who has been so immensely and continually praised and held up *ad nauseum* as a model to the younger men, that they at last, (though admiring him) are tired of it. One of them visits his grave; his thought is: 'You have had quite enough! We, too, should have our share!' " The anger is modified by the revelation that the great author also suffered "abuse, and false criticism, indifference, etc. It is only in death that he has gained universal praise."[10]

Woolson's own reputation has reversed this imagined situation. She was both a critical and popular success in her lifetime, but is unknown to most readers in this century. Unlike those of other women writers of her time with whom she deserves to be ranked—Sarah Orne Jewett, Mary E. Wilkins Freeman, Kate Chopin—her works have only now begun to be re-evaluated and made widely available. James's huge shadow, made even larger by his biographer Leon Edel, has a great deal to do with her eclipse. Although Woolson's five novels and four volumes of stories reveal a superb stylist and important innovator in American realism, Edel's influential biography of James dismisses her writing as "prosy and banal . . . without style, and with an extreme literalness," lacking "ease and the richer verbal imagination . . . minute and cluttered." Edel similarly distorts her relations with James, presenting Woolson as desperately "reaching out to a man younger than herself" who was grateful for her devotion but evasive of the demands of a woman Edel calls an "elderly spinster."[11] The reality is less stereotypical and more complex.

When Woolson and James met in Florence in the spring of 1880, she was, at forty, an established writer with two volumes of short stories in print and her first novel, *Anne*, appearing serially in *Harper's*. Despite the reclusive tendencies she had developed while wandering for a decade in the South with her widowed mother, and despite her devastation over her mother's recent death, she had sought and obtained a letter of introduction to James from his cousin, Henrietta Pell-Clark. He was then, at thirty-seven, the author of stories, articles, reviews, and several novels, just beginning to write his first major work, *The Portrait of a Lady*. Despite his numerous social and professional obligations, "he found time to come in the mornings and take me out," wrote Woolson; "sometimes to the galleries or churches, and sometimes just for a walk in the beautiful green Cascine. . . ." Her pleasure in James's company was inseparable from her delight at having "attained that old-world feeling I used to dream about . . . the whole having, I think, taken me pretty well off my feet! Perhaps I ought to add Henry James. He has been perfectly charming to me for the last three weeks."[12]

By 1883 she could tell him that "the deepest charm of your writings to me" is that "they voice for me—as nothing else ever has—my own feelings; those that are so deep—so a part of me, that I cannot express them, and do not try to. . . . Your writings . . . are my true country, my real home. And nothing else ever fully is—try as I may to think so." She is not, as Edel asserts, thinly disguising her ardor for the man in ardor for his work. Although she came to love James, she saw his personal limitations as clearly as she saw his literary genius, and let him know it. Gently in letters: "It doesn't make much difference what you do as an individual—one has to forgive the author of 'Hawthorne' and the 'Portrait.' " Directly in her stories about women artists' struggles with male writers or critics who resemble James. And with an accuracy that must have devastated James when he read entries like this in her journals after her death: "Imagine a man endowed with an absolutely unswerving will; extremely intelligent, he *comprehends* passion, affection, unselfishness and self-sacrifice, etc., perfectly, though he is himself cold and a pure egoist. He has a charming face, a charming voice, and he can, when he pleases, counterfeit all these feelings so exactly that he gets all the benefits that are to be obtained by them." This portrait is remarkably similar to Violet Paget's fictive account of James, but must have been much harder for him to dismiss, for, as James wrote to a friend, Woolson was his "extremely intimate" friend to whom he was "greatly attached."[13]

James was deeply distressed when he heard that Woolson had died by falling from her Venice balcony while seriously ill, perhaps delirious, from influenza and typhus. But when he came to believe she had committed suicide, he wrote a friend that he was "sickened and overwhelmed" by the "picture of lonely unassisted suffering! It is too horrible for thought." He felt that in his egotism he had contributed to her death, as well as having failed to recognize that loving her would have saved him from that egotism. That is the situation he dramatized in "The Beast in the Jungle," whose germ he found in an entry in Woolson's journal—"To imagine a man spending his life looking for and waiting for his 'splendid moment'. . . . But the moment never comes"[14]—and whose climactic scene of revelation he set at a grave that resembles Woolson's in Rome.

James seems to me to have misunderstood his share of responsibility for Woolson's suicide. While she would have welcomed more active sympathy and support from him, she was no more capable than he was of sustaining an intimate commitment.[15] Nor would James's attentions have outweighed her ill health, financial worry, history of depression and approval of suicide as an "open door"[16] out of life. James's real offense against Woolson was his manipulative response to her writing. Although this seems to have been largely unconscious on his part, it damaged her both as woman and writer.

James's essay "Miss Woolson," despite the encouragement it offered her, was in fact his most harmful intervention in her career, because of its mixture of apt and misleading criticism. He rightly identifies some of the weaknesses of her work—her tendencies to hurry her characters into marriage, to look occasionally in the wrong place for a picturesque atmosphere, to be too "fond of irretrievable personal failures." And some of his praise is just, as when he points out Woolson's ability to convey "the *voicelessness* of the conquered and reconstructed South" in stories of "remarkable minuteness of observation and tenderness of feeling," and when he notes that she has been "the first to take . . . straight from their lips" the language of the newly freed slaves. He is perceptive too in noting that Woolson interests herself "in the 'inner life' of the weak, the superfluous, the disappointed, the bereaved, the unmarried" (271–72).

But he also condescends to her work in ways that recall the way male artists manipulate the talented Marion Fancourt in "The Lesson of the Master." Perhaps from personal knowledge of Woolson's tendency to depression, James attributes the "dreariness" of her presentation of the postwar South and the "irretrievable personal failures" she finds there not to the actual conditions of the South she saw during the 1870s but to her personal "taste in the way of subject and situation" (272). Similarly, he trivializes her commitment to realism as "a fruitful instinct" (276) rather than the conscious literary philosophy that appears in her reviews, journals, and letters.

Much more damaging than this, however, is his awarding high praise for the wrong reasons to Woolson's best novel, *East Angels*. He applauds Woolson for making credible a heroine who "immolates herself—there is no other word—deliberately, completely, and repeatedly, to a husband whose behavior may as distinctly be held to have absolved her. The problem was a very interesting one, and worthy to challenge a superior talent—that of making real and natural a transcendent, exceptional act, representing a case in which the sense of duty is raised to exaltation." He identifies self-sacrifice with "a certain heroism" as perhaps the only heroic behavior available to women, since it persuades the reader that "a woman *may* look at life from a high point of view" (277–78). But this is a spectacular misreading of Woolson's novel. *East Angels* is not an endorsement but a sustained critique of self-sacrifice, which was in turn the main pillar upholding the temple of woman's limited "sphere."

Some of James's tangled motives for this misreading emerge as he expresses discomfort with women's presence on the literary scene, while seeming to congratulate them on their success. He begins his essay by contrasting women's continuing struggle for admission to "various offices, colleges, functions, and privileges" with their success in gaining "admission into the world of literature: they are there in force; they have been admitted, with all the honours, on a perfectly equal footing. In America, at least, one feels tempted to exclaim that they are in themselves the world of literature." On the covers of American and English periodicals, "these monthly joints of the ladder of fame the ladies stand as thick as on the staircase at a crowded evening party" (270).

Despite his genial tone, it's clear that James would prefer that the ladies remain at parties and leave the periodicals to the men whom they have all but pushed off the ladder. He is sure that Woolson shares this opinion, that except for the "strength of the current which today carries both sexes" to write books, she would not be "competing for the literary laurel" because she believes that women are "by their very nature only too much exposed"— he doesn't say to what—even in their confinement in the home. He praises the "spirit singularly and essentially conservative" that he finds in her work, and assures his readers that while "she has not, I take it, a love of bolts and Oriental shutters," she would never "lend her voice to the plea for further exposure—for a revolution which should place her sex in the thick of the struggle for power" (271).

James might have had some trouble reconciling this "essentially conservative" Woolson with the woman who agrees with James's sister Alice that women are well suited to practice medicine because the "feminine mind" is by no means "inferior to the masculine. . . . But it has been kept back, & enfeebled, & limited, by ages of ignorance, & almost servitude."[17] The distance between this Woolson and the one James describes indicates more than wishful thinking on his part: it points to his need to manipulate her. His essay on her work warns her against struggling for power, against competing with him, against exposing her feelings. At the same time it praises as "distinguished natures" her characters who "try and provide for the happiness of others (when they adore them) even to their own injury" (278). This remark seriously misrepresents the novel he is discussing, *East Angels*, in which the heroine carefully provides for the happiness of her husband whom she loves no more than he loves her, while bringing misery to the man she adores by consciously sacrificing him along with herself. James's misplaced praise makes most sense as an invitation to Woolson to "distinguish" herself by sacrificing her sense of herself to his preferred idea of her and her work.

James's desire to coerce Woolson into being a "conservative," uncompetitive woman also leads him to misrepresent two of the scenes he rightly identifies as the high points of Woolson's achievement in *East Angels*. He ends his essay by asserting that these episodes resemble each other in sharing "the stamp of the author's conservative feeling, the implication that for her the life of a woman is essentially an affair of private relations" (271). But in one of these episodes, the heroine refuses private relations for the sake of her ideal of herself, and in the other, a New England woman confesses that she has ardently prayed for a Northern victory while pretending to support slavery more than the Southerners among whom she has had to live. To call these women's political and philosophical passions "private relations" is to substitute the wish for the fact.

The two defects which James singles out in *East Angels* are also remarkable, since the novel seems to me to have more serious defects than those James names, and since the ones he chooses oddly misread the book. One is that the characters in *East Angels* are "too detached, too isolated, too much on a desert island . . . they have a certain shipwrecked air" (276). This is a surprising complaint, since in *The Europeans* James had similarly stranded his Wentworths, Actons, and Brand in a Puritanical Boston with no more alternatives than one another until the European cousins arrive.

James also complains that in Woolson's novel "the complications are almost exclusively the complications of love," which he finds "characteristic of the feminine, as distinguished from the masculine hand. . . . In men's novels, even of the simplest strain, there are still other references and other explanations; in women's when they are of the category to which I allude, there are none but that one" (276–77). James is here ignoring or deliberately misunderstanding the center of the novel, which is not love but a woman's desire for autonomy and freedom. In this respect, Woolson's Margaret Harold is very much like James's own Isabel Archer, as well as in her refusal to escape from a miserable marriage to the passion offered her by a good but overbearing man. Unlike Isabel, however, Margaret conceals her preference for autonomy over love behind a veil of principled self-sacrifice sufficiently thick, apparently, to have misled Henry James.

Just a year before she met Henry James, Woolson twice reviewed his comic novel *The Europeans* in the anonymous Contributors' Club of the *Atlantic*. Her account is at once witty—"Mr. James has advanced in his art; in *this* story of his there is absolutely no action at all"—and perceptive: "When we have once recognized the quality of a man's talent, why not take what he can give, and not ask for something different? Let us do without a story in Mr. James's novels, and enjoy instead something certainly as admirable in its way . . . keen observation and fine discrimination of character" as well as "delightful style"—a fair account of James's early work. She also has a number of specific complaints. She faults James for seeing "only [the] ludicrous points" of the earnest Mr. Brand: "During the war, the Brands had a chance . . . nobody minded their big feet on the plain of battle. . . . They headed the colored regiments. . . . The whole nation was in earnest then; the Brands found their place." She objects that Gertrude's character is "like a tune which the composer has as yet but briefly jotted down. *He* knows it; but *we* do not," and that the amiable painter Felix is "a shadow." But she recognizes that some of James's "finest art" has been lavished on that solemn Puritan, Mr. Wentworth, and that the Baroness Eugenia fails to make her fortune in America because "in our raw American atmosphere, delicate and congenial lying has not yet been comprehended as one of the fine arts . . . the American world was not equal to the accomplishments of her fine organism."[18]

This is as close as Woolson comes to naming the international theme of the novel, but certainly it impressed her. Shortly after writing these reviews, she moved to Europe and lived in England, Italy, and Switzerland for the rest of her life. Although her fiction only occasionally exploits the confrontation of European and American cultures, her own international adventure seems to have sharpened her sense of the clash of cultures she had experienced while living as a Northerner in the post–Civil War South.

From her earliest writings in the 1870s, Woolson had been interested in the confrontation of different cultures and social classes. Her earliest stories, set around the Great Lakes, confront cultured visitors with half-breeds, miners, hunters, trappers, and visionaries, while her Southern stories bring Northern visitors to abandoned plantations, military cemeteries, and impoverished Florida towns.[19] Although her first two novels used Southern settings, not until *East Angels* did she explore at length cultural conflicts between Northerners and Southerners, both black and white, just after the Civil War. As James noted, one of the best things in *East Angels* is the characterization of Mrs. Thorne, a former New Hampshire schoolteacher stuck on an impoverished Florida plantation, who feels she must pretend to admire slavery even more than the Southerners do, until her passionate abolitionism bursts out of her when she is dying. Other cultural conflicts appear between newly freed slaves and their former masters, and between blacks and Northerners. For example, an elderly ex-slave resists Mrs. Thorne's efforts to raise the productivity of an orange grove that had always been allowed to rot comfortably, but he feels sufficiently identified with the white family's pride that he subtly prevents an assignation that would damage it. An admirable black youth responds to the efforts of a Vermont seamstress to teach him how to read by setting spells to protect himself from her witchcraft. These relations are more than local color, more than comedy of manners. The ex-slaves resemble the women they serve in their training in dependency and submission, and in their emotional and economic inability to leave the scene of their bondage. And the different mores of individuals from different regions and social groups in the aftermath of a war between those regions offer material for confrontations which are more than comic, although often very funny.

Woolson not only enlarges on the cultural contradictions she found in James's novel, but also develops possibilities she saw merely sketched in James's characters. (She gives herself ample space to do so; her novel is nearly four times as long as James's.) Her version of James's amusing European painter, who is like Felix a wanderer with no fixed income and a collector of eccentric human specimens, remains as shadowy as Felix despite his American versatility as civil engineer, surveyor, and inventor. But Woolson significantly develops the character of the girl he loves, while recalling James's Gertrude in the name of her own Garda Thorne. She develops the Boston girl's latent hedonism into a talent for self-amusement with no more resources than a hammock and a pet crane. Gertrude's bluntness becomes Garda's startlingly frank acceptance of herself and her desires, a self-knowledge which Gertrude only begins to develop when she comes to reject her Puritanic family's efforts to erase her "peculiar" temperament. Gertrude's father, James's wonderful Mr. Wentworth, who "looks as if he were undergoing martyrdom, not by fire, but by freezing,"[20] Woolson divides into two brilliant characterizations: Garda's transplanted New Hampshire mother, a true Puritan, and a Southern doctor who is a self-appointed guardian of Southern propriety. With these characters, Woolson corrects what she saw as James's tendency to see only the ridiculous side of Mr. Brand. She makes them wonderfully eccentric—Mrs. Thorne displaying her Northern superiority by pronouncing every letter when she speaks so that her "T's snapped like a drop of rain falling into a fire,"[21] Dr. Kirby displaying his Southern superiority by his elaborate rhetoric and his canary-like postures—but at the same time makes them dignified and even heroic.

Besides expanding Mr. Wentworth into male and female, Southern and Northern, characters, Woolson compresses Mr. Brand and Robert Acton into the novel's hero, Evert Winthrop, who combines Brand's authoritarian certainty that he knows what's best for the woman he loves with Acton's experience of the world beyond the novel. Like Brand, Evert proposes to one woman while really loving another. Like Acton, he fails to win the woman he loves, though not for lack of ardent effort.

Woolson further expands *The Europeans* by dramatizing what James left off stage. She has asked what would have happened if Eugenia's invisible husband, Prince Adolf, had thought better of repudiating his wife, and come back to her expecting to resume his marriage. She gives the Prince's name and aristocratic presence to a young Cuban named Adolfo Torres, whose overwhelming sense of his aristocratic origins in the midst of his poverty leads him to behave with hilarious stiffness. The Prince's function as an absent husband she gives to Lanse Harold, who has twice left his wife to pursue a married European woman.

James's superb Baroness Eugenia, the queen of artifice who occasionally surprises herself by experiencing her performance of her feelings as genuine, loses considerable charm but gains immense complexity in Woolson's Margaret Harold. Margaret is also a repudiated wife, also evasive and secretive about her real feelings and intentions, but she conceals herself and manages others in ways very different from Eugenia's. Woolson's analysis of Margaret's convoluted conscious and unconscious motives, and her critique of the social codes governing women which underlie both sets of motives, turns her novel from a comedy of manners into an ironic tragedy which revises not only *The Europeans* but also its generic comic plot.

James's novel might have been a prototype for the comic genre as Northrop Frye described it in *The Anatomy of Criticism*. The essential features of that plot are that a pair of young lovers overcome the rigidities of blocking characters who have the power and prestige to give the force of law to their ideas of what is right. The young couple evades or breaks the absurd laws of their elders, and either transforms the rigid old society into something more humane and flexible, or escapes from it.[22] James sets up four pairs of lovers: the immature Clifford and Lizzie, the spontaneous Felix and Gertrude, the deluded Brand and Charlotte, and the evasive Eugenia and Acton. Felix and Gertrude break Mr. Wentworth's law, "the doctrine . . . of the oppressive gravity of mistakes" (46), with its supporting statutes requiring that one guard against temptation, excitement and "peculiar influences" (49). But they convert him only insofar as he consents to their marriage, and finally finds himself listening for an "echo" of their gaiety (178). They can live freely and happily—ever after, as far as we know—only by escaping to Europe. Brand and Charlotte ardently support Mr. Wentworth's laws, so their marriage does nothing to alter the rigid old society. Clifford and Lizzie integrate themselves into the older order. Acton, the man who's been to China and should have other ideas of life than Mr. Wentworth's, succumbs to the Wentworth doctrine of safety first by marrying instead of the complex Eugenia "a particularly nice young girl" (178). Because Eugenia fails to overcome Acton's suspicions of her, she fails to make her fortune, and the Americans lose their chance for transformation and freedom from absurd constraints.

Woolson takes on some of the basic assumptions of the generic comic plot by her treatment of the blocking characters. But in *East Angels*, the selfishness and rigidity of the older generation are not the real obstacles to the desires of the younger. Although Aunt Katrina prevents Margaret from ever drawing a free breath, and Dr. Kirby tries to prevent Garda from being educated in the North, we eventually learn that Margaret has freely chosen her bondage to Aunt Katrina, and that Dr. Kirby's commitment to preventing women from developing dangerously broad views is overwhelmed by his fundamental generosity.

The real obstructing function of the blocking characters is taken over in Woolson's novel by two of the lovers themselves. This is her most radical revision of the comic plot, and it directs her novel toward psychological analysis even while it lets her sustain her social criticism. Evert initially blocks his own love for Margaret by telling himself that no matter what her husband has done, Margaret should be loyal to him because it is "a wife's part to forgive" (134) and a husband's to "command" (77). He abandons his allegiance to the first part of this patriarchal law when he falls in love with Margaret and wants her to divorce Lanse and marry him. Although she has long loved Evert, Margaret recognizes the threat his imperiousness poses to her desire for freedom. She responds by constructing an ambitious plot to block Garda from marrying Lucian, in order to marry her to Evert, thereby blocking herself from acting on her love for Evert. (The complications of Margaret's scheme are so elaborate that they nearly swamp the novel.)

Garda's total frankness saves her from marrying Evert when she discovers they don't love each other, and her total disregard for conventional behavior evades Margaret's efforts to keep her away from Lucian. The young lovers, like Felix and Gertrude, marry and live ecstatically in Europe, allowed at least to glimpse a new and freer society. But Woolson is revising both *The Europeans* and its comic genre, so her novel cannot end here, where James's did. She kills Lucian off, and marries Garda to the absurd Adolfo Torres. They will live out their lives in the ironically named town of Gracias-a-Dios without transforming it.

Nor will the more mature lovers be more successful. In constructing Margaret's behavior and motivation, Woolson transforms a comic convention—what Frye calls the "ritual bondage" of a blocking character to the law of his or her "ruling passion" (168)—and transforms her own novel from a comedy of manners into a tragedy of character. Margaret's bondage to her ideal of herself appears both in her own language and in metaphors of bondage spoken by characters who collaborate in her self-enslavement. Aunt Katrina says that Margaret is "not free—free, that is, to make engagements" (239) that would compete with her demands that "Margaret must read her to sleep; Margaret must sit in a certain place, and sit still; she must not leave the room . . ." (268). Her husband, similarly exploiting Margaret's masochism, exclaims "what a fettered, restricted existence you women— the good ones—do lead!" (436). Margaret herself finally protests against her self-imposed "slavery" to Lanse and his aunt, and the worse slavery of her suppression of her real feelings: "Expected to bear everything in silence," unable to "breathe or think as I please—as I really am," she admits she's afraid of dying "without ever having been myself—my real self— even for one day" (497–8). Her fear will be realized. Locked in her self-imposed bondage, she tells Evert at the end of the novel, "I shall never change; and I should never yield" (590).

But neither he nor she comprehends the law she is actually obeying. When Lanse first leaves her after a few months of marriage, she writes him, "I feel as though I must have done wrong, and yet I don't know how" (417). To avoid this free-floating guilt, she has constructed her identity on strategies of repression and self-control. Feeling unlovable and worthless and therefore guilty, she seeks a sense of innocence and worth in self-sacrifice. At the same time, because her society enshrines self-sacrifice as the highest womanly virtue, she can conceal behind its impenetrable shield her unwomanly longings for freedom and autonomy—freedom which marriage to the imperious Evert, however much she loves him, would destroy. She prefers the lesser bondage of her loveless service to Lanse and his Aunt Katrina.

Unlike the younger lovers, Margaret and Evert have the capacity to transform their society into something more honest and responsive to real human needs, but they waste their lives in alienating conformity to the laws governing male and female behavior. Margaret devotes herself to meeting every trivial need of her husband and his aunt, while Evert bitterly devotes himself to making money. Since both of them had certain heroic capacities, their falls have tragic dimensions. Frye describes tragic heroes as "the highest points in their human landscape" whose tragedy inheres in their ultimate isolation, rather than in their betrayal by some villain, "even when the villain is, as he often is, a part of the hero himself" (208). Because they have accepted some compelling logic—such as Macbeth's accepting the logic of usurpation, Lear of abdication, Hamlet of revenge—their "comparatively free life" is tragically narrowed and their chance for a higher destiny is lost (212). Margaret, who is surely capable of a higher destiny than catering to a husband and aunt who don't need or love her, sacrifices a life of significant action and thought to the logic of self-sacrifice.

Central to tragedy is the hero's lost "opportunity for freedom" (213), which affects his whole society since he is its "supreme authority" (217). Such definitions suggest why women are rarely portrayed as tragic heroes: their opportunities for freedom are not great to begin with, and they can exercise authority only in a very narrow sphere. Margaret's freedom is limited to a choice between two ways of losing her liberty, and she chooses a bitterly confining servitude over a possibly enslaving passion. In making Margaret a tragic hero, then, Woolson revises the genre by suggesting that when the tragic hero is a woman, her tragedy inheres in the severe limitations of her choices.

James may have glimpsed Woolson's efforts to create a female tragic hero when he described Margaret as "conceived from the germ as capable of a certain heroism—of clinging at the cost of a grave personal loss to an idea which she believes to be a high one" (190). But his need to see Woolson as a conservative woman, his need to praise as "heroism" any sacrifices she might make for him, led him to misread her own character as well as her fictional characters. Woolson responded to the misreading of herself by adopting the pose of the "admiring aunt" in relation to the "proud salmon of the pond," an evasion of her feelings that assuaged her anxieties about intimacy as well as James's.

Her response to James's account of her fiction was equally damaging. He had stated that "*East Angels* is a performance which does Miss Woolson the highest honour, and if her talent is capable, in another novel, of making an advance equal to that represented by this work in relation to its predecessors, she will have made a substantial contribution to our new literature of fiction" (275). But she did not "advance." She abandoned her unappreciated talent for psychological analysis in favor of sensational melodrama, and she eventually abandoned her own struggle against depression by committing suicide. James bears some responsibility for both developments, for which he tried to atone in such late fictions as "The Beast in the Jungle" and *The Wings of the Dove*. The consequences of their relations—personally and professionally productive for James and destructive for Woolson—form part of the literary history of male and female writers.

Notes

1. Millicent Bell, *Edith Wharton and Henry James: The Story of their Friendship* (London: Peter Owen, 1966), 248.

2. Besides Millicent Bell's interpretation of Wharton's relationship with James, see R. W. B. Lewis, *Edith Wharton: A Biography* (New York: Harper and Row, 1975); Cynthia Griffin Wolff, *A Feast of Words: The Triumph of Edith Wharton* (New York: Oxford University Press, 1977); and Leon Edel, *The Life of Henry James*, 5 vols. (Philadelphia: J.P. Lippincott, 1953–72). Violet Paget deals astutely with James as a stylist in *The Handling of Words and Other Studies in Literary Psychology* (London: John Lane, 1923), and brutally with him as a hypocritical egotist in "Lady Tal" in *Vanitas: Polite Stories* (London: William Heinemann, 1892). The fullest account of her relationship with James is in Peter Gunn's *Vernon Lee: Violet Paget, 1856–1935* (London: Oxford University Press, 1964).

3. James first published his essay as "Miss Constance Fenimore Woolson" in *Harper's Weekly* 31 (12 February 1887):114–15, and reprinted it, slightly cut, in his *Partial Portraits*

‎

(London: Macmillan, 1888). I reprint the essay in *Women Artists, Women Exiles: 'Miss Grief' and Other Stories by Constance Fenimore Woolson* (New Brunswick: Rutgers University Press, 1988), 270–79. References in the text are to this edition.

4. Cheryl B. Torsney corrects Edel's construction of "the legend of the spinster chasing the lion over a continent" and his "convention-laden male fantasy" that Woolson killed herself out of unrequited love for James in "The Traditions of Gender: Constance Fenimore Woolson and Henry James," in *Patrons and Protégées: Gender, Friendship and Writing in Nineteenth-Century America*, ed. Shirley Marchalonis (New Brunswick and London: Rutgers University Press, 1988), 165, 166. In *Constance Fenimore Woolson: The Grief of Artistry* (Athens: University of Georgia Press, 1989), Torsney expands that analysis. Two articles examine the literary borrowings of Woolson and James: Rayburn S. Moore, "The Strange Irregular Rhythm of Life: James's Late Tales and Constance Woolson," *South Atlantic Bulletin* 41 (1976):86–93; and Sharon Dean, "Constance Fenimore Woolson and Henry James: The Literary Relationship," *Massachusetts Studies in English* 7, no.3 (1980):1–9. Edel discusses ways "The Altar of the Dead," "The Beast in the Jungle," and *The Wings of the Dove* embody James's struggle with his memories of Woolson (vol. 3, 387; vol. 4, 135–9). Elizabeth Kennedy's *"Constance Fenimore Woolson and Henry James: Friendship and Reflections"* (diss. Yale 1983) is perceptive and more balanced than Edel on both the literary and personal relationship.

5. See Woolson's "The Street of the Hyacinth," "At the Chateau of Corinne," and "Miss Grief" in *Women Artists, Women Exiles*. I discuss these stories in the introduction to that volume and in "Women Artists as Exiles in the Fiction of Constance Fenimore Woolson," *Legacy* 3 (Fall 1986):3–15. See James's "The Lesson of the Master," "The Author of Beltraffio," "The Death of the Lion," and "The Middle Years," for women who destroy the work or the lives of male artists. In "The Lesson of the Master," the destruction is mutual: here, a writer blames his wife for forcing him to write profitable tripe, while a woman whom men admit has a "superb artistic intelligence" learns that male artists will not take her talent seriously, but will use it to manipulate her and male rivals. Women who are themselves artists are consistently mediocre in James's fiction: see "Greville Fane," "The Next Time," and "The Figure in the Carpet."

6. Letter of 12 February 1882, in Leon Edel, ed., *Henry James: Letters*, vol. 3 (Cambridge, Mass.: Harvard University Press, 1974–1984), 528.

7. Much of Woolson's early fiction revises Cooper to clear an imaginative space for her own work. In "Castle Nowhere," "The Lady of Little Fishing," and "St. Clair Flats," all collected in her first volume of stories, *Castle Nowhere: Lake-Country Sketches* (1875), she parodies Cooper's views of the wilderness, its pure hero Natty Bumppo, and his idealized female character, the half-witted Hetty Hutter of *Deerslayer*. These stories are reprinted in *Women Artists, Women Exiles* and discussed on pages xxv–xxx.

8. Letter of 30 August 1882, in Edel, *Letters*, vol. 3, 544.

9. Letter of 12 February 1882, in Edel, *Letters*, vol. 3, 529.

10. Quoted in Clare Benedict, ed., *Constance Fenimore Woolson* (London: Ellis, 1929), 127–28.

11. Edel, *Life of Henry James*, vol. 3, 203, 87.

12. Benedict, 184–5.

13. Letters to James of 7 May 1883, in Edel, *Letters*, vol. 3, 551; 12 February 1882, in Edel, *Letters*, vol. 3, 529; Benedict, 135; Edel, *Life of Henry James*, vol. 3, 360.

14. Edel notes that the story reflects James's relationship with Woolson in his *Life of Henry James*, vol. 3, 357; Benedict, 144–45.

15. Woolson was traumatized by the deaths of five older sisters before she was thirteen. I discuss Woolson's complex and crippling family attachments in *Women Artists, Women Exiles*, x–xvii.

16. Woolson heavily marked a passage in her copy of *The Teaching of Epictetus* that justifies suicide:

. . . When, it may be, that the necessary things are no longer supplied, that is the signal for retreat: the door is opened, and God saith to thee, *Depart*.
"Whither?"

To nothing dreadful, but to the place from whence thou camest—to things friendly and akin to thee, to the elements of Being.

Someone—probably her niece Clare Benedict—cut out the pages on death and suicide before donating the volume to the Woolson Collection at Rollins College; these pages may have been annotated in ways that seemed too revealing.

17.   Letter by Woolson to Katherine Loring, quoted by Jean Strouse in *Alice James: A Biography* (Boston: Houghton Mifflin, 1980), 260.

18.   *Atlantic*, 43 (January 1879):106–08; (February 1879):259. Rpt. in Benedict, 55–62.

19.   See such stories as "Castle Nowhere," "The Lady of Little Fishing," "St. Clair Flats," "Miss Elisabetha," "Felipa," and "In the Cotton Country," all reprinted in *Women Artists, Women Exiles*.

20.   Henry James, *The Europeans* (New York: New American Library, 1964; 1878), 34; hereafter cited in the text.

21.   Constance Fenimore Woolson, *East Angels* (New York: Harper's, 1886), 186; hereafter cited in the text.

22.   Northrop Frye, *Anatomy of Criticism: Four Essays* (Princeton: Princeton University Press, 1957), 163–80; hereafter cited in the text.

Constance Fenimore Woolson Rewrites Bret Harte: The Sexual Politics of Intertextuality[1]

Caroline Gebhard

I have such a horror of "pretty," "sweet" writing that I should almost prefer a style that was ugly and bitter, provided that it was also *strong*.
— Constance Fenimore Woolson[2]

The mechanics of amorous vassalage require a fathomless futility. . . . (If I acknowledge my dependency, I do so because for me it is a means of *signifying* my demand: in the realm of love, futility is not a "weakness" or an "absurdity": it is a strong sign: the more futile, the more it signifies and the more it asserts itself as strength.)
— Roland Barthes, *A Lover's Discourse*[3]

Four years after *The Luck of Roaring Camp and Other Stories* (1870) appeared, a young woman published a story in the *Atlantic Monthly* about an all-male camp deep in the woods that undergoes a miraculous transformation. In "The Lady of Little Fishing," Constance Fenimore Woolson rewrote Bret Harte's story of Roaring Camp.[4] This was not just any story she chose to rewrite. "The Luck of Roaring Camp" established the style that was Harte's trademark. And it was also the story that one may say without too much exaggeration started the literary equivalent of the California Gold Rush. Harte's enormously popular fiction helped initiate the production of a fabulous Wild West that still continues today.[5] Harte's Roaring Camp is, of course, no place for a lady. Indeed, the reaction of the young woman who first proofread the story nearly persuaded the publisher not to print it.[6] On his side, Harte of the *Overland Monthly* had little use for ladies meddling in fiction; Patrick D. Morrow notes, "Hardly a single female-authored book failed to elicit some snide comment."[7]

Yet the first to study his effects most closely and the first to seize upon the possibilities for reworking "The Luck of Roaring Camp" itself was nevertheless a well-bred young woman with literary ambitions. Descended from a distinguished Eastern family, which included one of America's best-known novelists, James Fenimore Cooper, Constance Fenimore Woolson was

This essay was written especially for this volume and is published here for the first time with the permission of the author.

217

a woman who impressed the men in her literary circle (which included the critic E. C. Stedman and later Henry James) as being a woman of taste and refinement. Yet she chose as one of her first literary models a writer who seems in every way the opposite of what one would expect to appeal to such a woman. Critics have generally interpreted Woolson's obvious borrowing from Harte's fiction as yet another case of a master-disciple relationship, reminding us of how often women are cast in the role of disciple to a male "master."[8] Close attention to the nineteenth-century literary context for Woolson's bold maneuver, as well as an examination of her revision of the male fantasy that Harte mines in "The Luck of Roaring Camp," however, suggests that the relationship between these two writers cannot be understood as a case of literary discipleship; rather Woolson's conscious intertextual play with Harte's text is better read as a woman writer's bid for both literary popularity and mastery.

Woolson's rewriting of the story that made Harte famous represents an American woman writer's attempt at the outset of her career to appropriate the style and success of a popular male writer for her own, quite different literary purposes. How different they were may be gauged by the tale Woolson made from her source, but before we can consider how "The Lady of Little Fishing" revises the male fantasy elaborated in "The Luck of Roaring Camp," we must first situate the moment of her response to Harte, in the context of late nineteenth-century literary culture and of her own struggle to succeed as a professional writer after the Civil War.

I

In 1870 on the strength of the sensation caused by "The Luck of Roaring Camp" and a few other pieces published in the *Overland Monthly*, William Dean Howells offered the brash Western writer an unheard-of $10,000 for the *Atlantic Monthly*'s exclusive rights to his fiction for one year. The celebrated contract confirmed that he had scored not only a phenomenal popular success but also a critical one. To see why contemporaries were so taken by Bret Harte, it is only necessary to quote Howells: "Readers who were amazed by the excellent quality of the whole magazine were tempted to cry out most of all over 'The Luck of Roaring Camp,' and the subsequent papers by the same hand, and to triumph in a man who gave them something new in fiction."[9] The "something new" was not only Harte's locales—"the revolver-echoing cañon, the embattled diggings, the lawless flat, and the immoral bar"—but also his ability to render these places and the people in them who were formerly beneath literary notice not only inoffensive, but positively charming to middle-class tastes, especially to masculine tastes. Howells interprets Harte's literary coup as primarily a triumph of those masculine tastes, supposing that women generally would not "find his stories amusing or touching" because of the "entirely masculine temper" of Harte's sensibility. He imagines that "perhaps some woman with an unusual sense of humor would feel the tenderness, the delicacy, and the wit that so win the hearts of his own sex," but he assumes that Harte's brand of humor and "the robust vigor and racy savor of the miner's vernacular" must "chiefly commend itself" to a masculine mind.

There is no doubt, however, that Woolson not only admired Harte's work, she made use of it. In "Misery Landing," her hero takes to the woods, armed with Thomas à Kempis, French and German philosophy, and last, but not least, a volume of Bret Harte. In *Castle Nowhere* (1875), her first volume of short fiction, she chose to reprint this story and four others that deliberately echo Harte. "Castle Nowhere" and "St. Clair Flats" employ male narrators who adopt a narrative stance similar to Harte's to relate their encounters with society's outcasts in fantastic, remote settings. The fourth tale, "Peter the Parson," though much bleaker than anything Harte ever wrote, recounts an instance of frontier justice in a mining camp, a subject Harte had treated earlier.[10] The last, and often praised, story in the volume, "The Lady of Little Fishing," is, as I have noted, a recognizable revision of Harte's most famous tale. But it was not, I think, his "ferocious drollery" that interested Woolson, for unlike Harte's stories, Woolson's tales of encampments on the outskirts of civilization have a somber feel. Whether or not Howells was right in surmising that Harte primarily appealed to male readers, it is clear that he appealed to Woolson, but most likely not for the reasons that Howells imagines.

Woolson's self-conscious adoption of a popular male writer rather than a popular female one as a literary role model is significant in view of the literary marketplace in post–Civil War America. The generation of women writers who had succeeded in dominating the marketplace in the 1850s through their immense popularity still enjoyed a large following in the 1870s. If Bret Harte and other Westerners were making inroads into the nation's magazines of high culture, E.D.E.N. Southworth and other popular women writers still held their own.[11] Woolson did not lack female literary models, and we must therefore read her readiness to admire Harte in conjunction with her desire to reject her countrywomen as literary precursors. In the early stages of her career as a writer, Woolson was anxious to dissociate herself from the sentimental subjects and style of expression associated with women.

How Woolson felt about the prospect of being relegated to a female literary sphere is clear from her anger as a young woman; she later remembered "how sore" she felt when her "demi-god"—one of her male professors at school—delivered "an hour's eulogy of Miss Alcott's 'Little Women.'" She added that she thought such works "had their own sphere, and that it was a very high one," but it was not that of Shakespeare or Milton or of the great writers of fiction.[12] Her painful sensitivity about the commendation of particular types of women's writing suggests that she interpreted such extravagant praise as false, masking a fundamental disbelief in the power of women to write works of genius outside their "own" sphere.[13] Although her first book was a prize-winning children's book, Woolson had no intention of becoming trapped within this traditionally female literary sphere.[14] "I have the idea that women run too much into mere beauty at the expense of power," she confided to a male poet and friend, admitting, "the result is, I fear, that I have gone too far the other way; too rude; too abrupt."[15]

When she began to publish, Woolson also worried that she would be rejected by the majority of readers because she refused to write as a woman was expected to write. Significantly, she imagined this rejecting reader as female. She once confessed that "a dear good aunt" of hers "unconsciously to herself" always represented to Woolson "the immense general class of readers." She was afraid that female readers like her aunt who confounded " 'Christian Reid' with the great Charles of the same name," who were "devoted to Mrs. Southworth," and who thought the books Woolson admired "queer" and "stupid" ("stupid", Woolson explains, was her aunt's verdict on *Middlemarch*) would have little patience with anything she cared to write.[16] For a woman who aimed at making a living as a professional writer, these were not idle fears. In the 1870s, her father recently dead, Woolson was beginning to depend on income from her writing; without it, she recognized that she and her mother "should be very much cramped . . . every day an anxiety."[17] She was never financially secure despite her critical success as a writer, yet she always saw her writing as something she did not primarily do for money. Her personal correspondence makes plain Woolson's dedication to her art. She once wrote her niece, "I don't suppose any of you realize the amount of time and thought I give to each page of my novels; every character, every word of speech and of description is thought of, literally for years."[18] Woolson at times bows to the old view that writing makes a woman unfeminine: "What *is* the reason that if we take up a pen we seem to lose so much in other ways?" Woolson once wondered, certain that her friend, Stedman, must be glad *his* wife was not a writer.[19] But she is not afraid to see herself as an artist in pursuit of greatness, an ambition that very few women in America would have owned a generation earlier.

It must be said, however, that Woolson is not fair to her female predecessors; as Nina Baym and others have suggested, the women of Woolson's generation owed a great deal to the example of women like Southworth whose successful careers as professional writers created the conditions for the literary ambitions of the women of the next generation. Nor is it fair to characterize the "women's fiction" these writers produced as nothing but " 'pretty,' 'sweet' writing."[20] Yet the very success of "women's fiction" threatened Woolson. To make a place for herself as a woman with high artistic ambitions, she felt compelled to reject the previous generation of American women's writing. Male writers, such as her contemporary Henry

James, engaged in similar revaluations and rejections, as is evident in James's commentary on Nathaniel Hawthorne. But for a woman, the rejection of a popular feminine literary mode meant risking disapproval and even courting literary oblivion. Readers brought up on the happy endings of women's fiction, she feared, would find her fiction "queer" or "stupid," and indeed, for one early story, she reports that readers and critics alike "showered" abuse upon her for her " 'brutal killing of Peter the Parson.' " Yet even such an overwhelmingly negative response as this, she asserted, could not make her abandon "an artistic and truthful-to-life point of view," though it violated " 'the plenty to eat and the happy marriage' " popular with the public.[21]

Woolson was willing to risk her readers' disapproval; her self-conscious adoption of the ultramasculine style of Bret Harte is part of her declaration of literary independence from the "feminine sphere" of literature. Harte struck her—and many of her contemporaries as well—as "new and unconventional."[22] To Woolson, Harte's writing seemed as far as it was possible to be from the "pretty and sweet" stories supposed the natural province of women. To a modern eye, Harte's tales easily reveal a strain of sentimentality not so different from that usually ascribed to nineteenth-century women's writing, but Harte's genius was to discover that the sentimental could be given new life if the heart of gold were put into unexpected places—the rough miner or the unreclaimed prostitute. But to Woolson who had grown up spending the summer along the Great Lakes, where the wild life of the fur trade had not yet been forgotten, the uncouth characters and rugged scenes of Harte's fiction represented freedom to a woman writer.

Woolson used Harte as a point of departure for her early work. But she adamantly rejected the idea that she was Harte's disciple. "In spite of all I said to you," she once explained to Stedman, "I do *not* plead guilty to imitating Harte." She added that Harte "was the sensation of the hour, that was all."[23] Woolson was also well aware that Harte did not fulfill his early promise as a writer; in a later letter to Stedman, she writes that she "felt she could not desert her old favorite," but she admits, "I am afraid to read 'Gabriel Conroy'; I skimmed a little of it, and it seemed so disappointing."[24] Yet critics have usually been content to read Woolson as Harte's disciple; very few have seen any complexity in her conscious use of Harte's work. This judgment is all the more ironic, in the light of these same critics' willingness to admit that in rewriting Harte's popular story, she "bettered" the work of her "master."[25] Joan Myers Weimer is the notable exception, arguing that Woolson in revising Harte's popular tale performs a radical critique of the assumptions that lie behind his fiction.[26] But Weimer does not acknowledge that in Harte's writing, Woolson found much to admire and much that she could use. Her transformation of "The Luck of Roaring Camp" into "The Lady of Little Fishing" offers a glimpse into the sexual politics of literary intertextuality, both as practiced in nineteenth-century America and as carried on in contemporary criticism.

It is telling that the relation of these two American writers, one a man at the height of his popularity, the other a woman in the process of defining herself as a writer, was never realized as a literary friendship and that the relationship, such as it was, remained one-sided, in the mind of the woman writer alone. According to her biographer Rayburn S. Moore, Harte's name "occurs frequently" in Woolson's correspondence, but she did not occupy anything like this place in Harte's life; indeed, he seems never to have taken notice of her existence.[27] The two apparently never met, despite their sharing a good friend in John Hay.[28] It is even more telling that twentieth-century critics, despite their often judging Woolson as the better writer, have persisted in seeing theirs as a relationship in which intertextuality works only in one way, from "master" Harte to "disciple" Woolson (later in her career, according to some critics, she graduates from being Harte's disciple to being Henry James's[29]). Woolson's rewriting of "The Luck of Roaring Camp," however, deserves to be read as a woman writer's daring gambit. She was not only interested in capturing for herself Harte's readership and his critical success; she rewrites his story to make it serve her needs as a woman and as a writer in late nineteenth-century America. Her pointed reiteration of Harte's narrative situation in "The Lady of Little Fishing" invites a comparative reading, but the crucial and all-important difference in Woolson's text—the insertion of "the Lady's" voice and with it female desire into Harte's male text—testifies to the ambition of her project: to rewrite nineteenth-century American culture from a woman's point of view.

II

"The Luck of Roaring Camp" has a long critical history. Nineteenth-century critics tended to see it as a story of "noble" pathos, praising its evocation of "the spirit of early California life." Twentieth-century critics have been less unanimous in their praise. Although Fred Lewis Pattee reads the story as an important contribution to the American short story, other critics, such as Cleanth Brooks and Robert Penn Warren, have discussed it as an example of the failure of sentimental writing. In the late sixties and seventies, critics seeking to rehabilitate Bret Harte defended the story as a well-constructed "parable," although whether the story is to be read as a parable of Christian values, Manifest Destiny, or Victorian progress, or even as a parody of these pieties, is contested.[30] But Woolson's revision of this story suggests that she interprets "The Luck of Roaring Camp" in terms of nineteenth-century sexual politics,[31] an interpretation moreover fully in line with many modern interpretations of "classic" American fiction. For example, both Leslie Fiedler and Judith Fetterley, though from opposite points of view, see canonical American literature as retelling a central male fantasy, the escape to a paradise without women.[32]

In Harte's story the fantasy takes the form of a regression to a golden summer of childhood, where there is no separation from the mother: men and baby live happily together, in a womblike valley high in the Sierras.[33] The instrument of the camp's transformation is the baby, and the deepest instinct, the means by which paradise is recaptured, the desire to merge with the mother. Harte's narrative is staged as a gentleman's monologue, with the reader imagined as a mirror of the narrator, a gentleman at his elbow, who can be trusted to see the story as he sees it, despite certain aspects in questionable taste (the introduction of the camp prostitute and her illegitimate baby). The humor of this story depends upon the gentleman's holding himself—and the reader—at a safe distance from "them." The high literary tone of the gentleman-narrator—"deaths were by no means uncommon in Roaring Camp, but . . . this was the first time that anybody had been introduced into the camp *ab initio*" (2)—assures us that we ought not to take the likes of French Pete, Stumpy, and Kentuck seriously, but rather we should enjoy the ludicrous spectacle of a bunch of rough men reduced to cooing over a baby.

Woolson instead sets up the tale as a dialogue between two male narrators, one, a young man in his twenties, and the other, a man in his fifties. In her tale, the instrument of change is not a baby, but a beautiful woman. Harte's story proffers the fantasy that the forbidden wish to return to the womb can—if only briefly—be satisfied. Woolson's tale, however, dramatizes that such wishes cannot really be satisfied, for they are always already subject to a reality principle. The very harshness of her setting, deep winter on an island in Lake Superior, contrasts with Harte's. Although Woolson's camp represents an imaginary space of freedom, where male and female might meet and love as equals, finally, however, Woolson's story does not offer us a wish fulfillment at all. Hers is a cautionary tale about the damage that erotic fantasies sanctioned by the dominant culture can do, especially when they are substituted for social relations between men and women that are always more complex than ideology admits or fantasy allows.

The dialogic frame of her story allows Woolson to explore the dominant configurations of male and female fantasies in nineteenth-century American culture from multiple points of view. The frame narrator, the young man who hears the tale, is a figure of the narcissism of the male. He is under the delusion that everything is there for his amusement. Choosing this voice to frame the tale is a brilliant stroke, for it both provides the reader a measure of the egocentric behavior of the young man in the narrated story as well as invites the reader to side with the fantastic tale over his callow certainty. Struck by the "stupendous" fact that he had not even been born when the story the older man tells took place, he is clearly too immature to grasp fully what he is about to hear. Yet Woolson also suggests that the other male narrator is limited as well. Like some American incarnation of the Ancient Mariner, he is stangely obsessed by the story he is telling; at the end, it seems clear that he returns to tell the tale because he has only now begun to understand what happened there. But he also represents the dominance of masculine desire in American culture as he lives to tell the story, and it is his version of the events that survives.

Male desire, however, makes up only half the story. Through the filter of a dialogue between these two men, Woolson gives speech and desire to a woman. Only the remembered words of "our Lady" enable the reader to make sense of the events. In this curiously mediated way, her female creator represents female desire. By making the woman's voice central to the story, however, Woolson breaks Harte's illusion of a self-sufficient all-male world and so provides an alternative vision to the meaning of the West in America. The space beyond the borders of civilization represented by the freedom of the all-male camp, as Woolson's tale attests, becomes all too easily the place where dominant, middle-class culture once more plays out its enslaving fantasies.

In her revision, Woolson subtly undermines Harte's version of the American fantasy of a happy, all-male existence uncomplicated by women by exposing that this fantasy depends upon women—upon women being silenced and excluded. Not only can there not be a story without a woman in it—even Harte's story, after all, needs a woman to produce the wonderful baby—but also Woolson insists, the woman *is* the story. When the frame narrator discovers that his companion was actually one of the builders of the ghost town, he is astounded:

> "Was n't a meeting-house an unusual accompaniment?"
> "Most unusual."
> "Accounted for in this case by—"
> "A woman."
> "Ah!" I said in a tone of relish; "then of course there is a story?"[34]

It might be argued that Woolson once more reinscribes the woman as object, as the body of the fiction, upon whom men write their desires, but Woolson deliberately complicates the dominance of what Laura Mulvey has called the male gaze.[35] The privileged position of the male gaze is undercut by being split between two male narrators, neither of whom moreover seems entirely worthy of the reader's trust. Unlike Harte, who gives his narrator literary airs that suggest he is superior to the story he tells, Woolson repeatedly shows up the pretensions of the frame narrator. "Ruins are rare in the New World; I took off my hat. 'Hail, homes of the past!' " the young man declares, when he comes across these unlikely remains of a town in the wilderness (3). His jejune posturing throughout forces the reader to realize how limited his perspective is. The second male narrator, who materializes out of nowhere, also invites the reader's doubts. His obsession with the story he tells suggests a rigidity that is as suspect as the young man's jocular familiarity.

In "The Luck of Roaring Camp," Harte excises the woman early in the story. "The less said of her the better," Harte's narrator comments, adding, "She was a coarse, and it is to be feared, a very sinful woman" (1). In his tale, the woman never says a single word; there is no place for a woman to speak or to signify what, if any, desires she might have. Harte portrays the men as "boys" who happily return to the innocent companionship of their own sex once the camp prostitute dies in childbirth. The feminine, displaced onto nature and removed from the realm of complex adult relationships, remains at a safe distance. But Woolson sees male-female relationships as the main drama, imagining no escape from eros, even in the most remote wilderness. True, the men on their island in Lake Superior do manage for a time to live a relatively simple life without women: "there was n't any nonsense at Little Fishing—until *she* came," as the old man puts it (6). But this is only illusory, for Woolson's narrative reveals that such "nonsense"— that is desire, that which is not entirely subject to reason—is what lies at the great heart of nature, and indeed the heart of all stories.

"The Lady" miraculously appears in the camp one night, heeding the call that she must preach the gospel in every camp on Lake Superior. The men enshrine her as a saint, giving her the best wigwam and surrounding it with pine saplings, as if she were a medieval virgin to be protected by walls and moats. Almost overnight, civilization flowers, with log houses and a church springing up where there had only been shanties. The old man recalls, "It seemed as though she was not of this earth, so utterly impersonal was her interest in us, so heavenly her pity" (8). But Woolson's story exposes male worship of a pure and pious womanhood as a fatal illusion. When their "Lady" falls in love with one of the trappers, she awakens to her own erotic desire. For her, it is a slow, tortuous process, like spring coming to the Great Lakes, and she does not fully comprehend what is happening to her. It becomes clear to the camp, although it is not yet clear to her, that their Lady is in love, and with the one young man who is oblivious to her. The men feel bitterly betrayed. She has shown herself to be "nothing but a woman." In a dramatic scene in the church, the men confront her with the truth. When the angry men have the man brought to her, the impetuous object of her desire rejects her: " 'What is she to me? Nothing. A very good missionary, no doubt; but *I* don't fancy women preachers. You may remember that *I* never gave in to her influence; *I* was never under her thumb. *I* was the only man in Little Fishing who cared nothing for her!' " (22). As he tries to leave, she prostrates herself at his feet, begging him to take her with him. He rejects her, leaving her to pine away and die. At the end of this story, the reader is not surprised to learn—although his listener is very surprised— that the man who has narrated these events of thirty years ago, the only man who has come back after all these years to find their Lady's grave, is the young man who once so absolutely refused her. What are we to make of this story of the Lady's humiliation?

Even though the men are made furious by the discovery that their Lady, too, is driven by carnal desire, this is not because the men have succeeded, as Harte's miners do, in actually banishing eros. The transformation of a camp of hardened men into the pure joys of collective boyhood that in Harte's story is dramatized as a real possibility is shown up in Woolson's story as a sham. Her tale shows us that desire has only gone underground; the men's fury is unleashed not because they have been truly reformed and are therefore hurt by her "betrayal," but because the exposure of her erotic need forces into the open what the men would prefer to hide from themselves: the true source of her power all along has been sexual, not spiritual. On both sides, erotic desire has been sublimated in a dangerous and idolatrous game: the Lady believes she is holy and above desire, and the men, who would have her so, worship her as a god.

On one level, then, the story unveils an allegory of how the Cult of True Womanhood operated in nineteenth-century American culture.[36] Absorbed in the business of making an aggressively capitalist enterprise pay off (as hunters and trappers, they participate in a not-so-symbolic rape of the wilderness), the men seize upon her as an ideal of womanhood to bless their godless activities. Safely shut up within her home/church, the Lady is allowed to wield her "influence," but only over domestic and spiritual matters, which the story suggests is a narrow realm indeed. The men attend church on Sunday and adopt more gentlemanly manners, but the business of killing and trapping goes on exactly as before. In making her into the icon of "Our Lady," the men mystify her actual position in relation to themselves, which is in reality analogous to the animals they trap and profit from, for she, too, has been converted into an object of symbolic value. She is not a human being to whom they must respond, or with whom they must play any of the difficult roles of brother, husband, or friend, but a conveniently distant object of desire. At one point, the Frenchman in the camp disabuses another trapper, who imagines that what he feels for their Lady is similar to what he would feel for a sister; relations with one's actual sister, the trapper makes clear, are never so simple. The Frenchman says of his own sister: "We fight like four cats and one dog; *she is* the cats" (37). As long as their Lady is content to remain an idol and the men are willing to sublimate their desire, civilization of a sort can prosper. But the cost of such a civilization erected upon women denying their bodies may be read in the tortured relations between the sexes that the story portrays as the norm.

Yet men are not wholly to blame for this arrangement, for women— especially "ladies," that is, middle-class women—Woolson suggests, are themselves complicit in a social order that chiefly values them as objects to display and desire. Under the delusion that her influence over the men is "heavenly," the Lady wills her isolation and seeks out her martyrdom as a saint. But she is the one, the story shows, who in the end pays the most dearly for her own participation in the process that turns her into an object and denies her an autonomous subjectivity. The cost of True Womanhood is the loss of physical and sexual vitality. In the beginning, the Lady is pale, bloodless, almost a ghost. The only sign of life—as with Hawthorne's Hester—is her hair, but only a little of it is allowed to glimmer through her white cap. But when she falls in love, her female sexuality emerges as she stands before them "crowned only by her golden hair" (16), more like Lady Godiva than the Virgin Mary. Woolson manages the climax with great power, as hatred, rape, and violence seem about to erupt as the Lady falls from grace and admits to desire.

But something else happens. The woman speaks and strikes the men "dumb," disrupting this male text of possession and desire. The Lady's discourse is that of the traditional masculine "amorous vassalage" that Roland Barthes analyzes so well in *A Lover's Discourse*, which in fact *requires* "a fathomless futility." Barthes reminds us that the lover's acknowledgment of dependency becomes "a means of *signifying* demand" for "in the realm of love, futility is not a 'weakness' or an 'absurdity': it is a strong sign: the more futile, the more it signifies and the more it asserts itself as strength."[37] Yet it is shocking that a woman, a "lady," would appropriate this discourse, and all the more shocking because her gesture of submission is nevertheless a claim to power.[38] Clasping her beloved's ankles, she lays her face on his shoes and begs him to "let me be your servant—your slave—anything— anything, so that I am not parted from you, my Lord and master, my only, only love" (22); paradoxically, however, she signifies her strength in this gesture of total erotic self-abasement, which, in its extremity and futility, not only bespeaks an enormous demand, but also testifies that she is the men's equal in desire.

The female author enables the woman to speak, but the radical import of her words is that in speaking her desire, she does not reveal herself as Woman, as Other; rather she reveals that men and women are the same. When the Lady positions herself in the male role of humble suitor at the beloved's feet, she inverts the hierarchy of social meaning based on a belief in the "natural" difference between the sexes: predatory, amorous males in pursuit of passionless female prey. By suing for her lover's favor, she shatters the image of woman as a cold and distant mistress, unwittingly laying bare the power relations implicated in the culture's discourse of romantic desire. This role reversal betrays that this discourse is grounded in male power over women, in which "true" women, like slaves, are presumed to have no autonomous desires that might give rise to desires at variance with the dominant order. This is why Woolson represents the Lady's erotic speech act as so potentially disruptive; the spectacle of women desiring as men desire threatens to overturn a hierarchy based on female subordination and thus to remake the dominant social order. The potency of this threat explains the extraordinary measures the men take to erase all traces of what happened: "They tore down her empty lodge and destroyed its every fragment; in their grim determination they even smoothed over the ground and planted shrubs and bushes, so that the very location might be lost" (23). But Woolson proposes, contrary to Harte, that women can never be wholly silenced, entirely erased.

Nevertheless, no good comes of the Lady's attempt to express herself as a desiring subject. She suffers the same fate as the silent prostitute in Harte's story: abandonment and death. "The Lady of Little Fishing" comes uncomfortably close to supporting the ideology of True Womanhood: for women who fall through sexual desire, the consequences are betrayal and death. And yet Woolson's story resists any simple reading, for both desire and danger are confirmed. The very structure of the story commemorates a woman speaking: what is left after everything else has been destroyed is a voice that tells of woman's desire. The Lady remains, however, an enigmatic sign of contradiction: at once chaste and betrayed, dying and asking forgiveness from the men, but never renouncing desire, she hovers at the boundaries of True Womanhood, both fallen and unfallen, desiring and pure, false missionary and true woman.

III

Despite Woolson's radical rewriting of Bret Harte's "The Luck of Roaring Camp," however, she draws back from the most radical possibilities. Although she has inserted a woman's voice into Harte's text, she has also changed Harte's prostitute, "Cherokee Sal," a lower-class woman of a different race, into a middle-class, white woman missionary. And though she mostly avoids Harte's tendency to render the lower class as humorous grotesques, she, like Harte, has made the lower-class woman invisible; the prostitute, mute in Harte's tale, has been dropped out of her story entirely. Yet her intertextual play with Harte's structure and style in "The Lady of Little Fishing" represents Woolson's effort to fashion a bold, new literary language for herself. Her apprentice tale is stunning in the sheer array of speech that she tries out, although it must be admitted that the attempt to reflect the Euro-American conquest of the West is sometimes strained. The Frenchman talks like a bad cartoon; the Dutchman is hardly more successful. Woolson is at her best when she breathes into her characters the sound of colloquial American English: "Say, Frenchy, have you got a sister," one man says to another, and a little later, someone tells him, "Shut up your howling, Jack" (13). By turning the structure and the assumptions of Harte's famous story inside out, Woolson accomplishes in this best of her early tales what will become a characteristic double maneuver in her fiction: the deconstruction of the male gaze as blind and limited, and the oblique representation of women's suffering.

Woolson would soon drop Harte as a literary model, but she did not abandon her interest in representing sexual politics. In her later work, she dramatizes the toll on women in conventional relations between the sexes, exploring the woman who plays the part of the girl-wife in *For the Major* (1883), the woman who feels she must remain a true wife to the man who has deserted her years earlier in *East Angels* (1886), the woman who loves her batterer in *Jupiter Lights* (1889), and the woman undone by a romantic obsession in *Horace Chase* (1894).

Constance Fenimore Woolson's work richly deserves a new reading. Although she sometimes universalizes female experience in troubling ways, making middle-class, white women speak for all women, a feminist reappraisal must not underestimate the daring and subtlety of her fiction in post–Civil War America. In identifying with a male writer and setting herself apart from other writers of her sex, Woolson saw herself as choosing art over popularity and power over beauty. It was a deliberate and risky choice to make early in her career. Defending herself to her closest female friend for a supposed "want of morality" in a story she had published, she explained, "I want you to think of me not as your old friend, when you read my writings, but as a 'writer,' like anyone else. For instance, take 'Adam Bede' . . . Would you like to have a friend of yours the author of such a story? Dealing with such subjects? And yet it was a great book."[39] Later in her career, Woolson's fictions about women artists suggest that she had begun to confront the sexual politics not just of being a woman in the nineteenth century but also of being a woman writer; stories such as "Miss Grief" (1880) and "At the Château of Corinne" (1887) reveal how impossible it is for a woman to be read as a "writer like anyone else." Fifteen years after she championed Harte's fiction, her comment on Louisa May Alcott from the vantage of her own long struggle to succeed as an artist indicates that she had at last begun to read her female compatriots in a different light. Greatly impressed by Alcott's *Life and Letters*, she wrote, "What heroic, brave struggles. And what a splendid success."[40] One might with justice say the same of Woolson.

Notes

1. I wish to thank Julie Bates Dock, R. James Goldstein, and Paula V. Smith for their suggestions.

2. Constance Fenimore Woolson's letter to Mrs. [Arabella Carter] Washburn is quoted in *Five Generations (1785–1923*, ed. Clare Benedict, vol. 2 (London: Ellis, 1930), 21. Hereafter cited as *Five Generations*.

3. Roland Barthes, *A Lover's Discourse: Fragments*, trans. Richard Howard (New York: Hill and Wang, 1978), 82.

4. Constance Fenimore Woolson, "The Lady of Little Fishing," *Atlantic Monthly* 34 (September 1874):293–305. "The Luck of Roaring Camp" first appeared in the San Francisco journal Harte edited, *Overland Monthly*, 1st series, 1, no. 2 (August 1868):183–89. Fields and Osgood made it the title story of the first volume of Francis Bret Harte's collected tales, *The Luck of Roaring Camp, and Other Sketches* (Boston: Fields, Osgood, 1870).

5. Patrick D. Morrow has noted Harte's great influence upon popular film and television, in *Bret Harte*, Boise State College Writers Series 5 (Boise, Idaho: Boise State College, 1972), 7. For his most recent assessment of Harte's place in American literature, see "Bret Harte, Mark Twain, and the San Francisco Circle," *A Literary History of the American West* (Fort Worth: Texas Christian University Press, 1987), 339–58.

Other important appraisals include Margaret Duckett, *Mark Twain and Bret Harte* (Norman: University of Oklahoma Press, 1964); James K. Folsom, *The American Western Novel* (New Haven: College and University Press, 1966); Fred Lewis Pattee, *The Development of the American Short Story* (New York: Harper, 1923); George R. Stewart, Jr., *Bret Harte: Argonaut and Exile* (Boston: Houghton Mifflin, 1931), and Franklin Walker, *San Francisco's Literary Frontier* (New York: Knopf, 1939).

6. Harte tells how the printer did not return the proofs to him, but instead tried to convince the publisher of the *Overland Monthly* not to print a story "so indecent, irreligious, and improper that his proof-reader—a young lady—had with difficulty been induced to continue its perusal." See "General Introduction," *The Writings of Bret Harte*, vol. 1 (Boston and New York: Houghton Mifflin, 1896), xiii. Harte's youthful indignation at such female-inspired interference had softened over the years, and in this introduction, he stretched forth "the hand of sympathy and forgiveness" even to "the gentle proof-reader, that chaste and unknown nymph" (xv).

7. Patrick D. Morrow, *Bret Harte: Literary Critic* (Bowling Green, Ohio: Bowling Green State University Popular Press, 1979), 68.

8. See *Patrons and Protégées: Gender, Friendship, and Writing in Nineteenth-Century America*, ed. Shirley Marchalonis (New Brunswick and London: Rutgers University Press, 1988); for a feminist rethinking of Woolson's relationship with Henry James, see especially in this collection, Cheryl B. Torsney, "The Traditions of Gender: Constance Fenimore Woolson and Henry James,"

9. William Dean Howells, "Reviews and Literary Notices" (review of *The Luck of Roaring Camp, and Other Sketches*), *Atlantic Monthly* 25 (May 1870):633–35.

10. In Harte's "Tennessee's Partner," first published in the *Overland Monthly* and collected in *The Luck of Roaring Camp, and Other Sketches*, the hanging of Tennessee by the enraged citizens of Sandy Bar is softened by the sentimental ending, his partner's hope of meeting him in heaven. "Peter the Parson," Woolson's story of frontier justice, by contrast, emphasizes mob cruelty as the miners stone to death a frail and unpopular Episcopal priest.

11. "The most widely read writers of the post–Civil War decades, we should remember, were not Howells or James but domestic writers like Mrs. Southworth, Caroline Lee Hentz, and Mary Jane Holmes," writes Richard H. Brodhead, "Literature and Culture," *Columbia Literary History of the United States*, ed. Emory Elliott et al. (New York: Columbia University Press, 1988), 469.

12. Woolson's letter to Miss [Linda T.] Guilford is quoted in *Five Generations*, vol. 2, 42–43.

13. Woolson commented acidly that her friend E. C. Stedman had revealed that he did "not really believe in woman's genius," for the essence of his criticism of Elizabeth Barrett Browning is " 'She did wonderfully well for a woman' "; from Woolson's marginalia quoted in *Five Generations*, vol. 2, 93.

14. The Old Stone House (Boston: D. Lothrop, 1873); Woolson did not publish the book under her own name, but under the pseudonym "Anne March," perhaps an indirect

tribute to Louisa May Alcott and her novel of the March girls, but also a means of distancing herself from a genre perceived as female.

15. Woolson's letter to South Carolina poet Paul Hamilton Hayne is dated May Day, 1875, and is quoted in Jay B. Hubbell, "Some New Letters of Constance Fenimore Woolson," *New England Quarterly* 14 (December 1941):718. Hereafter cited as "Some New Letters."

16. Woolson's letter to Hayne is dated 16 January 1876, and is quoted in "Some New Letters," 728.

17. Woolson's letter to [Mrs. Samuel Livingston (Elizabeth Gwinn)] Mather is quoted in *Five Generations*, vol. 1, 229.

18. Woolson's letter to Katharine Livingston Mather is quoted in *Five Generations*, vol. 2, 52. Mary P. Edwards Kitterman, quoting Woolson's teacher, Linda Guilford, argues that Woolson felt that the " 'only way in which she could fulfill her soul destiny' was as a literary artist." See "Henry James and the Artist Heroine in the Tales of Constance Fenimore Woolson," *Nineteenth-Century Women Writers of the English-Speaking World* (Westport, Conn.: Greenwood, 1986), 54.

19. Woolson's letter to E. C. Stedman is dated 28 September 1874, and is quoted in Laura Stedman and George M. Gould, *Life and Letters of Edmund Clarence Stedman*, vol. 1 (New York: Moffat, Yard, 1910), 521–22.

20. Helen Waite Papashvily, *All the Happy Endings* (New York: Harpers, 1956) was the first to see discontent beneath the surface of nineteenth-century women's fiction, but Nina Baym must be credited with the first major reinterpretation of the tradition, *Woman's Fiction: A Guide to Novels by and about Women in America, 1820–1870* (Ithaca: Cornell University Press, 1978). "The flowering of this fiction," Baym writes, "created the ground from which, after the Civil War, a group of women who were literary artists developed" (298). Baym also argues that this women's fiction is not about romance and courtship, but about women learning to survive on their own. See also Mary Kelley, *Private Woman, Public Stage: Literary Domesticity in Nineteenth-Century America* (New York: Oxford University Press, 1984).

21. Woolson's letter to Samuel Mather is quoted in *Five Generations*, vol. 2, 23.

22. Woolson puts this praise of Bret Harte's fiction into the mouth of her male protagonist in "Misery Landing," *Harper's New Monthly Magazine* 48 (May 1874):866: "Strange that it should be so, but everywhere it is the cultivated people only who are taken with Bret. But they must be imaginative as well as cultivated; routine people, whether in life or in literature, dislike anything unconventional or new."

23. Woolson's letter to E. C. Stedman is dated 28 September 1874, and is quoted in Rayburn S. Moore, *Constance Fenimore Woolson* (New York: Twayne, 1963), 120–21. Hereafter cited as *Constance Fenimore Woolson*.

24. Woolson's letter is quoted in *Constance Fenimore Woolson*, 121.

25. Woolson is represented by Carlos Baker in *A Literary History of the United States*, ed. Robert Spiller et al., 4th rev. ed. (New York: Macmillan, 1974), as a lesser "imitator" of Bret Harte (868). Even her biographer Rayburn S. Moore views her as Harte's disciple, although he credits her in "The Lady of Little Fishing" with bettering "the work of one of her masters" (*Constance Fenimore Woolson*, 50). Although some critics have seen Woolson as improving upon Harte's story, very few have seen that she does more than make the characters or the ending more plausible. Fred Lewis Pattee, in *The Development of the American Short Story*, judges "The Lady of Little Fishing" as a "model short story" because it makes Harte's "grotesque situation" more "of a peep into the heart of life" when it reveals that "woman" is " 'the same the world over!' " (255). Claude M. Simpson also sees Woolson's story as more realistic than its predecessor because she resolves the story "by the strictly human device of disenchantment, where Harte resorted to chance calamity" (*The Local Colorists: American Short Stories 1857–1900* [New York: Harper, 1960], 130).

26. "Woolson directly criticized Harte's sentimental Victorian idea that a miner could

be brought to salvation by an innocent baby—or a pure woman," Weimer argues; however, she sees Woolson's famous uncle as her major male precursor, reading "The Lady of Little Fishing" as a rewriting of Cooper. See Joan Myers Weimer, "Introduction," *Women Artists, Women Exiles: "Miss Grief" and Other Stories*, by Constance Fenimore Woolson (New Brunswick and London: Rutgers University Press, 1988), 18 n., xxvi. Although I agree with Weimer that Cooper was an important precursor for his grandniece, I argue here that Harte's fiction, not Cooper's, is the primary source for "The Lady of Little Fishing."

27. *Constance Fenimore Woolson*, 120. Harte later gave credit to Joel Chandler Harris, George Washington Cable, Thomas Nelson Page, Mark Twain, Mary Noailles Murfree, and Mary E. Wilkins Freeman for following his lead in cutting "loose from conventional methods" in order "to honestly describe the life around them"; he neglects, however, to mention Woolson. "The Rise of the 'Short Story,' " *Cornhill Magazine* 7 (July 1899):102–110. That Harte omits her name here is significant; he may be indirectly accusing Woolson of earning the label "Imitator," a term he says "could not fairly apply" to the others mentioned.

28. See Alice Hall Petry, " 'Always, Your Attached Friend': The Unpublished Letters of Constance Fenimore Woolson to John and Clara Hay," *Books at Brown* 29–30 (1982–1983): 11–108. John Hay was responsible for Bret Harte's being promoted to the post of United States consul in Glasgow, Scotland, according to his biographer George R. Stewart, Jr. (*Bret Harte: Argonaut and Exile*, 269–70). Harte was a notoriously absentee consul. Woolson once commented in a letter to Hayne that Bret Harte "is *not* a nice person, I am told" (quoted in *Constance Fenimore Woolson*, 121).

29. For a feminist critique of this traditional reading of the Woolson-James relationship, in addition to Torsney and Kitterman cited above, see Sharon Dean, "Constance Fenimore Woolson and Henry James: The Literary Relationship," *Massachusetts Studies in English* 7 (1980):1–9. Dean was the first to note that James borrowed from Woolson's notebooks and fiction.

30. For early reviews of "The Luck of Roaring Camp," see Anon., "Notes," *Nation* 8 (13 May 1869):376; Anon., "New Publications," *New York Times*, (30 April 1870), 11; and Anon., "American Books," *Blackwoods Edinburgh Magazine* 110 (October 1871):422–30. Twentieth-century appraisals of the story include: Pattee, *The Development of the American Short Story*, 220–44; Cleanth Brooks, John Thibaut Purser, and Robert Penn Warren, *An Approach to Literature*, 3rd. ed. (New York: Appleton-Century-Crofts, 1952), 86–87; Allen B. Brown, "The Christ Motif in 'The Luck of Roaring Camp,' " *Papers of the Michigan Academy of Science, Arts, and Letters* 46 (1961):629–33; J. R. Boggan, "The Regeneration of 'Roaring Camp,' " *Nineteenth-Century Fiction* 22 (December 1967):271–80; and Morrow, "The Predicament of Bret Harte," *American Literary Realism, 1870–1910* 5 (1972):181–88, and "Bret Harte, Popular Fiction, and the Local Color Movement," *American Literary Realism* 8 (1973):123–31. In the last decade new readings of Harte's fiction have mostly been offered by German critics; see, for example, Klaus P. Hansen, "Francis Bret Harte: Ironie und Konvention," *Arbeiten aus Anglistik und Amerikanistik* 9, no. 1 (1984):23–37.

31. Jeffrey F. Thomas has noted that Henry Adams was the first to see Harte's fiction as an exploration of sexuality; Adams singled out Harte and Whitman as the only American writers who dared to treat sex as a force. "Bret Harte and the Power of Sex," *Western American Literature* 8 (1973):91–109. See also *The Education of Henry Adams*, ed. Ernest Samuels (Boston: Houghton Mifflin, 1973), 385. Like Adams, Thomas locates the "power of sex" mainly in women; unlike Adams, however, and unlike Woolson in her fiction, Thomas does not explore what it means for the woman herself to serve as the site of sexuality in American culture.

32. See Leslie Fiedler, *Love and Death in the American Novel*, 3rd. rev. ed. (New York: Stein and Day, 1982), and Judith Fetterley, *The Resisting Reader: A Feminist Approach to American Fiction* (Bloomington: Indiana University Press, 1978). Fetterley's more recent book,

Provisions: A Reader from 19th-Century American Women (Bloomington: Indiana University Press, 1985), attempts to redefine the field of American literature by offering new critical introductions to and selections from the work of nineteenth-century women.

33. Harte's description of the geography not only recalls the womb but is also linked with "the suffering woman" in labor: "The camp lay in a triangular valley between two hills and a river. The only outlet was a steep trail over the summit of a hill." "The Luck of Roaring Camp," *The Writings of Bret Harte*, vol. 1, 3. All quotations are from this edition and hereafter will be cited by page number in the text.

34. "The Lady of Little Fishing," *Women Artists, Women Exiles*, 5; all quotations are from this edition and will be cited hereafter by page number in the text. Weimer follows the text of the story as Woolson revised it for publication in *Castle Nowhere: Lake Country Sketches* (Boston: Osgood, 1875); I cite Weimer's volume because this is the first time in more than twenty years that a new and authoritative edition of Woolson's work is available to the general reader.

35. Laura Mulvey has analyzed how "the male gaze" controls the narrative perspective in film: "In a world ordered by sexual imbalance, pleasure in looking has been split between active/male and passive/female. The determining male gaze projects its fantasy onto the female figure." "Visual Pleasure and Narrative Cinema," *Narrative, Apparatus, Ideology: A Film Theory Reader*, ed. Philip Rosen (Columbia University Press, 1986), 203. The essay was first published in *Screen* 16, no. 3 (Autumn 1975):6–18.

36. See Barbara Welter, "The Cult of True Womanhood: 1820–1860," *American Quarterly* 18 (1966):151–74.

37. Barthes, *A Lover's Discourse: Fragments*, trans. Richard Howard, p. 82.

38. Weimer interprets the Lady's speech differently, as representing "the loss of dignity and verbal power," "Introduction," *Women Artists, Women Exiles*, p. xxvii. She elaborates this view in "Women Artists as Exiles in the Fiction of Constance Fenimore Woolson," *Legacy: A Journal of Nineteenth-Century Women Writers*, 3, No. 2 (Fall 1986), 3–15.

39. Woolson to Mrs. [Arabella Carter] Washburn, quoted in *Five Generations*, vol. II, p. 20. Woolson is defending "Castle Nowhere," the title story she wrote for the first volume of her collected fiction.

40. Woolson's letter to [Miss Linda T. Guilford] is quoted in *Five Generations*, vol. II, p. 43.

Getting Your Money's Worth: The Social Marketplace in *Horace Chase*

CAROLYN VANBERGEN

During the productive years that Constance Fenimore Woolson wrote novels, short stories, travel literature, and criticism (1870–1894), the most important American economic question was that of currency. For much of the nineteenth century American politicians, economists, and business people argued the merits of hard versus paper currency. The debate over varieties of values of course found its most heated expression in the Civil War, which Woolson often remarked was the central event of her life. Although the war infrequently figures in Woolson's novels, the split between North and South, between groups who value different commodities, is the central conflict of her novels. As this economic metaphor takes shape over her career as a novelist, three commodities emerge as predominant: money, self, and information, with their institutional faces of business, sex and marriage, and education or gossip. In her final novel, *Horace Chase*, Woolson explores ways in which her two main interest groups, men and women primarily, and northerners and southerners secondarily, can find ways of existing within a single social marketplace.

Although *Horace Chase* considers briefly the possibility of a separate female economy in the community of women exemplified by the Franklins and their female friends, most of Woolson's work backs the concept of a unified market, dominated by neither sex but honoring the currency of each. She seeks specifically ways in which women might become active in the mainstream economy, using male-dominated modes of exchange, and ways that the market might learn to use and accept female-dominated media. Men tend to favor money and self as modes of exchange, in that order, while women prefer information and self. Through the careful use of these goods, their production and exchange, characters can increase their social standing and power, which in turn grants them greater access to such stocks. Success in this social marketplace also guarantees the characters increased social autonomy; society forgives the foibles of a wealthy man, beautiful woman,

This essay was written especially for this volume and is published here for the first time with the permission of the author.

or shrewd authority more quickly than those of their poor, unattractive, uninformed counterparts.

The conflict of commodity values is manifest in the desire for control in relationships in *Horace Chase*, published first as a serial for *Harper's Magazine* in 1892. Since characters do not agree on the worth or marketability of their goods, there is little agreement about who if anyone should be dominant in relationships or how such dominance may be legitimately established. The overriding problem becomes one of control as men try to control women, wives try to control husbands, everyone tries to control money, their emotions, and even each other's minds. Ultimately we may even see Woolson struggling to control her narrative.

One of the most informative messages about the power relations between and within the sexes in the novel is found in the pattern of imagery associated with horses and horseracing. A study of the men and women in the story and their association with horses reveals the potency of the characters' sexuality and gender identity, and of their ability to control themselves.

Briefly, the novel traces the relationship of Ruth Franklin and Horace Chase. Chase, a self-made millionaire, meets the young woman at her mother's home in North Carolina and falls in love almost immediately. After they are married, Ruth too falls in love, with Chase's junior business partner, Walter Willoughby. The colorful cast of minor characters includes Ruth's invalid sister Dolly, her vain, do-gooder sister-in-law Genevieve, the local old maid Miss Billy, and her friend Maud Muriel, a pipe-smoking sculptress.

The person most closely associated with horses is the title character. Horace is renowned as an accomplished horseman and the owner of several enviable animals. He causes quite a stir in the small town of Asheville when his horses arrive and he and Ruth are seen riding together. Chase always insists on driving; even the mule-drawn railway car, which takes them to St. Augustine, arrives with Horace at the reins. He trusts no one else to drive a funeral procession through the mountains, at one point switching vehicles three times to guide each of them through a particularly dangerous curve. Obviously Horace is a man who needs to be in control, and his determined mastery over horses represents this as well as his wealth and buying power.

Horace's horses certainly symbolize his power to other characters in the novel. When he and the Franklins arrive at a resort, the entourage is mistaken for that of an even greater man:

> . . . the sojourners at the Warm Springs, . . . were assembled on the veranda of the rambling wooden hotel, after their six o'clock supper, when they saw two carriages approaching. "Phew! who can they be?" "What horses!"
> The horses were indeed remarkably handsome—two bays and a lighter-limbed pair of sorrels. . . . "Chase, did you say the name was? That's a hoax.

It's General Grant himself, I reckon, coming along yere like a conqueror in disguise," said a wag.[1]

Part of Horace's power, represented by his remarkable horses and acknowledged by this observer to be like that of a military conqueror, comes from his ability to do business, to drive a hard deal. Over and over again in *Horace Chase* horses are symbols for money and doing business, in other words for the dominant masculine economy. In the pivotal discussion between Walter Willoughby and Chase, where they strike the deal to become partners, Walter considers himself well seated in the race to make money:

> . . . he [Walter] had got his foot into the stirrup at last. The ride might be breakneck, and it might be hard; but at least it would not be long, and it would end at the wished-for goal. Between two such riders as Patterson [the third partner] and Horace Chase (Horace Chase especially; best of all, Horace Chase!), he could not fall behind; they would sweep him along between them; he should come in abreast.
>
> (242)

Woolson uses the racing metaphor again in a second business discussion, this one with Ruth's brother Jared when Chase offers him a job. In an ironic effort to clear himself of charges of greed for money, Horace reveals what it is that he enjoys about business and making money:

> "It's fun! To get down to the bed-rock of the subject, it's the power. Yes, sir, that's it—the power! The knowing you've got it, and that other men know it too, and feel your hand on the reins!"
>
> (269)

Not only does Chase admit to being a speculator and enjoying the game of making money, more importantly he confesses to loving the power of it with an enthusiasm we have not seen before. Horace Chase likes riding other men, likes knowing they feel his hands on their reins, as much as he likes riding, driving, and collecting his fine sorrels and bays. His name becomes a metaphor for his ambition; for Horace Chase life is truly a horse chase with money and power going to the winner.

Woolson further suggests that Chase speculates in more than business— that his marriage to Ruth is a kind of speculation. Although her family has strong reservations about the marriage, Horace is anxious for it to take place as quickly as possible. In business Horace goes after what he wants single-mindedly, and he courts Ruth with the same determination, taking her family on trips, finding a job for her brother, and buying her diamond rings (the first one after their initial meeting). In today's market it would be called a hostile takeover, with Horace steadily accumulating more and more stock and interest not just in Ruth but in her whole family, until they can do little to stop him from marrying Ruth, especially since Ruth always gets her way in the family, is a major stockholder, and wants to marry him. As a symbol of his successful conquest Chase buys two new horses for his use in Asheville after his engagement to Ruth.

In addition to representing money, horses also come to represent a second commodity, the self. Horace is not a man of obvious sexual attractiveness in the novel; nonetheless, his association with horses indicates his sexual power, being a traditional image of male sexuality. Horace is successful in all the traditional American male ways: he is decisive, self-made, self-taught, thoroughly independent. Men in the novel are judged and judge each other on the basis of their skill with horses. Chase and Commodore Etheridge find the local politician and scholar Achilles Larue unmanly because he cannot judge a horse (106). On the other hand, Horace Chase likes Malachi Hill because he can handle horses (282). Some of the text's humor derives from the fact that the women are attracted to Larue rather than Hill, an obvious mistake since Larue is about as powerful as his admirer Miss Billy. A man's horsemanship is a measure of his manliness and virility. Perhaps Horace should have paid more attention to the pleasures of horses enjoyed by his junior partner; for Walter Willoughby, the most potent male character, not only likes to drive horses but like his mentor likes to drive fast.

Horses are the exclusive property of men in this novel. Horace laughs at the idea of a woman taking care of his horse when he goes to a mountain farmhouse to find Ruth and Dolly (397). The important thing for men is both to own and to control the horses—you cannot trust anyone else to do it for you, especially not a woman. Horses become then a symbol of male domination over all forms of power and of final control of a woman's sexuality and power as well as the man's. In the same way that a horse must be broken to be controlled, a husband must domesticate his wife and control her. Chase, however, perhaps in his attraction to a challenge and respect for the fire in a horse or a woman, has not domesticated Ruth; he has treated her as a child and learns he must treat her as a woman at the end. That is not as liberating as it sounds in this case though, for it means entrusting her with the responsibilities of a woman (social activity, management of a household, and the raising of children), the limitations traditionally imposed by society in general and the husband in particular; it means no longer allowing her the caprices and freedom of a spoiled child. Ruth must learn to take responsibility for the commodities within her control. Her childlike irresponsibility, although attractive, has included mismanagement of her sexuality, followed by a necessary deception as she hides her affair with Willoughby from Chase.

Although Woolson herself was almost paralyzingly afraid of horses, her heroine Ruth Franklin Chase loves them. Ruth is fearless when it comes to horses and has ridden nearly every steed in Asheville. This love of horse flesh is the one thing she and Horace seem to have in common. The beginning of their courtship is marked by an impromptu horse race, which takes place when Chase's horses are shipped to Asheville.

The race causes lapses of propriety for several people: Ruth as a young woman of breeding should not be in attendance, as Commodore Etheridge makes clear; Malachi Hill forgets himself and his place as minister when he and his horse get involved in a race, especially one on which people have placed bets; the townspeople too find the race irresistible. They are attracted to it "like flies to honey." After the race, Ruth flees for refuge to Miss Billy's sitting room at the Old North Hotel. Apparently Ruth too acknowledges the possibly scandalous consequences of being seen at the race, so she goes to the protection of the most unscandalous person imaginable, the proper virgin of the town. The reaction to this race corresponds to expected reactions to sexual activity; people are drawn to it but are not supposed to enjoy it or be known to take part in it, especially unmarried clergy and well-born women.

The handling of horses, besides representing the need to control women, may also more generally represent the need for anyone to control emotion and passion. This can be seen in the women characters as well as the men. Walter Willoughby's reckless love of fast riding, indicative of his sexual passion, can also be seen in Ruth. She likes to ride, likes the excitement of the horserace, and likes it when the passions are set free.

Miss Billy, on the other hand, is afraid of passion and of excess, and she is very afraid of horses. This fear (and her relationship with Maud Muriel) are nicely illustrated in the scene where the two women attempt to cross the street in front of several large horse-drawn logging wagons. Maud crosses confidently in front of a huge team but Miss Billy panics halfway across

. . . finding herself hemmed in, [she] began to shriek wildly. . . . the whole procession, and with it the entire traffic of the main street, came slowly to a pause. The pause was not long. The energetic Maud Muriel, jerking up the heads of two of the leaders, made a dive, caught hold of her frightened friend, and drew her out by main strength. The horses whom she had thus attacked, shook themselves.

(60–70)

Maud Muriel's bold fearlessness in the face of teams of large workhorses complements her witchlike qualities: she lives alone, smokes a pipe, dresses differently from most of the women, and is an artist. Although we never see her ride, one can assume Maud Muriel to be a confident handler of horses. Equestriennes are traditionally seen as scolds who ride their men, or as witches whose evil and essentially sexual nature is expressed in their midnight rides to satanic assignations. In Woolson's first novel, *The Old Stone House*, a young woman who loves horseback riding primarily because it is forbidden to her is repeatedly called a witch and a brownie. In any case, the suggestions are socially dangerous ones. Whereas the men's interest in horses indicates their ability to control their passions and their women, Ruth and Maud's horse*man*ship indicates not only their wish to give into their passions but also their rebellious desire to wield control and power, to be players in the male market. The novel finds that kind of desire destructive to the female community in women like Ruth's sister-in-law, Genevieve.

In fact the Franklin household, minus the father and brother, as it is most often portrayed, functions very well as a productive female economy marked by a free exchange of information.[2] This version of the female economy is more or less successful because it is moderate and because it remains, for a time anyway, completely separate from other influences. The absence of access to the other two items of marketable value, money and sex, does not seem to bother the women as long as they remain separate from men, for those are the values more strongly associated with men.[3] When Horace Chase with his horses, money, and power infiltrates the female community, he changes the economy, introducing new values and resources that threaten to destroy the female family unit.

Ruth's passionate nature, however, makes her especially vulnerable to his temptations and makes it difficult for her to control her feelings, a skill necessary in the male economy and symbolized by men's ability to control difficult animals. Her mother and Dolly worry about her when she starts to laugh because they know how easily she can become hysterical. The strength of her feelings sometimes causes Ruth to become suddenly bright red followed by a frightening pallor. That passionate nature, coupled with her unfeminine and unusual interest in horses, signals that Ruth's passions include the sexual ones.

In addition to representing control and passion, for Ruth at least, horses are also associated with death. The night of a reception given to honor General Grant's visit to St. Augustine, Ruth plays the piano and begins to sing "The Stirrup Cup":

> My short and happy day is done
> The long and dreary night comes on;
> And at my door the Pale Horse stands,
> To carry me to unknown lands.
>
> His whinny shrill, his pawing hoof,
> Sound dreadful as a gathering storm;
> And I must leave this sheltering roof,
> And joys of life so soft and warm.
>
> (329)

She knows she will see Walter at the dance for the first time since he went to California a year before, and she seems to be saying that it will be the death of her. Woolson tells us that along with the courage to face Walter came a premonition that caused her to sing the song. It would take Ruth a total denial of her feelings, of her love for Walter, of the loss of her love for Horace, to be able to face Willoughby. In Ruth such a denial is equivalent to death; there has been little else to her besides her emotions, what Woolson calls her "essentially feminine" character (340). This passionate nature has led her from the "sheltering roof" of her family to the "gathering storm" of male-female encounter, where it appears Ruth has the will and resources but not the knowledge to participate in the complicated exchanges of self, property, and information.

This conflict of appraised market price and control causes Ruth to consider effecting her own death on two occasions: when she sings "The Stirrup Cup" and when Dolly tries to prevent her from telling Horace the truth. Such an act would be one of rebellion against the limitations of her life, an assertive act against all the denial that has gone before. It would also be a statement of ultimate control over her own life, and paradoxically of loss of control in the loss of the self. Like the sex act then, suicide would provide Ruth with a means of controlling others but at the cost of losing control of herself. If societal limitations deny her a full life, then she threatens to deny them the chance to work in her life any further.[4] In analyzing Lily Bart's part in Wharton's social marketplace and her eventual suicide, Wai-chee Dimock writes, "Where the marketplace is everywhere, in refusing to do business Lily is perhaps also refusing to live."[5] Like Lily, Ruth has found her goods undervalued, and she has not had the skill or will to manipulate the market into accepting them.

Whereas Dimock sees suicide as a complete victory for business, it seems to me that Ruth's threat at least contains a value of its own in its refusal to submit absolutely to the male standards. "The only way for a woman to attain a state of wholeness", Margaret Higgonet argues, "may be to move beyond the body."[6] This assertion is especially valid when the body symbolizes and contains the woman's fragmentation as both subject and object, producer and produced in the market. Because men have fixed the prices, Horace has been able to play out his fantasy of marrying the sweet little child-woman, but being the child-woman prevents Ruth from being an emotionally and sexually mature adult.

In her relationship with Walter, Ruth discovers a need for sexual expression, but frustratingly that relationship remains one where she has even less control over herself and her paramour. Clearly Ruth's attraction to Walter is sexually motivated. Although she does not go riding with him as much as she does with Horace, Ruth likes boating and dancing with Walter, two activities she compares to the exhilaration of riding. With Walter at least, she likes being dominated—with Horace they ride side by side on separate horses or she rides alone—but in dancing with Walter he holds her in his arms, leads, and at one time spins her so fast in a waltz she nearly faints.

While boating, too, she sits passively admiring his management of the sail and rudder.

It is worth closely examining a scene that demonstrates the excitement, tension, and passion at the heart of Ruth and Walter's relationship. On the day of a clambake on an island just off St. Augustine, Ruth, bored with the party and wishing to be alone with Walter, convinces him to take her sailing. They stop on another small island and Ruth decides to go hunting for alligators and bears:

> "I wish we could meet something, I wish we could have an adventure!" she said. "There are bears over here; and there are alligators too at the pools. Perhaps this trail leads to a pool?" The surmise was correct; the path soon brought them within sight of a dark-looking pond, partly covered with lily leaves. Ruth, who was first (for the old Indian trail was so narrow that they could not walk side by side), turned back suddenly. "There really *is* an alligator," she whispered. "He is half in and half out of the water. I am going to run round through the thicket, so as to have a nearer view of him."
>
> (217)

Walter follows her, believing Ruth to be so fearless that she might get dangerously close to an alligator. He finds her instead sitting in a swing laughing. He is annoyed at being made to appear more frightened than she. To make up for this he finds a young rattlesnake and presses Ruth to touch it with a stick and make it rattle.

> Hastily cutting a long wand from a bush, he gave it to her. "Touch him," he directed; "on the body, not on the head. Then you will see him coil!" . . . The wand came down slowly, paused, and then touched the reptile, who instantly coiled himself, reared his flat head, and struck at it with his fangs exposed. Walter, excited and interested, waited to see him strike again. But there was no opportunity for the wand itself was dropping. He turned. Ruth, her face covered with her hands, was shuddering convulsively.
>
> (218)

Ruth runs down the beach in terror, and Walter, confused at Ruth's response just when he thought her so fearless, runs after her. He finds her sobbing uncontrollably and realizes it is just like her laughing—nearly hysterical. But she assures him,

> "You must not mind if I happen to look rather pale," she said, timidly. "I am sometimes very pale for a moment or two. And then I get dreadfully red in the same way. . . . it doesn't mean anything. I can go now," she added, still timidly.
> "She thinks I am vexed," he said to himself, surprised. He was not vexed;

on the contrary, in her pallor and this new shyness she was more interesting to him than she had ever been before.

(219)

No, he is not vexed now that she is shaking and terrified, but he was when she made him look frightened at the alligator pond. Walter is clearly attracted by her weakness and repelled by her strength.

The dark pond, partly covered with lily pads, and reached by a narrow path, is a landscape of female genitalia, which Ruth in her swing of vines presides over like a goddess of femininity and fecundity. Walter senses nothing threatening about the scene, for the reputed alligator guardian is nowhere to be seen.[7] Maddened by her display of power and sexuality (without responding to her implicit invitation to join her in her bower), Walter sets out to give his own demonstration. The reptile used to represent his sexuality is, of course, the rattlesnake, which although a small, harmless baby is nonetheless real compared to Ruth's invisible alligator. His trick of essentially showing off his penis through the agent of the rattlesnake is enough to make Ruth remember her place as a weak and helpless female in the face of threatening male sexuality.

Ruth struggles to find the means and the men to participate in a full social economy that will allow her the freedom and value she had in her female-only family as well as the power, control and sexuality granted to men. Ruth enters the social marketplace with sex as her greatest asset, but she finds she cannot compete with an experienced speculator like Walter Willoughby.

Control finally becomes a problem for the author herself as in the final pages she tries to reassert Horace Chase as the main character, but Ruth will not yield the stage to him. The ending rests uncomfortably with the reader who has been asked to sympathize with Ruth but then must shift allegiance to her husband. We have seen so little of Chase's emotions that the ample delineation of them on the final two pages becomes somewhat embarrassing—"It was a strong man's anguish. . . . His face showed how profoundly he had suffered; it was changed, changed for life. . . . His rugged face had, for the moment, an expression that was striking in its beauty; its mixture of sorrow, honesty, and grandeur" (418–19).

This scene solidifies an image that has been shimmering on the surface for some time, the image of Horace as domestic heroine, complete with suggestions of his Christlikeness. His actions have been increasingly those of a caretaker for Ruth's whole family as he held them together financially and emotionally, especially after Jared's death. Now he acquires the splendor in suffering so often attributed to women like Alice Humphreys in *Wide Wide World*, Edna Earl in *Saint Elmo*, and in a more sophisticated sense Henry James's Isabel Archer. Although Woolson has always been sympathetic to the character of Horace, this elevation of his suffering still comes as an imposition, for it is Ruth and her suffering that have occupied the body of the work and the attention of the reader, and suddenly that focus is abandoned in favor of Horace's beatification. Furthermore, Horace's domestic grandeur fails to convince or comfort, since Woolson, through characters like Genevieve, has already convinced us of the potentially lethal effects of domestic control. As the narrator finds herself losing control of her characters and material at the end of the novel, she imposes this traditional domestic form as a means of enforcing order. But the embarrassment we sense at the melting of a strong character like Horace Chase ironically denounces the ending of all domestic novels, where a strong woman suddenly melts submissively into the arms of the hero. This too, Woolson urges, is unrealistic and embarrassing.

A more hopeful reading of this ending is possible, however, within the context of Woolson's metaphor of the social marketplace. Horace's transformation into the domestic heroine provides the opportunity for a sharing of values not seen before. Horace's feminization, the honesty of his emotional response, finds a corresponding change in Ruth. She grows from a belle-like character into something more dignified.[8] She now values her husband more completely, not just for his money. The emphasis on honesty as the quality that brings them together also puts the focus back on the female value of information and away from the male values of sex and money that Ruth has so long pursued in her romances first with Horace and later with Walter. Although readers are denied any vision of their life together after this crisis, Horace and Ruth may be the one couple in Woolson's novels for whom a successful partnership can be hoped.

Marriage is a certainty for Horace and Ruth, a union they have already formed, and for them, as for Margaret and Lansing Harold in *East Angels*, divorce seems unacceptable. Their final embrace then gives us a sense of closure without making the reader "a complicit participant in the conventions residing in the romantic ideal," for we know this resolution has not come, nor will it continue to come easily; the process of developing and maintaining a fair and equitable partnership is not finished.[9] A whole new method of determining value exchange remains to be constructed, a system where participants receive equal access to and remuneration for their currency. This is a hopeful ending, not a static "happily-ever-after" ending; both partners will make demands—sexual, social, and economic.[10] This is the model of a social economy Woolson has been struggling to produce in all of her novels, a marriage in which everyone gets his/her money's worth.

Notes

1. Constance Fenimore Woolson, *Horace Chase: A Novel* (New York: Harper and Brothers, 1894), 93; hereafter cited in the text.

2.   Several women characters try to use telepathy either to control or to read the thoughts of other characters: Maud Muriel and Miss Billy concentrate on trying to make Maud's sister-in-law spank her children; Dolly uses a planchette to produce automatic writing and to receive a mental message from her mother across several rooms. At the time she wrote *Horace Chase* Woolson was reading William James's *Principles of Psychology*, in which James frequently discusses the activity of automatic writing and the use of the planchette.

3.   Not every woman who finds herself only in female society, excluded from the larger market, is as content as the Franklin women are at the opening of the novel. These women and their careless attitude toward clothing specifically and "doing good" generally earn Genevieve's disapproval and pity. In their exclusively female environment her in-laws see the use of sex as a commodity as counterfeit; but since men genuinely value it as a form of currency, Genevieve's deliberate manner of dress meets with male approval. The men believe what they see, especially when it conforms to their standards of value, but the women, interested in what lies beyond appearances, know that Genevieve is different from her public manifestation. Her control of images, her ability to project the image demanded by men, gives her the ability to usurp some of the power usually granted only to men, the power of money and administration, though she loses the respect and friendship of women.

4.   Dolly and Maud Muriel also escape the constraints of the mainstream-male economy through retreat into disease and art, respectively. By not fulfilling male expectations of women, they succeed in at least guaranteeing themselves a degree of freedom, though Woolson clearly finds their solutions imperfect because of the losses necessary to gain that freedom.

5.   Wai-chee Dimock, "Debasing Exchange: Edith Wharton's *House of Mirth*," *PMLA* 100 (October 1985):788.

6.   Margaret Higgonet, "Suicide: Representations of the Feminine in the Nineteenth Century," *Poetics Today: International Journal for Theory and Analysis of Literature and Communications* 6 (1985):114.

7.   Any visitor to Florida will realize how rashly Walter dismisses the alligator, since nearly every body of water in the state contains at least one such resident, who is, however, infrequently seen because he becomes invisible when only inches below the surface.

8.   For a concise discussion of the belle and her economic implications, see Nina Baym, *Woman's Fiction: A Guide to Novels by and about Women in America, 1820–1870* (Ithaca: Cornell University Press, 1978), 28. Baym notes that in contrast to the domestic heroine "the belle has given herself to the marketplace."

9.   Joseph A. Boone, "Modernist Maneuverings in the Marriage Plot: Breaking Ideologies of Gender and Genre in James's *The Golden Bowl*," *PMLA* 101 (May 1986):374–88.

10.   According to Carolyn Heilbrun in "Marriage Perceived: English Literature 1873–1941," *What Manner of Woman: Essays on English and American Life and Literature*, ed. Marlene Springer (New York: New York University Press, 1977), it has been left to the modern novel to explore within the text the marriage that makes these demands (181). Woolson suggests such a union but leaves its accomplishment to her followers.

Index

◆